AF477784

Studies in
Modern French History

Catholicism and children's literature in France

MANCHEStER
1824

Manchester University Press

Studies in
Modern French History

Edited by
Mark Greengrass and Pamela Pilbeam

This series is published in collaboration with the UK Society for the Study of French History. It aims to showcase innovative short monographs relating to the history of the French, in France and in the world since c.1750. Each volume speaks to a theme in the history of France with broader resonances to other discourses about the past. Authors demonstrate how the sources and interpretations of modern French history are being opened to historical investigation in new and interesting ways, and how unfamiliar subjects have the capacity to tell us more about the role of France within the European continent. The series is particularly open to interdisciplinary studies that break down the traditional boundaries and conventional disciplinary divisions.

The Society for the
Study of French History

Catholicism and children's literature in France

The comtesse de Ségur
(1799–1874)

SOPHIE HEYWOOD

Manchester University Press

Manchester and New York

distributed in the United States exclusively by Palgrave Macmillan

Published by Manchester University Press
Oxford Road, Manchester M13 9NR, UK
and Room 400, 175 Fifth Avenue, New York, NY 10010, USA
www.manchesteruniversitypress.co.uk

Distributed in the United States exclusively by
Palgrave Macmillan, 175 Fifth Avenue, New York, NY 10010, USA

Distributed in Canada exclusively by
UBC Press, University of British Columbia, 2029 West Mall,
Vancouver, BC, Canada V6T 1Z2

British Library Cataloguing-in-Publication Data
A catalogue record for this book is available from the British Library

Library of Congress Cataloging-in-Publication Data applied for

ISBN   978 0 7190 8466 9   hardback

First published 2011

The publisher has no responsibility for the persistence or accuracy of URLs for any
external or third-party internet websites referred to in this book, and does not guarantee
that any content on such websites is, or will remain, accurate or appropriate.

Typeset
by Toppan Best-set Premedia Limited
Printed in Great Britain
by the MPG Books Group, Bodmin

In memory of James F. McMillan

Contents

List of illustrations

Acknowledgements

The project began life as a doctoral thesis at the University of Edinburgh under the supervision of James F. McMillan, who was a wonderful mentor. The resulting book is dedicated to his memory, for without his vision and encouragement it would never have seen the light of day. I would like to offer warm thanks to Robert Anderson, Robert Gildea, and Richard Thomson for reading the manuscript at various stages, and for their insightful comments. I am also grateful to the anonymous readers, Mark Greengrass, and Pamela Pilbeam for their excellent suggestions, and to the staff at Manchester University Press. Chantal Marsden, Joël Félix, and Claire Neuts provided much needed help with the French language, for which I am very grateful – although the mistakes that remain are entirely my own. I have benefited from the advice of many friends and colleagues, but I would like to thank in particular Frank Tallett and Nicholas Atkin at the University of Reading for their friendship and support. Professor Atkin's untimely death has been an immense loss for us all, and to the discipline as a whole.

Financial support was generously provided by the Carnegie Trust for the Universities of Scotland and the Institute of Historical Research. I would like to thank the staff of all the libraries and archives that I have used. I am particularly grateful to André Derval at the IMEC and Aldona Kucharska at Hachette Livre. I would also like to thank Iris de Moüy for kindly answering my questions.

I owe an immense debt to my parents Colin and Olena, who have provided unflagging support and excellent advice throughout. Special thanks must go to my mother for her many invaluable comments on the manuscript, which she read through with great skill and care. Finally, I would like to thank Jack Harrington for being a constant source of joy and inspiration.

List of abbreviations

AN   Archives Nationales
BN   Bibliothèque Nationale
HEF   Histoire de l'Édition Française
ICFV   Institut Catholique, Fonds Veuillot
IMEC   Institut de Mémoires de l'Édition Contemporaine
NAF   Nouvelles Acquisitions Françaises

All references to correspondence from the comtesse de Ségur to Olga de Pitray are taken from Vicomtesse de Simard de Pitray, née Olga de Ségur, sa fille (ed.) *Lettres de la Comtesse de Ségur née Rostopchine au Vicomte et à la Vicomtesse de Pitray* (Paris, Hachette, 1891).

All references to correspondence from the comtesse de Ségur to Émile Templier are taken from comtesse de Ségur, *Œuvres*, 1:lxi–cxlvi, edited by Claudine Beaussant (Paris, Laffont, 1990).

All other references to letters written by the comtesse de Ségur, unless otherwise indicated, are taken from Marie-José Strich (ed.), with a preface by Michel Tournier, *1799–1874 La Comtesse de Ségur. Correspondance* (Paris, Scala, 1990).

Introduction

'The holidays were drawing to their close, the children loved each other more and more.' According to Charles de Gaulle, this was the most melancholy line in all of French literature.[1] It was written by the children's author Madame la comtesse de Ségur, née Rostopchine. Although virtually unknown in the English-speaking world, in France Ségur is a national icon and a cultural phenomenon. Generations of children have grown up reading her storybooks. Alongside de Gaulle, the list of her illustrious devotees includes Proust, Simone de Beauvoir, Vladimir Nabokov, and François Mauriac, amongst countless others.[2]

A Russian-born aristocrat, Madame de Ségur took up writing books for children as a grandmother, at the age of fifty-five, in 1855. In the following fourteen years she produced twenty works of fiction and a Bible series, writing as the flagship author for Hachette's new *Bibliothèque Rose* collection for children. Her books went on to become best-sellers for young children in the twentieth century.[3] She was estimated by 1990 to have sold over thirty million copies in France alone, and was translated into many other languages as well.[4] New editions of her books in the 1930s testify to her wide audience, adults and children alike, of all social strata.[5] And this success has been enduring – these are not old classics left to gather dust on the shelves. Indeed, the comtesse is enjoying something of a revival in France, where her books are being marketed in conservative circles as good old-fashioned education treatises for beleaguered modern parents.[6] Following the hundred and fiftieth anniversary of the *Bibliothèque Rose* in 2006, sales of Ségur's *Petites filles modèles* (1858) are reported to have increased by 25 per cent, and are now selling twenty thousand copies a year. This has prompted Hachette to commission a reworking of the book, in which the model girls now have mobile phones and boyfriends.[7]

The comtesse wrote in many well-loved genres of children's literature: fairy tales in *Nouveaux contes de fées* (1857); domestic education in *Petites filles modèles*; animal stories for her donkey Cadichon's memoirs, *Mémoires d'un âne* (1860); the school stories contained within *Les deux nigauds* (1863) and *Un bon petit diable* (1865); children's Bible series (1866–69); and the very feminine hybrid of domestic and adventure stories, set on a desert island in *Les vacances* (1859) and in her native Russia for the *Auberge de l'ange gardien* (1863) and its sequel *Général Dourakine* (1863). She is considered to be one of the French authors of the so-called 'golden age' of Western children's literature in the second half of the nineteenth century. It was at this point that the industrialisation of the print trade and rising literacy rates combined with the expansion of the prosperous middle class. These middle-class families produced fewer children, upon whom money and attention were lavished. The changes in effect created a flourishing new market for children's books that publishers across Western Europe and North America were quick to exploit. Some of the most famous titles in children's literature were written in this period, such as Lewis Carroll's *Alice's Adventures in Wonderland* (1865), Johanna Spyri's *Heidi* (1880), Collodi's *Pinocchio* (1881–83), Louisa May Alcott's *Little Women* (1868), and Jules Verne's *Around the World in 80 Days* (1873).[8] Authors developed new strategies to appeal to children, demonstrating a greater respect for young readers, and a desire to reject older, more didactic forms of writing for children. Thus, although Ségur's books are underpinned by a strong sense of Catholic morality, and feature the hallmarks of religious didacticism – pious death scenes, a clear division between good and bad, and a careful delineation of social hierarchy according to gender and class – she is also notorious for her wickedly observed comic characters, and her predilection for violence.

In spite of her success in France and internationally, the comtesse de Ségur remains a little known figure in the English-speaking world. And while French scholarship on Ségur has been flourishing since the 1980s, only a handful of literary scholars in Anglophone academe have studied her work.[9] This is no surprise, for it follows a general pattern in the field of children's literature, which is still dominated by English-speaking research and, as such, reflects their concerns.[10] Penny Brown's recent two-volume history of French children's literature[11] offers an important and long overdue corrective, but much more remains to be done. Ségur is also rarely mentioned in studies of modern France, and she is noticeably absent from most textbooks on women's history. Given the comtesse's long reign over the classics of children's literature in France, her absence represents an important gap in our knowledge of French cultural history. This book aims to fill this gap, and ask what insights Ségur's life and works offer into nineteenth-century French culture, by reading them in their specific religious, political, and cultural contexts. As a modern, professional, and militantly religious author for children, Madame de Ségur is the French Catholic counterpart to many women writers from this period, such as Charlotte Yonge, Mrs Molesworth, and Louisa May Alcott to name but a few. Although sustained comparisons are beyond the confines of this book, which is a study in French history, it is hoped to offer an important contribution to the study of the history of children's literature, and to stimulate further research in this field.

There is a wealth of recent French-language material on the comtesse to build upon, as there has been a renaissance in French academic research on Ségur. Alongside the publication of her collected works in 1990,[12] she has been the subject of a series of pioneering monographs,[13] and in 2000 the *Cahiers Séguriens* journal was launched. In particular, literary scholars such as Laura Kreyder, Francis Marcoin, and Isabelle Nières-Chevrel have brought to light the complexity of the writings of the comtesse, as well as many of the fascinating issues surrounding her life and work. In contrast, this monograph is written from a historical perspective, which has led to the discovery of new source material (notably correspondence preserved in the Institut Catholique, Paris, and her reception in Catholic book reviews). To read her works in their historical contexts, this book uses the correspondence, family papers, memoirs, biographies, and published writings of the comtesse, her associates, and her family. This is complemented with an analysis of the reception of her works in the context of the new discourse on children's books generated by the Catholic missionary drive to propagate 'good books'.

Ségur wrote her books in a period of important cultural and religious change across Europe. In 1855, 38 per cent of conscripts were illiterate; this figure had dropped to 17 per cent by 1880. Although literacy rates varied greatly between regions, and according to gender and occupation, still, Ségur's generation was aware that mass literacy was fast becoming an inescapable social phenomenon.[14] This, along with falling book prices, advances in printing technology, and improved transport, ensured that the printed word was reaching more and more readers than ever before. Such changes in the way that populations had access to information were causing widespread alarm – sharpened especially by the revolutions of 1848, which were said to have been spread by pamphlets and print. Of particular concern were the consequences for such impressionable readers as the young and the lower classes. Would they be exploited or even brainwashed by the unscrupulous and the immoral? The Catholic Church was the most vehement critic of the expansion of education and popular reading, and the most effective force in exploiting their potential. The Papal encyclicals *Mirari vos* (1832) and *Quanta cura* with its *Syllabus of Errors* (1864) underlined the need for 'good' books to save society from the perils of 'bad reading', and the need for education to be religious as opposed to secular.

The Catholic Church was therefore to have a huge bearing on the market for children's literature when Ségur became an author, and on the direction of her writing, not least because of her own political and religious beliefs. The religion Ségur adhered to was highly politicised, and was undergoing an important modernisation process. James F. McMillan has argued that 'one of most profound changes of the nineteenth century was the transformation of European Catholicism into an essentially new religion'.[15] The revolutionary and Napoleonic era had destabilised the symbiotic relationship between Church and State. Monastic lands had been sold off, and civil war in France had led to religious violence in the early 1790s. Over the course of the century sympathetic regimes often restored the Church, but many changes remained irreversible. The revolutions in 1848, the wars of unification in Italy 1859–70, and the growth of State machinery further eroded the Church's traditional power base across Europe. It was weakened by the intellectual challenges of the Enlightenment and positivism, and churchmen regularly denounced the threat to religion and moral order posed by the uncontrolled spread of books and reading. At the same time, and partly in response to these dislocations, the nineteenth century witnessed a dynamic religious revival. At the grassroots level, active, lay-driven charitable orders flourished, particularly women's orders, and the century witnessed a surge in popular devotions, pilgrimages, and visions. From the top down, the papacy, particularly during the pontificate of Pius IX (1846–78), pursued a centralisation policy, designed to strengthen papal authority.[16] As an institution, the Church felt increasingly threatened. Joseph Byrnes speaks of a 'siege mentality'.[17] Nevertheless, this was also a period of great vitality for religious life in Europe.

Politically speaking, revivalist Catholicism accommodated a broad range of opinions, ranging from hard-line theocrats to more liberal currents. There was also bitter disagreement between 'gallicans' who sought to protect the national character of their Church, and 'ultramontanes' who looked over the mountains (*ultra montes*) to Rome for the preservation of traditional religious society as they saw it. In the 1850s and 1860s the balance tipped towards Rome. Under the aegis of Pius IX, a more militant, aggressively anti-liberal current came to predominate, culminating in the *Syllabus of Errors* in 1864 and the declaration of the dogma of papal infallibility in 1870. The *Syllabus* told believers that the papacy would not be reconciled with progress, liberalism, and modern civilisation, and depicted the Church in modern Europe as being locked in a deadly power struggle with the forces of Satan.[18] Such inflammatory rhetoric was typical of the debates in the second half of the nineteenth century. The escalating power struggles between Churches, States, and anti-clericals in Europe are now referred to by scholars as 'culture wars', in recognition of the all-encompassing nature of the debates.[19]

The comtesse de Ségur was located at the very heart of these 'culture wars' in France. She was head of a powerful ultramontane religious dynasty in the Second Empire, which played an important role in ensuring the spread of anti-liberal Catholicism. Her eldest son, Mgr Gaston de Ségur, a close friend of Pius IX, was a zealous missionary and a best-selling author of politico-religious tracts.[20] Her second son, Anatole de Ségur, was a writer of Catholic propaganda, a successful poet, and a politician. Her other children or their spouses were also involved in religious politics. Their 'family' also included the journalist Louis Veuillot (whom they called 'brother Louis', while he referred to the comtesse as 'maman Ségur').[21] Veuillot's newspaper *L'univers* was the principal voice for the new militant Catholicism of Pius IX, and Mgr de Ségur's tracts were also used to spread the new piety amongst the populace. It was through the press and the printed word that the 'new Catholicism', the new militant, Romanised, centralised, and defensive Catholicism, was diffused. In this way, the Ségur family and Veuillot were instrumental in setting the tone of French Catholicism. It was not just as 'maman Ségur' but also as a fellow writer that the comtesse de Ségur was involved in the activities of this influential group. She kept up a correspondence with Veuillot throughout her writing career, and worked closely with him and her sons in the production of 'good' books.

By writing books, magazines, and pamphlets, women like Ségur – laywomen authors of print culture for children – could find meaningful ways of contributing to their Church, that would at the same time provide them with opportunities for professional careers as writers, journalists (although they were not called this), and editors. Research into the role of women in the Catholic Church has been expanding and the lives of the women religious and bourgeois women engaged in charitable associations have been well documented.[22] However, as Carol E. Harrison has argued, Catholic women are still deprived of a voice in historiography.[23] This is not because Catholic women's voices from this period are hard to find. The 1850s experienced a great publishing boom, and in 1860–61 religious literature accounted for around 20 per cent of the market.[24] Numerous women authors were included in this cultural surge, and many were celebrities, championed by the Catholic establishment. Alongside the comtesse de Ségur, there were women such as Zénaïde Fleuriot, Victorine Monniot, Madame Craven, Mathilde Bourdon, and Josephine de Gaulle, to name a few. Although their names are familiar to historians of children's books and the education of bourgeois girls, the contribution that these women made to their Church remains obscure. Most importantly, Claude Savart's now classic study of religious publishing in nineteenth-century France did not include works of edifying fiction in his definition of 'religious literature'.[25] In one fell swoop he excluded most women authors from the religious publishing revival. By contrast, I argue that if we examine the book reviews and reports published by the Catholic 'good books' missions, and include the arguments put forward by leading lights of the militant Catholic right, then it becomes clear that edifying fictions, in the form of short stories (*contes*), novels, and recreational magazines were definitely mobilised in the fight to prevent 'bad reading'.

Children's literature was one of the principal genres considered to be suited to women authors, and so this was an area in which they could make their mark. It was a role of no small significance, because the next generation was believed by all to hold the key to regenerating the nation. Alongside wrangles over control of the schooling system, education more generally (books included) became one of the principal sites of the culture wars between the Church, State, and anti-clericals. As Savart himself tell us, books for children formed the main output of Catholic publishing houses in the mid-nineteenth century.[26] It was widely agreed by 'good books' reviewers that children needed more recreational forms of reading matter, and these were not simply permitted by the 'good books' campaign, they were positively encouraged. By focusing on the comtesse de Ségur, the most enduringly successful writer of this generation of women writers, this book examines how such women could carve out a professional identity for themselves, and challenge some of the old stereotypes surrounding Catholic women as being in the thrall of their priests.[27] It provides an opportunity to hear one of the most important 'voices' of this generation of pious women authors. Ségur was very much a woman of her time: her politics were reactionary, as was her religion, and at the same time she was entrepreneurial, and an enthusiastic adept of modern communications. In this way my book adds to the important research by historians of religion, who, over the past twenty years, have worked to nuance the idea that modern Europe was a secular creation. They point instead to the continuing role played by the Church in modern society, and argue that religion and secular–religious conflicts were an integral part of the modernisation process.[28]

A study of one woman is necessarily a partial view. Obviously Ségur cannot 'speak' for the many Catholic women in nineteenth-century France. Nevertheless, if we do not study exceptional women, then the voices in the religious history of this period will remain overwhelmingly male. Second, as Joan Walloch Scott argues, biography is an excellent tool for understanding and historicising how culturally constructed definitions of gender operate upon the individual in society.[29] It must be remembered that simply by entering into professional life the comtesse de Ségur was contravening the strict gender codes that underpinned nineteenth-century French society.[30] In post-revolutionary France, politics and the public sphere, which is to say both professional life and the space within which society and politics were debated and articulated, were considered the male domain. Women's vocation was in the domestic sphere; they were the so-called 'angels of the hearth'. Michelle Perrot describes these codes as the 'invisible barriers' that framed nineteenth-century society, and worked as a powerful exclusionary force for women who entertained ambitions beyond being a wife and mother.[31] In order to analyse Ségur as a politically engaged, professional author, and therefore a woman in the public sphere, this book draws upon the methodology of the feminist 'New Biography'. This school of research examines the lives of exceptional women who defied the rigorous separation of the public and private spheres.[32] Their case studies look at the identities that women had to fashion in order to gain public acceptance, and how the gendered codes that structured French society informed the vocabulary that women used to conceptualise their sense of self and their professional work. The New Biography therefore exposes the gaps between nineteenth-century rhetoric and reality. At the same time as moral discourse exalted women's role in the domestic sphere, more and more women were entering the public sphere as authors, educators, charity workers, and members of religious orders.

There are however tensions inherent in choosing the comtesse as a subject for a New Biography. Practitioners thus far have made their feminist agenda clear: to enter the public sphere in nineteenth-century France, they argue, was automatically an act of resistance to culturally accepted gender roles. Yet, as author of the best-selling *Petites filles modèles*, Ségur was one of the most successful creators of just such cultural norms. Relatively few women in the Second Empire used their careers in the public sphere as a platform to denounce their repression. In the case of the comtesse de Ségur the opposite was true, and in many ways she embodied a paradox – she was a conservative, who believed in the importance of women's role in the home, but in order to defend that belief she had to carve out a professional role for herself. Written from this perspective, a New Biographical study of the comtesse adds to the increasing diversification of feminist scholarship, for, as the historian Elizabeth Macknight explains, 'negative responses or lack of response to campaigns for women's rights form part of the historical narrative of feminism'.[33] My aim in this book is not to question the extent to which Ségur really believed in her own paradox, nor to portray her as a victim who had interiorised the norms that she in fact helped to create. Such interpretations rely too much on a rather convenient bad faith on her part, and too much on reading between the lines.[34] Rather, I hope this study of the difficulties and paradoxes the comtesse encountered in her professional career demonstrates the courage of those who dared to campaign openly for women's emancipation, when the patriarchal norms of nineteenth-century society operated such immense pressures on even the comtesse de Ségur, this most conservative of women.

The next question is then have there been any unintended consequences of the paradox of a conservative woman publishing in the professional sphere? What is her legacy? Charles Sowerwine argues for caution. In his view, although recent revisionist feminist scholarship is correct to show how many women could and did flout the cultural restrictions placed upon them in the nineteenth century, scholars are wrong to argue that this necessarily helped to undermine such strictures: 'the more women performed functions perceived as consonant with their nurturing vocation, the more they conformed to the very norms which justified their exclusion from the public sphere'.[35] Ségur, it could be argued, confirms Sowerwine's thesis, for although she defied conventions by entering public literary life, and engaging in political life through her family circle, she made her career out of producing the most successful gender scripts in modern France. For the past 150 years she has formed a crucial part of the reading matter of little girls in particular. Although she wrote for both boys and girls, she was increasingly interpreted in the late nineteenth century, and the twentieth century, as being primarily for girls. The phrase 'petite fille modèle' has entered into the French lexicon to describe a gentle, submissive, well-to-do young girl, and is regularly used by historians as shorthand for traditional gender roles. Certainly, Ségur's tales of model girls and their pious mothers were designed to reinforce gendered codes of behaviour in children. Simone de Beauvoir (b. 1908), whose philosophy of feminism, 'one is not born a woman, but becomes one', has proved so influential on gender history, was well aware of the importance of the comtesse de Ségur. Still, Beauvoir's writings on Ségur also reveal the deep respect she held for the comtesse as a very feminine writer.[36] I argue that this is no straightforward tale of heroines and villainesses, for the comtesse's legacy is a complex one, subject to constant reinterpretation and appropriation by the successive generations who have read her books. Many French scholars now agree that Ségur invented the cultural image of the 'modern' little girl, citing her famous heroine 'Sophie' from *Les malheurs de Sophie* (1858), a well-rounded character, capable of autonomous thought and much more than a 'model' female stereotype.[37] Given the current surge in sales of her *Petites filles modèles* (which also features Sophie), it is hard to argue that her creations do not have a place in modern girls' culture. But is this legacy wholly positive? Do Ségur's female characters represent a femininity that transcends the domestic ideal? How have they been read, reread, and reinterpreted by readers? Exploring the possible answers to these questions offers a way to nuance (without necessarily rejecting) Sowerwine's thesis.

This book has five thematic chapters. The first chapter develops the theme of biography. It examines the main accounts of the comtesse de Ségur's life, looking at the ways in which Madame de Ségur and the Ségur family fashioned an attractive image of her as a charming old grandmother and a model of Christian motherhood. It looks at the function biographies played in the political–religious conflicts of the period, giving special attention to the family narrative that formed the principal ideological filter through which stories of Ségur's life passed through before they reached the public domain.

Chapter 2 looks at the comtesse and the idea of children in France. It analyses constructions of childhood in her collected works, and asks how militant Catholic designs altered religious ideas of 'childhood' in the nineteenth century. Ségur's approach to writing for children, and her enthusiastic reception by the Catholic 'good books' movement, shows how the Church played a part in the modern revaluation of childhood that began with the Enlightenment.

The third chapter develops this notion of her 'modernity' further. It focuses on Madame de Ségur's relationship with her editor, Émile Templier, at the publishing giant Hachette. Using Ségur's dealings with Templier, and in particular her struggles against the censorship of her work, the first section examines how she developed a moral reputation for her public, which eventually gave her more authority in her negotiations with Hachette. The second section then looks at how she defended her work against the pressures of writing for a standardised collection, in which book length, illustrations, and even content were determined by the collection, rather than by the author. In so doing, this chapter traces the tribulations of an author in a time of the rapid industrialisation of the print trade.

Chapter 4 considers Ségur's involvement in her family network of militant, highly influential Catholic propagandists, and how this informed her writings and political thought. This chapter uncovers the private channels through which alliances were formed, and information was diffused. While lacking in ecclesiastical or political authority, the comtesse was nevertheless engaged in the politico-religious 'combat', firstly as matriarch of the Ségur family, and then as a writer.

The fifth and final chapter focuses on gender and legacy. It situates the comtesse in the school of 'governess' literature, as moral literature for children was called, and charts the emergence of a new, militant Catholic generation of 'governess' authors in the mid-nineteenth century. It then looks at their readership and subsequent reception, in order to ask what their legacy was, and in particular whether we can trace any unintended consequences of their work as professional writers, editors, and journalists. It concludes with an assessment of the longer-term, adult feminist reception of Ségur and her colleagues, to locate their place in the collective memory of French feminine culture.

The main aim is therefore to bring to light an important writer of the nineteenth century, and to show how the study of her life and works can make a contribution to several areas of study: the history of children's literature, more specifically Catholic children's literature; the history of gender and religion; and the history of print culture. As a New Biography of a conservative woman and creator of an image of so-called 'traditional' femininity, this book provides an important contribution to understanding of the role women authors could play in nineteenth-century French religion and culture. It examines the legacy her work had for subsequent generations of girls. The rediscovery of Ségur's writings that is now clearly under way in France is a further reminder that she was a deeply paradoxical author, whose writings both endorsed and transcended the apparent conventionalities of her gender and politics. This book explores why that was so.

Notes

1 Alain Larcan, *De Gaulle inventaire. La culture, l'esprit, la foi* (Paris, Bartillat, 2003), pp. 267–268. All translations are by the author, unless otherwise indicated.

2 See Laura Kreyder, *L'enfance des saints et des autres. Essai sur la comtesse de Ségur* (Fasano, Schena, 1987), pp. 213–224; Armelle Leroy, *La saga de la Bibliothèque Rose* (Paris, Hachette, 2006).

3 On sales, see Annie Renonciat, 'Fortune éditorial de la comtesse de Ségur (1857–1939)', *Cahiers Robinson*, 9 (2001), 213–222; Valérie Legros, *De l'histoire à l'Histoire. Lire la comtesse de Ségur*, thèse de doctorat, Université de Rennes II, 1996, Unpublished; Appendix II below.

4 Guy Schoeller, cover text, comtesse de Ségur *Œuvres* (Paris, Robert Laffont, 1990), p. 3.

5 Renonciat, 'Fortune éditorial', p. 218.

6 Cf. Natacha Polony, 'Famille: le retour de l'autorité et des pères', in the right-wing broadsheet *Le Figaro*, 15 February 2010, or Hachette Jeunesse editor Charlotte Ruffault's comments reported in 'Les petites filles de Ségur revisitées', *L'hebdo*, 21 April 2010.

7 'Les petites filles de Ségur revisitées'; Rosalind Elland-Goldsmith, *Les nouvelles petites filles modèles* (Paris, Hachette, 2010).

8 Ganna Ottevaere-van Praag, *La littérature pour la jeunesse en Europe occidentale (1750–1925)*, (Berne, Peter Lang, 1987), pp. 185–291; Emer O'Sullivan, *Comparative Children's Literature*, translated by Anthea Bell (London and New York, Routledge, 2005), chapter 6.

9 See works by Penny Brown, Rosemary Lloyd, Kiera Vaklavik, Élise Noetinger, Valérie Lastinger, Ruth Carver Carpasso, Claire Malarte-Feldman, Claudine Giachetti and Lisette Luton.

10 O'Sullivan, *Comparative Children's Literature*, p. 11; recent publications are working to redress the balance, for example Peter Hunt (ed.) *International Companion Encyclopaedia of Children's Literature* (London, Routledge, 2004).

11 *A Critical History of French Children's Literature 1600–Present* (London, Routledge, 2008).

12 Comtesse de Ségur, *Œuvres*, 3 volumes, edited and annotated by Claudine Beaussant, (Paris, Robert Laffont, 1990).

13 Kreyder, *L'enfance des saints et des autres*, (1987); Marie-France Doray, *La comtesse de Ségur: une étrange paroissienne*, (Lyon, Rivages, 1990); and Francis

Marcoin, *La comtesse de Ségur ou le bonheur immobile* (Arras, Artois Presses Université, 1999).

14 Robert Anderson, *Education in France 1848–1870* (Oxford, Clarendon Press, 1975), pp. 18–19, p. 144; Colin Heywood, *Childhood in Nineteenth-Century France. Work, Health and Education among the classes populaires* (Cambridge, Cambridge University Press, 1988) pp. 68–71, 85–89.

15 James F. McMillan, 'Louis Veuillot, *L'univers* and the Ultramontane Network in Nineteenth-Century France', in Bates David and Gazeau Véronique, (eds) *Liens personnels, réseaux, solidarités en France et dans les îles Britanniques (XIe–XXe siècles)* (Paris, Publications de la Sorbonne, 2006), pp. 221–236, p. 221.

16 Christopher Clark, 'The New Catholicism and the European Culture Wars', in Clark Christopher, and Kaiser Wolfram, (eds) *Culture Wars. Secular–Catholic Conflict in Nineteenth-Century Europe*, (Cambridge, Cambridge University Press, 2003).

17 Joseph F. Byrnes, *Catholic and French Forever. Religious and National Identity in Modern France* (University Park, Pennsylvania State University Press, 2005), p. xx.

18 Austin Gough, *Paris and Rome: The Gallican Church and the Ultramontane Campaign 1848–1853*, (Oxford, Clarendon Press, 1986); Bruno Horaist, *La dévotion au pape et les catholiques français sous le pontificat de Pie IX (1846–1878) d'après les archives de la Bibliothèque Apostolique Vaticane* (Rome, École Française de Rome, Palais Farnese, 1995).

19 Clark and Kaiser (eds) *Culture Wars.*

20 On Gaston de Ségur, see Anatole de Ségur, *Mgr de Ségur. Souvenirs et récit d'un frère*, (Paris, Bray et Rétaux, 1882); Marthe de Hédouville, *Mgr de Ségur, sa vie – son action 1820–1881*, (Paris, Nouvelles Editions Latines, 1957); Émile Poulat and Jean-Pierre Laurant, *L'antimaçonnisme catholique*, (Paris, Berg International, 1994), pp. 105–167.

21 On Veuillot, see Eugène and François Veuillot, *Louis Veuillot*, 4 volumes, (Paris, Victor Rétaux, 1899–1913); James F. McMillan, 'Rediscovering Louis Veuillot: The Politics of Religious Identity in Nineteenth-Century France', in Harkness Nigel, Rowe Paul, Unwin Tim and Yee Jennifer, (eds) *Visions/Revisions: Essays on Nineteenth-Century French Culture*, (Bern, AG, Peter Lang 2003) pp. 305–322; Gough, *Paris and Rome*, chapter 5.

22 Claude Langlois, *Le catholicisme au féminin. Les congrégations françaises à supérieure générale au XIXe siècle* (Paris, Les Éditions du Cerf, 1984); Hazel Mills, 'Negotiating the Divide: Women, Philanthropy and the Public Sphere in Nineteenth-Century France', in Atkin Nicholas, and Tallett Frank, (eds) *Religion, Society and Politics in France since 1789*, (London, Hambledon Press, 1991), 29–54; Ruth Harris, *Lourdes. Body and Spirit in the Secular Age* (Harmondsworth, Penguin, 1999); Caroline Ford, *Divided Houses. Religion and Gender in Modern France* (Ithaca, Cornell University Press, 2005).

23 Carol E. Harrison, review of Caroline Ford, *Divided Houses*, *H-France Review*, 94 (2006).

24 Claude Savart, *Les catholiques en France au XIXe siècle. Le témoignage du livre religieux*, (Paris, Beauchesne, 1985), pp. 189–251.

25 *Ibid.*, p. 50.

26 *Ibid.*, pp. 440–442.

27 On the subject of stereotyping of Catholic women, see Ford, *Divided Houses*, introduction.

28 Harris, *Lourdes*; Clark and Kaiser, *Culture Wars*; James F. McMillan, 'Catholic Christianity in France from the Restoration to the Separation of Church and State, 1815–1905', Gilley Sheridan, and Stanley Brian, (eds) *World Christianities c. 1815–1914* (Cambridge, Cambridge University Press, 2006), pp. 217–232.

29 Joan Walloch Scott, *Gender and the Politics of History* (revised edition, New York, Columbia University Press, 1999), p. 44.

30 For an excellent overview of the historiography, see the essays by Charles Sowerwine and Karen Offen in Forth Christopher, and Accampo Elinor, (eds) *Confronting Modernity in Fin-de-Siècle France. Bodies, Minds and Gender* (Basingstoke, Palgrave Macmillan, 2010).

31 Michelle Perrot, 'Preface', in Corbin Alain, Lalouette Jacqueline, and Riot-Sarcey Michèle, (eds) *Femmes dans la cité 1815–1871* (Grâne, Créaphis, 1997), pp. 9–16.

32 Jo Burr Margadant (ed.) *The New Biography. Performing Femininity in Nine-teenth-Century France*, (Berkeley and Los Angeles, University of California Press, 2000).

33 Elizabeth C. Macknight, 'Why Weren't They Feminists?: Parisian Noble Women and the Campaigns for Women's Rights in France, 1880–1914', *European Journal of Women's Studies*, 14 (2007), 127–141; James F. McMillan, 'Wollstonecraft's Daughters, Marianne's Daughters, and the Daughters of Joan of Arc: Marie Maugeret and Christian Feminism in the French Belle Époque', in Orr Clarissa Campbell, (ed.)*Wollstonecraft's Daughters. Womanhood in England and France 1780–1920* (Manchester, Manchester University Press, 1996), pp. 186–198.

34 For further discussion of the ways in which Ségur has been depicted vari-ously as a 'victim', or a 'proto-feminist' who subverted her own moral mes-sages, see Chapter 5.

35 Sowerwine, 'Women's Citizenship and Republicanism in France, 1789–1944', in Forth and Accampo, *Confronting Modernity*, pp. 25–35.

36 Simone de Beauvoir, *Mémoires d'une jeune fille rangée*, (Paris, Gallimard, 1958), pp. 29, 42, 70–71, 77–78; see also *Le deuxième sexe* (Paris, Gallimard, 1949), 2:37.

37 See Chapter 5.

1

Life stories

My very dear children,
Here are the tales you so loved to hear, and I had promised you I would
publish.
When reading them, dear little ones, think of your old grandmother, who,
to please you, has renounced her obscurity and exposed to the censure of
the public the name of the

COMTESSE DE SÉGUR,
née Rostopchine[1]

In this dedication to her first book, the comtesse de Ségur introduced
herself to the public. It contains all the crucial ingredients of her
brand that was to prove so popular. She evokes a delightful picture of
two little girls, sitting listening rapt as their grandmother tells them
stories. What could be more innocent and charming than for the comtesse to give in to her little darlings' desire to see these stories in print?
Yet this is no ordinary grandmother. With dramatic flair, she builds up
to her grand announcement: that the illustrious comtesse de Ségur,
daughter of the formidable General Rostopchine, is entering into the
public arena.

This chapter introduces the biographical details of the comtesse de
Ségur's life, in order to examine how and why this dear, if rather contradictory, old grandmother figure was constructed for the public. Her life

as a celebrity and an aristocrat was automatically considered of public interest; moreover she was a writer who presided over a family of writers and therefore there has been preserved a substantial amount of material with which to reconstruct her life stories. As can be seen from this opening quotation her identity was carefully packaged for popular consumption. The comtesse de Ségur was a master storyteller, and some of the most attractive stories she told to her public were about her self.

Undertaking to write a person's life in the wake of the postmodernist rejection of the unified self is fraught with pitfalls, if indeed it is possible at all. In 1986 Pierre Bourdieu spoke ominously of the 'biography illusion'.[2] He argued that identity is fluid, and contingent on time, place, and a variety of historically specific factors that are all subject to change. The one fixed point in a person's life is their name (and, even so, this is only true for men). The medium of biography was exposed as a creative exercise which seeks to impose a single, coherent narrative upon the disorder of multiple and contradictory selves that a person constructs in the course of their life. Besides the epistemological complications, biography had fallen out of favour with historians, as it was associated with an outmoded vision of history centred upon the stories of great events and great men. For a long time, in spite of the perennial popularity of the genre with the general public, many historians viewed biography's rightful place to be hidden away under a sub-heading of literature. Nevertheless, developments from the 1980s onwards; notably the focus on individual stories in microhistory, and the growing interest of social historians in how individuals fashion identity within the social constraints imposed upon them by their gender, race, religion, income, or occupation, have allowed for a resurgence of biography. Some social historians now embrace the idea of multiple selves, seeing this not as a problem but rather as a key to deconstructing the workings of prescriptive roles upon a person. This is the methodology currently favoured by researchers looking at women in the public sphere, and is known as the New Biography.[3]

In spite of the rhetorical division of the spheres along gender lines, many women did enter the public sphere in the nineteenth century in France, out of necessity or desire. To do so, they had to carefully negotiate the strict gender norms set out by society, to avoid being accused of transgressing decency. Although all those in the public eye had to present a legible persona,[4] for women in the nineteenth century the personae available to them were strictly limited. The New Biography therefore provides a useful set of tools with which to read the personae constructed by and about the comtesse de Ségur throughout her public life. Ségur, like many of the women represented in the New Biography, acceded to professional opportunities through her insistence upon her respectable domesticity. However, the majority of New Biographies have focused upon women who were in some way subversive. The comtesse de Ségur is an unusual choice because she was a deeply committed Catholic, and so belonged to a community that believed in the importance of self-abnegation, particularly for women.[5] This chapter argues that it is precisely because of how she combined her faith and conservatism with her ambitions as a writer that Ségur is an important subject for such a study, because of the questions she raises about religion, gender, and the self in exemplary life stories.

Biographies as sources

The selves which Madame de Ségur fashioned must be considered in conjunction with the normative role which such life stories were supposed to perform in this period. Her books but also her 'real' biographical life were to reinforce each other, to present a 'model' life. The illusion that this was her 'real' life functioned to underline the message that this was a model of behaviour intended for the reader to imitate. Alongside her own self-fashioning we find biographies of the comtesse by her sons and daughters, which fitted into a wider biographical project of the Ségur family that they were constructing. They all worked hard to ensure the continuation of the image of the comtesse de Ségur as a devoted grandmother surrounded by her grandchildren, and matriarch of a Catholic dynasty. Cécile Dauphin and Philippe Lejeune suggest that family biographies obey several of the rules of autobiography, because of the close involvement of the author in the subject they are writing about. The authors identify themselves as a member of the family, and alert the reader to the fact that this is a history not of *a* family but of *their* family. As such, their interest lies less in literary concerns, more in writing the family identity as they wish it to be preserved.[6] In the dedication quoted at the beginning of this chapter, the comtesse boldly announced that she was exposing the name of the comtesse de Ségur, née Rostopchine, to public censure. Her use of the impersonal 'the', rather than referring to them as 'my' names emphasises that first and foremost they were the names of her father and her husband. Family honour was at stake. This was the critical filter through which all information about the comtesse in the public domain has passed.

The idea that the life stories of great men and women should inspire others has been central to the genre of biography. In Christian culture, biography, in the form of the lives of saints, plays an important part in religious instruction. As a Catholic celebrity, the comtesse de Ségur's life was swiftly put into print to inspire others following her death. Exemplary versions of her life were enshrined in a series of biographies written by her sons and daughters. Their motivations for preserving the family memory were primarily religious.[7] Her daughter Olga also produced two volumes of edited correspondence.[8] These texts form the bulk of the information on the comtesse de Ségur's private life. They were also the major point of reference for subsequent biographers, and so were crucial in the construction of the 'official' image of her. A great deal (though by no means all) of the source material on the comtesse de Ségur has passed through this second, ideological filter. According to the family ideal, the comtesse de Ségur's life and vocation can be summed up in the phrase 'God and my children', the legend which she had inscribed on her tombstone.[9] They emphasised her role as an exemplary Catholic grandmother, who turned to writing almost accidentally, as an extension of her maternal role. The second concern of these family biographies, beyond sanctifying their mother's life, was to glorify the new Catholic generation of the Ségur family.

As the book trade expanded from 1830 onwards, Church authorities and moralists concurred that real-life examples of Catholic lives were far more appropriate than any other form of writing (notably novels or fairy tales). The Jesuit Father Marquigny explained, 'the imaginary adventures of these exceptional people [characters in novels] which are designed to arouse our enthusiasm, do not have the penetrating influence of authentic deeds'.[10] The Catholic Church recognised the missionary potential of private spiritual writings, and many ecclesiastics or Catholic editors published the so-called 'secret' diaries of pious women.[11] The lives of saints such as St François de Sales, or the *Imitation of Jesus Christ* were religious best-sellers in the nineteenth century,[12] which also saw the publication of a whole series of contemporary diaries, letters, and biographies. Faced with what many Catholics saw as the threat of modernisation, these life stories were to provide not just a blueprint for the life of the modern Christian but a precious weapon in the struggle against anti-clericalism and dechristianisation. It was important to make private piety public.

However, writing an exemplary life of a woman who had been a writer and revelled in finding her own voice was no easy task, and gave rise to contradictions. The pious concerns of her family created a dualistic image of the comtesse, for there was always tension between the holy image they sought to perpetuate and the myriad selves which the comtesse had projected, consciously or not, through the medium of her books and writings. Paradoxically for somebody who traded so heavily on a loving grandmother image, her books feature countless examples of older women prone to losing their temper and administering brutal beatings to little children. While the comtesse always identified herself with the gentle, Catholic grandmother figures in her books, she became indissolubly associated in the popular imagination with the excessive violence of her other female characters. The content of these tales that 'grandma' was reading to the nation's children was often far from reassuring. Ségur had a vivid imagination, and delighted in encouraging children's interest in blood and gore. This dualistic image was further exacerbated by her father's reputation, and her exotic status as émigrée from Russia, a land considered 'barbarous' in the French imagination. The suspicion that there was a darker side to the nation's grandmother dogged her career from the very outset.

The volume and variety of material Ségur produced as a writer allows the study in detail the self-fashioning of a Catholic woman; in other words of a woman who was supposed to have annihilated all notion of self. Coupled with the fact that she was a celebrity, prompting interest from a range of critics, this gives rise to a number of contradictory narratives to the official exemplary grandmother image that she and her family emphasised. This is the first 'New Biography' of such a woman. It allows us to nuance, or at least add flesh to the symbols of maternity, silence, suffering, and self-abnegation that formed the ideal of religious womanhood in this period.[13]

Childhood

> It is singular how it is so easy to forget for many years something that is so clearly remembered after.[14]

So mused little Sophie on the forgetting and remembering of her sad childhood in *Les vacances*. Scholars have highlighted the poignancy of this idea in the mouth of Sophie, the comtesse's semi-autobiographical character.[15] Sophie is the heroine of her Fleurville trilogy, which comprises *Petites filles modèles* (1858), *Les malheurs de Sophie* (1858), and *Les vacances* (1859). Ségur announced that these works were based upon real life, the 'model' real life of her family in Normandy which she was recording for the profit of her readership. Privately she admitted that they were also in part based upon her own childhood, and that she was using literature to confront ghosts from the past. She was obliged by the conventions of the day to mask her reminiscences in a subtle play of fiction and memory. In the prudish mid-century, the idea that a pious woman aristocrat would write her childhood memories with anything other than exemplary aims in mind was unthinkable. Michelle Perrot emphasises that the notion of an individual self was contrary to the values of this aristocratic society, which placed the family before the individual, and preached Catholic self-abnegation to its women.[16] Memoirs were written by great men, or perhaps society women, and recorded important events. Writing about something as banal as one's childhood on the other hand was a dubious practice that had been invented by Rousseau, a hate figure in *bien-pensant* circles. That George Sand had recently turned her hand to remembering her childhood no doubt confirmed the disreputability of the undertaking. Moreover, the comtesse felt that her childhood had been anything but exemplary. She appears to have used her own experiences to try to warn a new generation not to resort to corporal punishment. This was not an appropriate subject in the century that particularly idealised the relationship between mothers and children. Jules Vallès's *L'enfant* (1879) would cause outrage because of its frank portrayal of his mother's violent methods of disciplining her son.[17] Even in a fictional guise the violence in her books caused problems with the censor for the comtesse.[18] However, the heavy restrictions upon writing her story did not prevent the comtesse from weaving a web of childhood past and present in order to revisit her own memories, and in so doing fashion her identity as an author with a specific agenda on childcare.

It is often noted that many children's authors experienced traumatic childhoods. Madame de Ségur was no exception.[19] The future comtesse de Ségur, née Sophie Rostopchine,[20] was born into the highest ranks of the Russian aristocracy in 1799. Her godfather was Tsar Paul I. The comte Rostopchine was a prominent figure in Russian high society. Tolstoy characterised him as a flamboyant, witty socialite, and, ultimately, the embodiment of all that was decadent and weak in Alexandrian Russia.[21] Thanks to Rostopchine's favour at court, the family was extravagantly rich, and owned several properties, of which the most impressive was the country estate at Voronovo, just outside Moscow. The comte Rostopchine devoted much of his wealth to embellishing this enormous palace, whose estate comprised several thousand serfs.[22] Despite such an illustrious setting, by all accounts the comtesse de Ségur's childhood was miserable.

Her daughter explained that Ségur entitled her semi-autobiographical book *Les malheurs de Sophie* (usually translated as *Sophie's Misfortunes*) with this in mind: 'the author often portrayed herself in the book. My mother's childhood was very unhappy due to the extreme rigours she underwent.'[23] The comtesse Rostopchine was a singular woman. Anecdotes of her alleged brutality abound.[24] Her daughter Sophie de Ségur's storybooks portrayed her in a deeply ambiguous manner, while the writings of her other daughter, Nathalie Narichkine, and granddaughter, Lydie Rostopchine,[25] painted her as violent, vindictive, and dangerous.

Apparently inspired by Rousseau's *Émile*, the comtesse Rostopchine felt that her children should be brought up to reject luxury or comforts of any sort, and learn how to look after themselves. She forbade her children to drink or eat anything between allocated meal times. The worst torture was thirst, particularly in summer, and the children resorted to drinking from the dog's bowl. The elder sister Nathalie recalled harsh Russian winters spent without being allowed boots, hats or gloves: 'how we managed to stay alive with the regime our mother made us follow is something I cannot understand'.[26] In contrast, in Ségur's *Les malheurs de Sophie* the guilt is projected on to the child. Madame de Réan, the mother, is portrayed as distant, and rather severe, but she is always in the right. The incident with the dog bowl for example is transformed from a survival tactic into a childish prank. To amuse her friends who are coming to celebrate her birthday, Sophie wants to set up a little tea party. When her mother refuses to give the child real tea and cakes, the girl decides to make an ersatz tea instead, using water from the dog bowl, chalk for sugar lumps, and white paint for milk. Her plan fails when the guests spit out her tea in disgust, and a fight ensues. The moral of the tale is that Sophie ought not to have disobeyed her mother. The problem that Ségur faced when disguising difficult childhood memories in the form of educational books for children becomes clear. The adult's moral perspective must prevail.

This example illustrates how problematic the Fleurville books are as a source for Ségur's childhood, but it is also fascinating to see Ségur's process of reconstructing her early life. The dedication to *Les malheurs de Sophie* announced 'these are the true stories of a little girl that grandmother knew very well when she was a child',[27] although this is also a clue for the discerning reader that the protagonist and the author are the same. Both are called Sophie, they share the same birthday, and a description of Sophie resembles a portrait painted of the author around the same age:[28] 'she had a fresh, bonny face, so gay, with very lovely grey eyes, a snub nose that was a bit big, a large mouth always ready to laugh, and blond hair that was not curled and cut short like a boy's'.[29] Biographers have therefore made extensive and often uncritical use of these stories to illustrate their accounts of Ségur's childhood. This is to do a terrible disservice to the comtesse as an author. If the tragic tale of little Sophie and her terrifying stepmother Madame Fichini have had such widespread appeal, we must also attribute this to Ségur's unerring sense of what made for good copy. The wicked stepmother Madame Fichini certainly owed a literary debt to fairy tales. So, while evidence suggests that hers was indeed a traumatic childhood, we must qualify this notion with the fact that the comtesse was also a talented storyteller with a view to selling books.

Following Philippe Lejeune's definition of what constitutes an autobiographical text, it is clear that to take Ségur's Fleurville trilogy as strictly autobiographical or realist material is a highly questionable procedure, for the Fleurville trilogy does not fulfil the conditions of the 'autobiographical pact'.[30] Her use of the form of fiction immediately excludes the comtesse's Fleurville books from being considered strictly autobiographical, and the pact she establishes with her readers is rather coy about whom these 'true stories' are about. Moreover, the books do not respect the chronology set out in the dedication to *Les malheurs de Sophie*. The trilogy is set firmly in Normandy in the 1850s, so how could grandmother have known Sophie during her childhood, when this girl is growing up in the present? Her friends are Camille and Madeleine de Malaret, who, we already know from the dedication to her first book, and also that of *Petites filles modèles*, are the comtesse's granddaughters and 'they really do exist'.[31] That these books are set in the present is further emphasised by her use of family Christian names, and thinly disguised surnames (for example, Ségur becomes Rugès), as well as place names near her home in Normandy. The comtesse de Ségur deliberately blended fiction and reality in her books. Given the subject matter of the books, it is rather surprising that she pretended to realism at all, particularly in the use of her family's names.

However, Ségur made it clear that some of this material was written about her self, and she had an important purpose in mind when doing so. Running through the Fleurville trilogy is the suggestion that beneath the veneer of even the most respectable families could lie repressed misery and violence. Most importantly, in *Petites filles modèles*, the sequel to *Malheurs*, Sophie is now an orphan, and her stepmother Madame Fichini has instigated a very brutal regime. The child is beaten mercilessly.

Madame de Ségur laid a great deal of importance on the notion that Madame Fichini was 'real'. She told her editor that he might have been shocked by Madame Fichini's brutality, but that she had based the character on a real mother. Further, she was not a stepmother but a biological mother, and Ségur had not exaggerated this woman, rather she had softened her cruelty for her readers.[32] Remarks made by a family friend, Élise Veuillot, in private correspondence with her brother Louis Veuillot, suggest that the comtesse did not conceal from her entourage that the monstrous Madame Fichini was linked in her mind to 'grandmother Rostophine'. Élise Veuillot reported a row that had taken place between herself, the comtesse, and the comtesse's daughter, Olga, over how to discipline Olga's unruly son Jacques. The comtesse warned Olga that, if she continued to beat her son, then 'Olga will be like grandmother Rostopchine, Madame Fichini will be her portrait, she will have her book'.[33] Not only did the comtesse use her mother as a kind of ogress to frighten her children with but she also threatened her family with literary retribution if they did not stop spanking their children. Such impassioned interference caused further ructions between parents or guardians and their charges. Élise complained that her nieces were disobedient because they knew that the comtesse would rush to their defence. The harmonious scene set out in the comtesse de Ségur's dedication, depicting herself telling stories to her granddaughters Camille and Madeleine de Malaret, was not so straightforward in the privacy of the family home. Élise Veuillot observed: 'maman Ségur is writing the sequel to *Petites filles modèles* that Monsieur de Malaret curses, swearing that the book will mean he will still have to spank his girls at fifteen years old'.[34] The incident also indicates the emotional charge invested in her memories that she committed to paper. By setting her own memories in the present, the comtesse emphasised that violence against children continued.

The comtesse was also engaging with the wider debate on child protection that was heating up in the latter half of the century.[35] 'Mme de Ségur is of a more modern school', wrote the journalist Louis Veuillot in his review of *Petites filles modèles* for his Catholic newspaper *L'univers*; 'she even displays a certain irritation with parents that use corporal punishment'. Veuillot was also a close family friend (and kept well informed by his sister), and he hinted that this hatred of corporal punishment stemmed from her own experiences as a child: 'in truth I do not know how education was directed in the Rostopchine household; but the switch must have played a role . . . here is the proof that it does not repress the passion and beauty of the mind. Throughout the book, one can see the author.'[36] For the journalist, the comtesse was in fact living proof of the efficacy of corporal punishment. The practice was still common in nineteenth-century France. It was considered acceptable to spank a disobedient child, or beat them with a switch.[37] However, attitudes towards child rearing were slowly changing, following the ideas of Rousseau, who advocated a more rational approach to discipline. The republican Ernest Legouvé argued in 1867 that corporal punishment belonged to an earlier, more barbaric age, that of the discredited *ancien régime*.[38] Two years later, the liberal Bishop Dupanloup condemned corporal punishment, saying that it bred rebellion against authority.[39] Anti-clerical polemics denounced the violent treatment of children by Jesuits, and their allegedly perverse love of spanking little boys – forcing the order to modify its regulations in 1858, although corporal punishment remained permissible.[40] Similarly, the Christian Brothers' manuals advised against beating children, but the practice evidently continued and in 1856 parents of nine novices withdrew them from classes after accusations of mistreatment.[41] Veuillot became embroiled in debates in the late 1860s over whether corporal punishment should be used in schools. He energetically insisted that to spare the rod was to spoil the child. It was only at the very end of the century that the State began to intervene in the family. Protective legislation to remove children from brutal parents was enacted 1889 and 1898, although parents still had to the right to lock their children up in correctional institutions if they saw fit.[42] The comtesse was steadfastly on the reforming side.

In light of the terrible family dramas that play out in her Fleurville books, it is difficult to reconstruct an idea of the comtesse's relationship with her father. Certainly, the father in *Les malheurs de Sophie* is perpetually absent, before being swiftly killed off in *Petites filles modèles*. However, absent fathers were normal in the nineteenth century, indeed over the course of the century they became more and more distant from the home.[43] It has not escaped modern biographers' attention that one scene where Madame Fichini is horsewhipped by her husband is suggestive of feudal society, whereby the master of the house was perfectly within his right to use the rod to punish his servants, children, and wife.[44] Travellers' anecdotes revelled in describing the brutality of Russian feudalism, which became notorious in the Western European imagination. However, there is no indication that the comtesse was writing about scenes which had taken place within her own family. Her sister Nathalie Narichkine merely noted in passing that, while his children were desperately drinking from the dog's bowl, Rostopchine was very busy, looking after his horses.[45]

The General Rostopchine was a charismatic figure. His children appear to have worshipped him as a hero, but also as a fond father when he was around. Olga describes how her mother had 'the cult of memory', especially for her father.[46] 'Our childhood was spent listening avidly to moving tales of the governor general of Moscow, the great patriot'.[47] General Rostopchine wrote affectionately about his daughters, describing how 'Sophalette, with her constitution like a sturdy countrywoman, is our jester. She is very intelligent and loves making up little stories that nobody can understand.'[48] The tone of General Rostopchine's letter was that of a proud, indulgent father. He described the young Sophie Rostopchine as talented, funny, and afflicted, like him, with a short temper. He greatly respected his daughter's early talent for storytelling, and encouraged her to pursue her studies.[49] Hers was a family in which learning was respected and encouraged. The young Sophie spoke reverently of her mother as a 'learned lady', for the comtesse Rostopchine had produced several religious treatises. They received an extensive, Western European education, as her mother was steeped in the philosophers of the Enlightenment, while her father apparently had been greatly impressed by Madame de Genlis. Their governesses were usually English.[50] Sophie Rostopchine spoke four languages fluently.

Religious questions and conversions were central to her family's story. The Rostopchine family situation became complicated once the comtesse Rostopchine converted to Catholicism, and began to keep company with Jesuit émigrés.[51] Biographies disagree as to when was the exact year of her conversion, but it was at some point during the Napoleonic Wars, when France and all things French were fast falling out of favour in Russia. She kept her new faith secret for many years, for this bold move threatened to cause the breakdown of her marriage. Once made public it caused a huge rift within the family.[52] Rostopchine, who had embraced the cause of Russian nationalism, was appalled to discover his wife was willing to renounce her native religion. She was a determined woman, however, and preferred to risk letting her marriage founder rather than compromise her new-found faith. Henceforth the comtesse Rostopchine's aim was to save her family's souls no matter what the personal cost. Nathalie described how their mother bored the children silly with her pious books, refusing to read them anything else.[53] The only one of her progeny she succeeded in convincing to renounce their Orthodox faith was Sophie, although she apparently also managed a deathbed conversion for her youngest daughter, Lise. The comtesse Rostopchine became close to the counter-revolutionary Catholicism emerging in nineteenth-century Europe. She and her sisters attended the salon of the seminal Catholic thinker Joseph de Maistre in St Petersburg, which he immortalised in *Les soirées de Saint Petersbourg*. Nathalie Narichkine underlined the families' closeness, recalling how Maistre's son Rodolphe had asked for Sophie Rostopchine's hand in marriage[54]. She was too young, however. These were the first in a series of conversion narratives that the Ségur family biographies delighted in telling.

Exile

The 1812 war against the invading Napoleonic Army was to change everything. Under General Rostopchine's governorship Moscow had been burned to prevent it falling into Napoleon's hands.[55] In the bitter aftermath the family's star fell. Rostopchine went into self-imposed exile in 1816, taking water cures in German spa towns. He wrote wistfully to his daughter of Moscow, 'that superb city that gave me a little celebrity, a lot of bad blood, and cost me my health'.[56] He and his family moved to Restoration France in 1817. The comte Rostopchine was a celebrity in Europe in this period, as one of Napoleon's most colourful foes, and the family was received in Paris with great interest – he complained of being an object of curiosity, like 'a sea monster or an elephant'.[57] The General's notoriety was to inform public (and private) perceptions of his daughter. General Philippe de Ségur, one of Napoleon's generals in the 1812 campaign, spoke highly of him as 'a good husband and excellent father', commenting on his cultivated wit and the pleasure of his company; 'however, like some of his compatriots, he combines modern civilisation with the energy of antiquity'.[58] In the popular press he was an ogre, a barbarous arsonist who was descended from the fearsome Eastern despot, Genghis Khan. He had encouraged this reputation, and cultivated the family legend that the line had been founded in the sixteenth century by Boris Rostopcha, a Crimean who moved to the Russian court, and claimed to be a descendant of the great Mongol conqueror.[59] While he elicited admiration as the man who had successfully resisted Napoleon, the name Rostopchine had a distinct whiff of dangerous exoticism.

Sophie Rostopchine never returned to Russia. Once the family had moved to Paris, her mother engineered with Madame Swetchine (another Russian émigrée converted to Catholicism) a French Catholic match for her daughter. This was imperative, for in converting to Catholicism she had compromised her chances of finding a Russian suitor. She was effectively in religious exile. By a strange twist of fate, she married a nephew of the General Philippe de Ségur. Sophie Rostopchine was wedded to Eugène, comte de Ségur, on 14 July 1819, by the cardinal de la Luzerne in his private chapel.[60] The bride brought an enormous 300,000 francs dowry.[61] When the Rostopchine family returned to Russia in 1823, Sophie remained. This exile would be permanent, and she would never return to her country of origin even to visit. However, owing to her father's immense fortune, her exile was not ignominious. She had married into one of the great noble families of France.

Marriage and motherhood

In comparison with the great number of pages in the family biographies devoted to the comtesse's life as a mother, they have little to say on her married life. The Chanoine Cordonnier's study of her life as an exemplary Catholic admitted, 'she is more easily represented as a mother than as a wife'.[62] Mgr de Ségur's biography referred briefly to 'the liberal milieu, to say the least, in which she had found herself following her marriage'.[63] The number of less sympathetic sources who refer to the marital discord, and the silence of family and subsequent *bien-pensant* biographers on the subject, would suggest that this was not a happy marriage. Or, at least, it did not remain happy. It had initially been a fertile union, producing a total of eight children of whom seven survived. This would indicate that the spouses had been attracted to each other, at least in the 1820s when the first seven were conceived. Overall, the problem when trying to reconstruct the comtesse's early years as a wife is that the bulk of documents have been edited by her descendants, who were keen to paint a picture of the Ségurs as a Catholic family. The comte Eugène de Ségur was a liberal, even a libertine, and remained impervious to attempts to convert him to the extreme new form of Catholicism the rest of his brood were to adopt. He features little in their biographies; Anatole de Ségur happily donated papers to the Bibliothèque Nationale that cast the comte and his relatives as venal; while the comtesse's books ruthlessly kill off or punish husbands and other men who do not conform to the Catholic model. Most of her writing dates from after the collapse of the marriage, and following her conversion to Catholicism, so it is far from positive. We may readily agree with Cordonnier that Ségur's identity as mother and matriarch of the Ségur brood eclipses that of her identity as a wife.

Eugène de Ségur came from the less successful branch of the Ségur family,[64] which was more or less ostracised by Parisian society by 1819 owing to the father's suicide, widely believed to have been precipitated by his wife's infidelities. The new bride's dowry was to provide much-needed funds for repairing the damage. Their lack of finances was fairly common amongst the aristocracy of the nineteenth century, who had seen their lands confiscated and their privileges revoked during the revolution. Still, this marriage of necessity bucked the trend in the social elite of the nineteenth century, described by Margaret Darrow, whereby the groom was often older, took greater initiative in choosing his bride, and assumed a more dominant role in the marriage generally.[65] The Ségur marriage had been arranged by the bride's family, and the comte was barely older than his future wife. The large discrepancy in wealth meant that she considered some of their assets to be rightfully hers. Most notably their large country estate, Les Nouettes, in Aube (Orne), Lower Normandy, had been a wedding gift from Rostopchine to his daughter.

The couple lived most of the year in Paris, established at 91 rue de Grenelle, in the heart of the faubourg Saint Germain. This address in what was known as *le faubourg* signalled that the Ségurs belonged to the exclusive upper echelons of the French nobility.[66] Between 1820 and 1835, the couple produced Gaston (b. 1820), Renaud (b. 1821, d. 1822), Anatole (b. 1823), Edgar (b. 1825), Nathalie (b. 1827), then twins Henriette and Sabine (b. 1829), and finally Olga (b. 1835). Theirs was an unusually large family for the *faubourg*. Although there were examples of large families in the upper aristocracy, the norm was to have around four children. This was a marked increase from the eighteenth century, when such women rarely had more than two children.[67] The comtesse d'Armaillé recalled how their grandmother, the comtesse Octave de Ségur, gave fashionable children's tea parties, and listed the illustrious guests and their offspring who graced them with their presence, 'then a troop of children from the faubourg Saint-Germain. They were Eugène de Ségur's.'[68] Her caustic tone suggested that to arrive surrounded by a bevy of children was hardly elegant.

Motherhood dominated over thirty years of the comtesse de Ségur's adult life. Between the ages of twenty-one and fifty-five she was either pregnant, nursing, or overseeing the children's upbringing. Nineteenth-century noblewomen were much more involved in their children's lives than in previous centuries. Motherhood was central to their identity and status. Later, in her books, Ségur would castigate any mother who rejected the joys of mothering for the superficialities of society. Women's lives therefore increasingly revolved around their children, and this altered the face of feminine sociability. The comtesse de Boigne referred to children as 'the tyrants' of Restoration salons.[69] The comtesse d'Armaillé described the social whirl which surrounded noble children: 'it was the done thing to amuse children and organise gatherings; a relic from the fashion at the court of Louis XVI and the era of Berquin. Every winter there would be put on for us little balls and little shows at our friends' parents' houses.' The comtesse d'Armaillé noted however that the practice fell out of fashion, as such events tired the children out too much and were hard work.[70] Being an elegant, but also devoted, mother of eight children in the faubourg Saint Germain was no easy task. When Ségur began to write books, she wrote for children, on the basis of her authority as a mother, who knew and loved children. Family biographies emphasised that she was a devoted mother, who loved children, almost to a fault.

Motherhood also meant the physical reality of seven pregnancies. By the time Madame de Ségur gave birth to her final child she was aged thirty-six, and it left her with difficulties walking, speaking, and subject to migraines for a further period of ten years. Olga remembered 'our poor mother, whey-faced, her eyes dull, her forehead bathed in a cold sweat, her face distorted by suffering! She could barely utter a word, in spite of her courage.'[71] Portraits of the comtesse trace the effects of illness. A painting of the comtesse in her youth, by Oreste Kiprensky in 1823, depicted a lively young woman, with large blue eyes, high cheekbones, and dark blonde hair curled in ringlets framing her face. Her daughter described her as tall and slender.[72] Her eldest son Gaston was a talented artist, and painted many pictures of his family. In portraits of his mother he always gave her a simpering look, possibly meant to convey maternal love, or emphasise her tenderness. The eyes seem more hooded, and contrast starkly with the alert expression that Kiprensky saw earlier. A drawing of the comtesse by Achille Deveria from the 1830s portrayed her reclining in a chair – almost slumped – looking into the middle distance in a romantic, melancholy pose. When Gaston painted her in the same period, her shoulders are hunched, and wrapped in a voluminous shawl, indicators of her ill-health. The family biographies abound in descriptions of how these repeated births and the strains of looking after such a large family caused their mother great suffering. They emphasised how Ségur struggled on, sacrificing her health to them as a sign of her great devotion to her maternal duties. The comtesse proudly told her daughter how during seven births she had not cried out once.[73] Hazel Mills has shown how in nineteenth-century Catholic writings the obsession with motherhood surpassed even that with virginity. The sufferings of motherhood expiated the sins of Eve, and the chaste, devoted mother was the new paragon of feminine virtue. Above all, she suffered in silence, and spoke very little.[74]

As to the relationship between the comte Eugène and the comtesse Sophie de Ségur, the family papers concerning this marriage suggest it was beset with problems, hinging on the question of money. Long reams of correspondence detail the sorry tale of the loss of her dowry, after the Moscow bank it was held in went bankrupt in 1826.[75] Eugène entreated his grandfather, who had been ambassador to Russia in Catherine the Great's reign, to write to the Tsar. Meanwhile the comtesse tried to persuade her family to give her money, constantly reiterating her need as mother of a steadily growing family. She pleaded with her brother, saying she could not afford to be in Paris with her husband, and so was stranded in their country residence, on her own with five children.[76] Most published memoirs and family correspondence cast the comtesse as the victim in this situation. Although Eugène's grandfather reassured the comtesse that 'we have lost the dowry, but kept the treasure', the comtesse d'Armaillé noted that his kindness contrasted greatly with the 'morose' response of her husband and mother-in-law.[77] This is confirmed by a letter from Sophie de Ségur's mother-in-law, Madame Octave de Ségur, complaining to her son about the Russian family's dissolute behaviour, and how they were spending what she considered to be Eugène's money.[78] According to the liquidation of Eugène de Ségur's estate, the Rostopchine family paid the lost dowry almost in full, Sophie de Ségur sold all her diamonds, whereas Madame Octave de Ségur never paid them the sum promised in the couple's wedding contract.[79]

The comtesse certainly worked hard to encourage this interpretation of her marriage as one of financial discord in which she was the victim. She wrote to her family in Russia repeatedly to complain about her husband's behaviour. Her sister Nathalie noted, 'I do not think that Eugène is as mean as Sophie portrays him; he is avaricious, to be sure, but he is an exemplary father. He loved his wife as no other husband has done.' After visiting them in 1838, Nathalie changed her mind, accusing Eugène at one point of cutting his wife off financially in an attempt to force the Rostopchine family to send more money.[80] Their marriage was, by the 1830s, in evident trouble, and by 1854 they were living virtually estranged, as divorce was illegal. The comtesse Rostopchine repeatedly wrote to her daughter in this year, advising her at least to try talking to Eugène.[81]

The year 1854, one year prior to her debut as an author, proved pivotal. In November 1854 the comte de Ségur proposed to sell the Normandy chateau, a property Madame de Ségur considered to be her own. She was furious: 'it is rather indelicate to sell in spite of my opposition, in spite of that of your brothers and sisters, an estate that is mine, that my father gave to me'.[82] The French civil code cared little for her opposition, or that of his children. All the legal power rested in Eugène's hands. However, the property was not sold. Perhaps the comtesse's indignant refusal to even speak to her husband any more worked. A few years later, during a visit to her eldest daughter's new home in London in 1856, the comtesse took great interest in how the English system worked: 'women reign over their homes and can transmit titles and peerages along with their fortune to children'.[83] These problems concerning money and power certainly appear to have marked the comtesse. This was partly what inspired her to try to find professional work, and so win herself a measure of independence from her husband. Once she had reached a position of authority as a successful author, the comtesse tried to help young women in distress on several occasions. In one instance she worried about protecting a young woman translator from 'paternal fury'.[84] She was only too aware of women's vulnerable legal position.

Society gossip portrayed them as an odd couple. Eugène de Ségur was a handsome, highborn aristocrat, but disadvantaged by his parents' behaviour and lack of money, while Sophie de Ségur was a rich foreigner, reputed to have an uncontrollable temper. He was known to have mistresses, and there were rumours of terrific arguments. The comtesse d'Armaillé recalled how on one occasion Madame de Ségur arrived at their house seething with rage, with her thirteen-year-old son Edgar in tow. She refused to let them take him into another room, 'I want the child to hear us', and then went on to detail Eugène's indiscretions with governesses and chambermaids.[85] Her behaviour scandalised the family, and went against all the advice to women in conduct manuals, which was to suffer such sorrows in silence.[86] Further, her values did not seem to fit with those of the Ségur family, and served to irritate her husband. The preface to the comtesse d'Armaillé's memoirs, written by her granddaughter, depicted d'Armaillé as a rather cold, distant woman, who retained an aristocratic distance from her offspring: 'she never kissed me, that was not the done thing, she would just point at my little chair with her knitting needle: "sit there!" . . . Her rule was never to talk down to children. She always spoke to me as if I was twenty years old.'[87] D'Armaillé's memoirs suggested that the comtesse de Ségur did not conform to the family's conception of how one ought to behave: 'she remained rather lively and careless in her remarks; ill at ease with her mother-in-law and jealous of her husband'.[88] Madame de Ségur on the other hand ridiculed the aristocratic manners the Ségur family prized. Her short story *On ne prend pas les mouches avec du vinaigre* (1865) suggested that keeping children at a distance according to the aristocratic ideal was cruel. Her books for children laid great emphasis on emotional declarations of joy, friendship, and love.

Olga de Pitray described her father as distanced from the family. This was the accepted norm in the century that exalted the mother's supremacy over the hearth. The role of the father was fixed in the public sphere, meaning that he was much less involved in his children's upbringing. Thus, while Eugène de Ségur possessed the authority to send his sons to boarding school against his wife's will, he played very little part in the daily education of his children. Naturally, then, the children's behaviour often resembled that of their mother. This served to alienate the comte from the family circle: 'we were all, like him [Gaston] given to "joyous laughter" (we got this from our mother). My father, although he liked to have fun, was not one for "joyous laughter", which invariably would irritate him and make him frown.'[89] This tendency for Eugène de Ségur to feel isolated from his wife and their offspring became greatly exaggerated once she and the younger generation rediscovered Catholicism, and Gaston de Ségur moved to assume the headship of the family.[90]

Like many of her (not so *bien-pensant*) contemporaries, Madame de Ségur's view of marriage was rather jaded. Patricia Mainardi's cultural history of marriage lays the blame squarely on legal changes that had taken place during the revolutionary period, which were then further exacerbated by the abolition of divorce in 1816.[91] However, unlike the docile wives in conduct manuals, Ségur used her books to make her displeasure clear. Following her husband's death in 1863, she set to writing *L'auberge de l'ange gardien*. This novel featured several romantic marriages 'of inclination', but also the General Dourakine, who declares that he had been married once, and would have given anything to be unmarried one year later. When her granddaughter Camille de Malaret made a disastrous match with a man who badly abused her, the comtesse's low opinion of men and marriage was confirmed. She unleashed a torrent of vitriol in a letter to console Madeleine de Malaret, Camille's sister. The force of her feeling was eloquently expressed in language most unbecoming for a lady, particularly the grandmother storyteller writing to her granddaughter, otherwise known as one of the *Petites filles modèles*: 'down with husbands; these nasty creatures were created by the good Lord to exercise women's patience and to ensure that their [women's] entry into heaven ... is all the more assured! ... only one tenth ascend to heaven (I am referring to men). The rascals! They roundly deserve their fate.'[92]

Foreigner

The comtesse was a Russian living in France, a foreigner. During the Crimean War, 1854–56, the press and satirists were filled with anti-Russian sentiment. One caricature by Albert Adam depicted cossacks and tartars as wild beasts, captured by the French army and caged in the zoo, while the cartoonist Daumier invented the Russian General Oursikoff (from the French 'ours' meaning bear), a buffoon who got himself into all sorts of ridiculous situations. Although Russians in Paris generally enjoyed good relations with the French, these images permeate descriptions of the comtesse – as they blended with those of her father.[93] Her fictional General Dourakine, a Russian soldier from the Crimean War, suggests that the comtesse was acutely aware of this view of her fatherland and father – with his name meaning 'stupid' and his clownish antics he bears a distinct resemblance to Oursikoff. Critics were not slow to associate Dourakine with her father, the General Rostopchine.

According to local legend in Normandy, the comtesse de Ségur was considered an eccentric, colourful figure. Jean de la Varende, novelist and 'chronicler of the rustic nobility',[94] collected gossip about the comtesse from his uncle: 'a great she-devil who walked around in boots and who had a great yellow face like a real cossack', who was reputed to have 'stormed out of a Church crying "Vive Sebastopol!" during the Crimean war, dragging a string of children behind her'.[95] La Varende then immortalised her in a novel, *La centaure de Dieu* (1938). The comtesse appears as a tall, savage but warm-hearted foreigner dressed in bright yellow and purple: 'she spoke very quickly, multiplying and rolling her Rs, in a deep voice'. He portrayed the Ségurs' marital discord as something of a local joke, like the comtesse's resulting furies: 'she caused amusement with her outlandish tempers, which reverberated round the house and gardens'. The reputation of General Rostopchine's daughter preceded her, Varende suggested. One society host was alleged to have joked 'hide the matches!' before she came to visit.[96]

The comtesse, along with family and friends, also cultivated the Rostopchine family legend. She also wrote two fictions set in Russia, in which, rather paradoxically one might have thought, she portrayed her native country as a barbaric and dangerous place. Similarly, the family excused the comtesse's legendary temper by blaming it on her eastern heritage.

Olga de Pitray described the comtesse as a woman who was utterly devoted to her loved ones, but merciless in equal measure to those she considered her enemies, citing the example of how, when the comtesse met one of her friend Louis Veuillot's detractors, 'she had assumed a formidable physiognomy (I was there) and her stare was worthy of the granddaughter of Genghis Khan'.[97] Veuillot affectionately called her 'the terrible tartar'. Paradoxically for a mother who tried to object publicly to corporal punishment, Ségur suffered from accusations of excess and violence – many of the family biographies felt it necessary to deny categorically that she ever raised a hand against a child or flew into rages. Gaston protested that 'the passion with which she sometimes expressed her sentiments and impressions was never more than an excessive frankness . . . *Never*, as far as my memory allows, never did I see her get angry or even impatient.'[98] Her great-granddaughter Arlette de Pitray, writing just after La Varende's *Centaure de Dieu* was published, insisted, 'never, absolutely never did her marzipan-scented hands administer anything other than caresses to the cheeks of her children and grandchildren'.[99] The family's attempts to cover over the glaring problem of their ancestor's temper made little difference. The family friend Charles Baille was so frustrated by Gaston de Ségur's biography of his mother that he felt moved to publish a corrective in his book on Mgr de Ségur, whom he accused of being 'blinded by filial love', in which he detailed examples of the comtesse's tantrums.[100] Élise Veuillot's letters mentioned the comtesse's flashing eyes. Upon learning that Élise had spanked her niece, Madame de Ségur, 'her expression became ferocious, shooting me looks that would have terrified me, if I was easily scared'.[101]

The reputed characteristics of her father, coupled with perceptions of Russian brutality, were exciting and sensational, and so hard to suppress. Olga insists that the comtesse hid from her celebrity, but that once famous her father's reputation preceded the comtesse: 'everyone knew that she was the daughter of the illustrious Rostopchine, patriotic arsonist of Moscow'.[102] Contemporary accounts described her variously as a 'yellow-faced Cossack', with 'Kalmouk' cheekbones.[103] Her predilection for portraying violence in her books served to confirm suspicions. The comtesse d'Armaillé's granddaughter recalled, how, 'while reading me chapters from the *Général Dourakine* or the *Bon petit diable*, she [the comtesse d'Armaillé] would signal her ill humour by pointing out certain excessive passages and say "scratch the Russian, you will find the bear" which made a great impression on me'.[104] This was a paraphrase of Napoleon's famous 'scratch the Russian, and you will find the tartar'.

Conversion

The most important element of the comtesse de Ségur's story told by her descendants has thus far been missing, and that is religion. This is because, once married, Madame de Ségur's Catholicism became rather lukewarm, in the 'liberal milieu' which her husband inhabited. Although the family maintained links with Madame Swetchine, who held a famous Catholic salon during the Restoration and the July Monarchy in Paris, the family biographies make no mention of her, and this society does not appear to have had any discernable religious influence on the comtesse de Ségur. All this was to change when her eldest son Gaston discovered the Catholic faith in 1838 and began a concerted mission to lead his family back into the fold, starting with his mother. Thus began the process that would transform the comtesse into the devout old lady of letters who became so beloved of the Catholic establishment in the Second Empire and beyond.

The comte and comtesse de Ségur had allowed their children to grow up with minimal religious education. When Anatole de Ségur described the 'dire' effects of the school which he and his brothers attended, he swiftly glossed over the point that, if the children had little contact with the Church during their youth, then surely the parents must also share some of the blame.[105] The family received the news of Gaston's conversion with trepidation, and his decision to enter the priesthood in 1842 with utter horror. His conversion marked a turning point not just for the comtesse but also for the history of the Ségur family as a whole. By the 1850s, thanks to his determination, Gaston had succeeded in convincing his mother and most of his siblings to turn to God.

The religion they embraced was a new strain of Catholicism that had emerged as an important force in early nineteenth-century Europe.[106] In a reversal of their father's politics, the young Ségurs subscribed to the most militant, political form of this new Catholicism, known as 'intransigent ultramontanism', which had been developed initially by thinkers like the comtesse Rostopchine's friend, Joseph de Maistre. The intransigents felt that modern, liberal European society was deeply flawed, and needed to be brought under the authority of the Pope, who would restore order and harmony. It was in this period that the Ségurs developed a close friendship with the influential journalist Louis Veuillot and his family, all fellow converts to the new Catholicism.

In 1852 Gaston de Ségur was made auditor of the rote and sent to Rome on a diplomatic mission to convince the Pope to preside over Napoleon

III's coronation ceremony. The mission failed, but he would stay in Rome in this capacity until 1856. He resigned because he had gone blind two years previously, and no longer felt able to fulfil his duties. His sojourn in Rome was crucial in confirming Gaston's ultramontanism, and he developed a firm friendship with Pius IX. It was here that Madame de Ségur's faith was also greatly strengthened. According to Gaston's account of his mother's conversion, this renewal of faith was like a rebirth. The illness which had blighted her existence for many years was miraculously cured. Upon her visiting Rome in October 1852 to April 1853, Gaston claimed that her health was completely restored. The comtesse's faith continued to deepen. In 1858 she had a chapel installed in her château, and in 1866 she joined a Franciscan tertiary order.[107] The theme of conversion runs through all the family biographies. For example, Gaston revelled in detailing his grandmother Catherine Rostopchine's great courage, like an early Christian martyr, in openly practising her faith in the teeth of state repression.[108] Meanwhile, Anatole, writing in 1882, used Gaston's conversion as an opportunity to denounce the effects of an education without God, in other words to warn about the spiritual devastation that the Third Republic's laic school laws would cause.[109]

This was the lens through which Gaston de Ségur saw his life, and, by extension, that of his mother. His siblings followed suit, to a greater and lesser extent. Their religion was the ideology that shaped the comtesse de Ségur's later years in life, and, as these were the years in which she entered the public sphere, they are by far the best documented. As stated in the introduction to this chapter, religious concerns were paramount when writing biographies, or presenting family documents to the public. All of the comtesse's correspondence that the family published dates from after her conversion, or relates to her relationship with Gaston. Anatole reprinted the letters she wrote to Gaston when she learned of his desire to enter the priesthood for example. Moreover, her books recast her childhood in the mould of Second Empire France, allowing her to introduce a Catholic morality that was missing from her early years.

Grandmotherhood

Looking back over her life at the age of sixty-nine, the comtesse de Ségur characterised it as 'my long maternal career', to which she attributed, and in particular to her son Gaston, 'the happiness of all my life as a woman.'[110] Then, aged seventy-two, she wrote the public conclusion to her second, literary career. It was inextricably linked in her mind to that of her maternal career. She brought a close to the family saga that had played out in her books by dedicating her swansong to the next generation, her great-grandchild, Camille de Malaret's newborn son. As Ségur explained, she had dedicated her first book to Camille, and so it was fitting that 'it is to you that I dedicate my last and twentieth work, which also happens to be the number of my grandchildren . . . I bless you as I end my literary career.' This second phase of her maternal career had ensured she was educating not only her own family but a much wider audience, whom she also acknowledged in this final farewell: 'pray for me when I am no longer of this world. I ask my readers to do the same.'[111] This was 'grand' motherhood, an important shift in her life hitherto lived.

Madame de Ségur took up the pen at a turning point in her life, when her children were all grown up and no longer needed her in the same way. She faced the prospect of losing her status in society, based on her biological utility as mother. She was in a rather morbid frame of mind. In March 1854 Ségur wrote to Gaston, 'what is the use of an old woman in this world; once she has become a grandmother for all her children, her role is well and truly over, she is indispensable to no-one'.[112] Her letter shows that Ségur was particularly preoccupied with the day-to-day consequences. Where would she live? What would she spend her time doing? 'One feels the futility of existence.' Growing old was a distressing process, she admitted to her daughter: 'ageing is unattractive. One has wrinkles, one worries about smelling bad'.[113] Ségur concluded, 'long live youth! Down with the old! Out of the door with the old. Their door, is the tomb.'[114] However, the ageing woman, while she was considered useless, was also granted more freedom. The same letter to Gaston in 1854 suggests her hopes. Her main concern was to be able to visit him in Rome, and 'to live as I please'. She was about to enter a new stage in her life.

Becoming a writer gave Madame de Ségur the financial independence from her husband that she so desperately wanted. There was real psychological importance in earning her own wage. When first negotiating an advance payment with her new editor, she explained, 'you are aware Sir, that in a marriage [*communauté conjugale*], the husband's purse does not always open at his wife's demand; it was this that gave me the inspiration and the will to begin writing'.[115] The phrase 'communauté conjugale' is a legal term, used in marriage contracts to designate the distribution of wealth within the union. Ségur underlined the contractual nature of her marriage, alluding to her husband's abuse of his legal hold over her. Financial reward was one of the major considerations the comtesse mentioned when she talked about her writing, and in her business dealings with her editor. Her need for financial independence should be under-stood perhaps first and foremost as a consequence of marital difficulties, which had as its corollary a negative impact upon her performance of class, motherhood, and her role as a charitable patroness. After having handed in her manuscript to Hachette, she wrote of 'my victory'.[116] This victory gave her independence: 'I went to the store on the rue Bonaparte where I bought some round-ended scissors, knives, coloured candles and balloons . . . I found it greatly amusing to buy them with the money I had earned.'[117] She could go out and buy presents for the grandchildren without having to ask permission. Michelle Perrot lists the three main venues for elite women's sociability as the Church, the tearoom, and the department store.[118] If the comtesse's husband kept a tight rein on the purse strings, this resulted in a further lack of control over her own sociability, and ability to fulfil her role as grandmother. As Chaline points out, within Catholic women's charitable organisations, one of the major areas of women's sociability, a social hierarchy can easily be traced, and the deciding factor was the ability to afford the rather steep subscription fee.[119] When Ségur asked for an advance on her payment from Hachette, she explained this was because she needed money for charitable works: 'I write to give to the poor'.[120] While this could perhaps be partly explained as an accepted formula to cover her embarrassment at having to ask for money, it was more than likely that she did use the money to give to charity. Her need for financial independence translated as a need to maintain her class identity as well. Her letters to her family had cited money as one of the main reasons why she remained in Normandy with the children, which effectively barred her from the nerve centre of aris-tocratic society.

However, it should be noted that it was Eugène de Ségur who used his connections to gain employment for his wife. His position as president of the Eastern Railway Company brought him into contact with Louis Hachette, who was negotiating the railway station kiosk monopoly, and the comte took this opportunity to suggest his wife as a possible author for their new collection.[121] As her legal representative in the eyes of the law, he was required to give his permission to let his wife sign a contract with Hachette and receive payment from them.[122] There is also no indica-tion that Eugène objected to her enjoying her new income as she pleased, when he would have been within his rights to do so. By 1859 he had given his legal endorsement of his wife's new liberty in a letter to Hachette, renouncing any claim to her earnings. A co-operative husband was imperative for any woman hoping to operate in the public sphere, to treat with institutions, or sign contracts, as fathers and husbands had absolute right of control over women. Furthermore, the comte de Ségur allowed his wife to publish books under her real name, that is to say his family's name. This was something many women authors were denied by their husbands, George Sand being the most famous case.[123]

The ability to 'live as she pleased' was to prove one of the perks of growing old. Although she found the ageing process frustrating, the comtesse learned to enjoy the new-found freedom of time and lifestyle, now that she was released from having to look after children all day every day. It allowed her to begin her writing career, an activity that evidently improved her health and self-confidence. She could also travel on her own. A woman of a certain age was permitted far greater liberty of movement, without a chaperone, as she was considered beyond scandal.[124] The comtesse spent her advanced years constantly on the move. Her role as grandmother, whose children were dispersed across France and Europe, gave the comtesse the chance to travel to London, Rome, or Brussels, not to mention the miles she covered within France, often alone. But there was more to her itinerant lifestyle than simple maternal duty, whatever she might say to her editor or daughter. Gaston wryly thanked his sister for giving him news about their mother, unreachable, as she was off, manuscript in hand, 'on the express train route from les Nouettes to Hachette'.[125] Her travel had another function; that of a professional going to work, the famous author off to negotiate contracts with her editor.

Most importantly, her freedom allowed her the time to write her books and letters. Although she loved her grandchildren, she complained when their parents left her in charge of them, as they prevented her from writing – 'I lost my best writing hours of the day'[126] – and from leading her own life: 'in spite of myself, I am counting the days that separate me from the centre of my life and activity'.[127] When Eugène de Ségur fell seriously ill in late 1859, and social conventions dictated that the comtesse should return to his side to nurse him, she was displeased at his imposition on her new life. She constantly referred in her letters to Olga to feeling imprisoned, and suffocating in their Parisian apartment. Her frustration is palpable: 'I will be forced to stay confined in Paris, because of your father.'[128] Eugène de Ségur's illness had proved trying for both of them. It meant that the couple were forced to live together once more. This was a far from ideal situation; they argued over everything. He died at his brother's house in 1863. A great obstacle had been removed, as her daughter admitted: 'it was a wonderful day for her when she found herself free to manage the house and when she could direct everything, exactly as she wished'.[129] This meant a rather austere regime, with her time entirely given over to her books, correspondence, and keeping up with the Catholic newspaper *L'univers*: 'apart from two half-hour inspections outside, I have been constantly writing constantly; it is five o'clock in the evening . . . I ate at midday and, to save time, I read my newspapers while eating.'[130] Her nephew wrote in 1864, 'my aunt is doing very well, the calm and regular life that she leads suits her in every way and her health has never been better. She has just finished a new book that she is going to deliver to M. Hachette; she has another one at the printers.'[131] In the years following her husband's death, the comtesse's literary output was suddenly increased. During his illness she had struggled to produce more than two manuscripts per year; in 1860, she had only managed one. After his death, she produced at least three, sometimes four works each year, including the laborious grandmother's Bible series.

Several of these books considered the vagaries of ageing. The bulk of analysis on Ségur's constructions of self has focused on the character Sophie. This has been to the detriment of her later books, which feature characters where Ségur mused on the absurdities of getting old.[132] In her correspondence Ségur communicated her frustration with the ridiculous predicament of being young at heart, but weighed down by her ageing body; she threatened to celebrate good news by 'demonstrat[ing] my great pleasure with leaps and bounds; fortunately the weight of my age and the weight of my body are holding back my joyous enthusiasm and keeping me on the ground as befits an old grandmother and a respectable mother'.[133] The General Dourakine expressed similar sentiments. His lumpish corporality is a constant source of irritation to him, and he curses 'my fat belly, my thick waist, my heavy legs. I have my amour-propre, as I told you previously, and in the company of a young girl and a young lady I do not wish to be taken for an invalid, a gout-ridden, decrepit old man.'[134] Ségur wickedly mocked his approaching senility, as he constantly suggests ridiculous, but good-hearted ideas. He protests, 'have I not reached the age of reason? At sixty-three years old do I not know what I am doing?'[135] (In French this joke had more piquancy, for going senile was referred to as 'tomber en enfance', which literally meant to regress to the state of early childhood prior to the age of reason.) Needless to say the comtesse was herself sixty-three years old when she wrote the book.

Writing meant more to the comtesse than simply earning money or filling her time; she attacked her task with gusto, devoting as much time and energy to it as she could. Writing had given her a voice and a new identity. Now she was famous, people listened to her, and appreciated her ideas. Louis Veuillot sang her praises in *L'univers*, her favourite newspaper. As a child she had venerated her mother's intellectual work. While motherhood earned a woman a certain status in society, writing made the comtesse into a woman of letters. She drew a clear distinction between her life before becoming a writer and after. It gave her a new confidence, and she was not going to be silenced. She wrote her first letter to Louis Veuillot, stating emphatically, 'I will speak, I want to speak'.[136] The dedication to her first book, quoted at the beginning of this chapter, characterised her former domestic existence as 'obscurity'. The idea of silence appeared in a letter to her editor in 1864, when Ségur reflected on the prospect of becoming 'mute again as I was for fifty-six or fifty-seven years'.[137] When she grew too old to write, depression took hold: 'everything tires me. Everything makes me sad. It is the *weight of age* [her italics] that is dominating me and crushing me. This is why grandmother is mute.'[138]

By the early 1870s the comtesse was seriously ill. While her daughter looked after her in Brittany, Madame de Ségur watched with horror as first the Prussians invaded, and then Paris descended into bloody civil war. Although grandmother was no longer publishing material, she was far from 'mute'. She poured out streams of invective in letters to friends and family, fulminating against the Prussian invaders, followed by the Communards and the 'wicked cowardice' of Thiers, president of the new Republic. 'Let God rid us definitively of these abominable visitors, without forgetting to sweep away the reds.'[139] She frightened her grandchildren with tales of Prussian brutality. Her dearest wish was that the monarchy would be restored under Henry V. Gaston was working fervently towards this end, publishing pamphlets, and corresponding with the pretender. He was also sheltering with his mother in Brittany, revolutionary Paris being too dangerous for a reactionary priest like Mgr de Ségur. On their return to Paris the comtesse moved in with her son. She was too feeble to join his counter-revolutionary activities, and became truly 'mute'. By 1873 she was bedridden. She died in Paris on 9 February 1874, aged seventy-five.

Her last agonising months were meticulously recorded by Gaston de Ségur, in the curious book on his mother, *Ma mère*, which he published the year following her death. Dedicated to immortalising the Christian deaths of both his sister Sabine and his mother, this short book feels incredibly intimate as he lays their pain bare on the page. No detail is spared. The famous author is reduced to a frightened old woman, 'become thin and senile'.[140] His graphic depiction of the mortification of the flesh accorded with the Baroque sensibilities of the cheap devotional literature popular in the nineteenth century.[141] Lengthy passages repeat cries of fear, pain, and Christ-like resignation in the face of death. These are what the historian Kselman calls 'textbook illustration[s] of the good death as described by clerical manuals'.[142] Gaston clutches a crucifix which has been blessed by two Popes, and then sanctified by the dying breaths of various members of the Ségur family; Lourdes water performs miraculous cures, he even uses it to drive away the demons tormenting his mother on her deathbed. The doctor admits defeat before the superior healing powers of Lourdes water. Gaston attributes healing powers to her embalmed heart. The book was originally intended only for the family, but he was convinced to publish these painful memories, in the 'hope that the Christian families where the charming and well-loved books by my good mother penetrated, will be happy to know more about her and to learn about the source from which flowed her pure and gracious waters, that nourished the spirit and hearts of their children'.[143] This book demonstrates just how far the family's religious concerns dictated the details of the comtesse's life that were released to her public. Not only the story of her life but also of her death could play an important role in winning back souls for the Catholic Church. And there was evidently a market for this version of the comtesse's life: by 1893, it had reached twelve editions.

Ségur's second public career coincided with her role as grandmother. At the age of fifty-five, she decided to renounce the obscurity of her domestic identity, and assume a new professional role as an author. In this way, she became a modern woman, who relished the independence this new-found income gave. It was only once she was an old woman, and her biological career had ended that she found the freedom of movement and time that allowed her to do this. It gave her a new, positive identity, 'this title of grandmother, gentle and sacred, my mother wore it like a crown'.[144] She dedicated her books to her numerous grandchildren, who also provided the subjects for many of her writings. Her writing process, her authorial identity, her public image, and the books themselves were all linked in her mind with her grandchildren. This new career allowed the comtesse to prolong her biological maternity beyond its natural end, extend it even, by reinventing this role: a subsequent hagiographer developed this idea of the 'bonne' maman (or 'grand' mother) he felt Ségur embodied in her later years.[145] Telling bedtime stories, and then publishing them so that many more children might benefit was much more than simply an extension of her maternal role: she became the nation's grandmother. Small children would come up to her in the street and ask to kiss her hand. Gaston described how many of her young readers were distraught when their beloved comtesse died: who, they wanted to know, would write them stories now?[146]

Conclusion

'I will speak, I want to speak.' These determined words, uttered by the woman considered by many commentators to be a paragon of Catholic maternal virtue, and written to none other than Louis Veuillot (a man who declared he had married an illiterate woman on purpose), demonstrate the strength of feeling that motivated the comtesse de Ségur to take up the pen. The comtesse depicted finding her voice as a triumph, and she expressed pleasure in her new found financial independence, as well as her fear of becoming voiceless once more. In her mind there was a clear distinction between the silence of motherhood and the voice that she found in her second, literary career. The silent suffering of motherhood had been an important achievement however, and one which the comtesse would later insist upon, for it confirmed her identity as a Christian 'femme forte'. Clearly there were tensions between her twin identities of the long-suffering, silent mother and the woman determined to speak. And yet the two were intertwined, for, if the comtesse de Ségur had such a strong desire to write, it was because she wanted her ideas on motherhood, childcare, and religious education to be heard. Moreover, this idea that writing for children and motherhood were both expressions of the same maternal instinct was entirely accepted by contemporaries. The specific knowledge that women possessed as mothers gave them valuable skills in the struggle to regenerate France as a Catholic nation. Madame de Ségur's status as a mother gave her the authority to contribute to debates on corporal punishment, education, and childcare which had much wider political import.

Madame de Ségur used her fictions as a vehicle to write stories about her 'self'. She revisited memories of childhood traumas, and wrote them into the present, creating a literary challenge to modern parents who dared to inflict corporal punishment on their children. That she disguised her autobiography in fiction suggests the problem of creating a sense of 'self' through exploring her childhood, or expressing her anger at her failed marriage, in the context of a community that did not admit such a concept. Furthermore, by rewriting her Russian memories and her identity as a mother into Second Empire France she endowed them with a religious morality that they did not originally have. As a child she had been brought up according to Enlightenment precepts, and as a mother she had brought her children up without any meaningful religious instruction. This perhaps explains the strange mixture of sympathy and censure with which the comtesse treated her younger selves. Still, we should be slightly wary of the obsession with violence and dysfunctional families in her books, or her colourful claims about her husband in her correspondence. One might be tempted to conclude that her childhood was as terrifying as that of the fictional Sophie, or her husband an utterly villainous man; if, that is, we let ourselves be seduced by the stories by Madame de Ségur, the talented author.

She obliterated her role as wife from her life stories. Catholic discourse in effect allowed for this, as the ideal mother was a chaste mother who modelled herself on the Virgin Mary. The family were happy to paint their father out of the picture, for his values were an affront to their own. In examining the roles she assumed, and the various personae that were attributed to her, we also lay bare the process of elimination attempted by her family in order to construct the image of the 'nation's grandmother'. This was all the more important because the comtesse was the matriarch of the Ségur family. Family biographies aimed to create a corporate identity. The new Ségur family was militantly Catholic, and Eugène de Ségur did not fit their story. Their conversion to the new Catholicism was the dominant narrative in the Ségur family story, and determined many of their editorial choices. However, it was impossible to impose this identity completely on the comtesse de Ségur, no matter how much she and her family attempted to do so. Her Russian identity made the comtesse a dangerous outsider to some, and an exotic figure in the eyes of her public. Ségur's legendary temper added fuel to the rumours that the 'nation's grandmother', as styled in her dedications and the family biographies, was a myth. Moreover, her denunciations of corporal punishment and child abuse of different kinds translated into an obsession with violence that haunted many of her books, and served to further exaggerate her dualistic reputation.

Notes

1 *Nouveaux contes de fées* (1857), *Œuvres*, 1:2.
2 Pierre Bourdieu, 'L'illusion biographique', *Actes de la recherche en sciences sociales*, 62/63 (1986), 69–72.

3 Margadant (ed.), *New Biography*, pp. 1–32; for a full discussion of the New Biography, see Introduction, above.

4 Carol E. Harrison, *The Bourgeois Citizen in Nineteenth-Century France. Gender, Sociability and the Uses of Emulation* (Oxford, Oxford University Press, 1999).

5 On this problem, see Phyllis Mack, 'Religion, Feminism and the Problem of Agency: Reflections on Eighteenth-Century Quakerism', *Signs*, 29 (2003), 149–177.

6 Cécile Dauphin, Pierette Lebrun-Pézerat, and Danièle Poublan, *Ces bonnes lettres. Une correspondance familiale au XIXe siècle* (Paris, Albin Michel, 1995); Philippe Lejeune, *Le pacte autobiographique* (Paris, Éditions du Seuil, 1975, 1996).

7 Mgr de Ségur wrote about his mother and sister in *Ma mère. Souvenir de sa vie et de sa sainte mort* (Paris, Tolra, 1875). The second son Anatole produced *Mgr de Ségur. Souvenirs et récit d'un frère*, 2 vols (Paris, Bray et Rétaux, 1882), *Sabine de Ségur, en religion sœur Jeanne-Françoise* (Paris, Tolra et Haton, 1870) and *Vie du comte Rostopchine. Gouverneur de Moscou en 1812* (Paris, Bray et Rétaux, 1871). The youngest daughter Olga de Pitray wrote *Mon bon Gaston, souvenirs intimes et familiers par sa sœur Olga* (Paris, Gaume, 1887), and *Ma chère maman (Comtesse de Ségur, née Rostopchine) pour faire suite à Mon bon Gaston. Souvenirs intimes et familiers* (Paris, Gaume, 1891).

8 Olga de Pitray (ed.) *Lettres de la comtesse de Ségur née Rostopchine au vicomte et à la vicomtesse de Pitray* (Paris, Hachette, 1891), and *Lettres d'une grand'mère: la comtesse de Ségur à son petit-fils Jacques de Pitray* (Paris, Librairie H. Oudin, 1898).

9 Pitray (ed.) *Lettres de la comtesse de Ségur*, avant-propos.

10 P.E. Marquigny de la Compagnie de Jésus, *Une femme forte. La comtesse d'Adelstan. Étude biographique et morale* (Paris, Jacques Lecoffre, 1873), p. 15.

11 Michelle Perrot, 'Une jeune fille du faubourg Saint Germain', in Caroline Brame, *Le journal intime de Caroline Brame*, with essays by Michelle Perrot and Georges Ribeill (Paris, Éditions Montalba, 1985), pp. 170–171.

12 Claude Savart, 'Le livre religieux', *HEF*, 3:406–407.

13 Mills, 'Negotiating the Divide'; Michaela di Giorgio, 'La bonne catholique', in Duby, Georges, and Perrot, Michelle (eds) *Histoire des femmes en occident* (Paris, Plon, 1991), 4:169–194.

14 *Œuvres*, 1:434.

15 Isabelle Nières-Chevrel, '"Les vacances" de la Comtesse de Ségur ou en finir avec le malheur de Sophie', *La revue des livres pour enfants*, 131–132 (1990).

16 Perrot, 'Une jeune fille du faubourg Saint Germain', p. 171.

17 Theodore Zeldin, *France 1848–1945* (Oxford, Oxford University Press, 1979–80), 1:336–337.

18 See Chapter 3.

19 See Ségur family biographies listed above, and Rostopchine papers, NAF 22834. Marthe de Hédouville and Marcel Orbec edited *Les Rostopchine. Une grande famille russe au XIXe siècle* (Paris, Éditions France-Empire, 1984), a translation of Rostopchine family correspondence. See also Nathalie Narichkine, née Rostopchine, *1812 Le comte Rostopchine et son temps* (Saint Petersbourg, Société R. Golicke et A. Willborg, 1912); Lydie Rostopchine, *Les Rostoptchine* ([1919] 1984).

20 I have chosen to use the French spelling of her Russian surname, as this was how the comtesse signed her books, and have adopted this policy with all the Russian names.

21 Leo Tolstoy, *War & Peace* (1865–69, this edition London, Penguin Classics, translated by Anthony Briggs, 1995).

22 Paul Loyrette and Marie-José Strich, *Sur les pas de la comtesse de Ségur. Le voyage en Russie de Louis-Gaston de Ségur* (Paris, Gallimard, 2005); Narichkine, *1812*, pp. 68–69.

23 Olga de Pitray, *Mon bon Gaston*, p. 156; see also Narichkine, *1812*.

24 Marthe de Hédouville, *La comtesse de Ségur et les siens* (Paris, Editions du Conquistador, 1953).

25 Lydie Rostoptchine, *Les Rostoptchine*.

26 Narichkine, *1812*, p. 85.

27 *Œuvres*, 1:272.

28 Portrait of Sophie Rostopchine by Salvatore Tonci, c. 1805.

29 *Œuvres*, 1:289.

30 Lejeune, *Le pacte autobiographique*.

31 *Œuvres*, 1:119.

32 Letter to Templier, 16 March 1858.

33 Letter from Élise Veuillot to Louis Veuillot, 26 July 1858, ICFV, Carton 18, Envelope G.

34 Letter from Élise Veuillot to Louis Veuillot, 23 July 1858, ICFV, Carton 18, Envelope G.

35 Jean-Claude Caron, *A l'école de la violence. Châtiments et sévices dans l'institution scolaire au XIXe siècle* (Paris, Aubier, 1999).

36 Louis Veuillot, 'Les contes de Madame de Ségur', 31 December 1859, *L'univers*.

37 Colin Heywood, *Growing Up in France: From the Ancien Régime to the Third Republic* (Cambridge, Cambridge University Press, 2007), pp. 161–165.

38 *Les pères et les enfants au XIXe siècle* (Paris, Hetzel, 1867), pp. 73–75.

39 Mgr Dupanloup, *L'enfant* (Paris, Douniol, 1869).

40 Caron, *A l'école de la violence*, pp. 97–99.

41 Sarah Curtis, *Schooling the Faithful. Religion, Schooling, and Society in Nineteenth-Century France* (De Kalb, Northern Illinois University Press, 2000), p. 100.

42 Michelle Perrot (ed.) *A History of Private Life* (Cambridge, MA, The Belknap Press of Harvard University Press, 1990), 4:157–159.

43 Hugh Cunningham and Michael Morpurgo, *The Invention of Childhood* (Radio 4 series, BBC Audiobooks 2006), episode four.

44 Ghislain de Diesbach, *La comtesse de Ségur, née Rostopchine* (Paris, Perrin, 1999), chapter one.

45 Narichkine, *1812*, p. 85.

46 Olga de Pitray, *Ma chère maman*, p. 76.

47 Olga de Pitray, *Mon bon Gaston*, p. 14.

48 Letter from the comte Rostopchine to the comte Voronzow, quoted in Ségur, *Rostopchine*, p. 126.

49 Of their correspondence only Rostopchine's replies remain, in NAF 22834, published in part, in Anatole de Ségur, *Souvenirs et causeries*.

50 Narichkine, *1812*, p. 17.

51 Mgr de Ségur, *Ma mère*, p. 6; Daniel Schlafly, 'De Joseph de Maistre à la "Bibliothèque Rose" le catholicisme chez les Rostopcin', *Cahiers du monde russe et soviétique*, 11 (1970), 93–109.

52 Narichkine, *1812*, pp. 99–100.

53 Narichkine, *1812*, p. 100.

54 *Ibid.*, pp. 115, 227–228.

55 Tolstoy, *War & Peace*; cf. the Rostopchine family's response, *L'incendie de Moscou raconté par Rostopchine et par Mme Narichkine, sa fille* (Paris, Editions Historiques Teissèdre, 2000).

56 Letter dated 1816, reprinted in Anatole de Ségur, *Souvenirs et causeries*, p. 258.

57 Quoted in Nicolas Ross, *Saint-Alexandre sur-Seine. L'église russe de Paris et ses fidèles des origines à 1917* (Paris, Cerf, 2005), p. 116.

58 Philippe de Ségur, *La campagne de Russie. Mémoires du General Cte de Ségur* (1824, this edition Paris, Nelson, c. 1910), pp. 161–162.

59 François Gasnault and Alexeï Kisselev (eds) *Paris – Moscou, un siècle d'échanges 1819–1925. Documents inédits des Archives de Paris et de Moscou* (Paris, Archives de Paris et Musées de Paris, 1999), p. 25.

60 Mgr de Ségur, *Ma mère*, pp. 18–19.

61 Wedding Contract AN Minutier Central ET/ CXVII/ 1098.

62 Charles Cordonnier, *Silhouettes familiales. La Comtesse de Ségur L'idéale Grand'mère* (Paris, Librairie J.-M. Peigues, 1931), p. 209.

63 Mgr de Ségur, *Ma mère*, p. 32.

64 Laura Kreyder, '"Défendu de grimper aux arbres" ou la généalogie chez la comtesse de Ségur', *Cahiers Robinson*, 9 (2001), 85–97.

65 Margaret H. Darrow, 'French Noblewomen and the New Domesticity', *Feminist Studies*, 5 (1979), 41–65, see p. 50.

66 Anne Martin-Fugier, *La vie élégante, ou la formation du Tout-Paris 1815–1848* (Paris, Fayard, 1990), pp. 109–117.

67 Darrow, 'French Noblewomen', pp. 48–51, and p. 60 appendix table 3.

68 Comtesse d'Armaillé (née Ségur), *Quand on savait vivre heureux (1830–1860) Souvenirs de jeunesse, publiés par la comtesse Jean de Pange* (Paris, Plon, 1934), p. 19.

69 Quoted in Darrow, 'French Noblewomen', p. 51.

70 D'Armaillé, *Quand on savait vivre heureux*, pp. 19–28.

71 Olga de Pitray, *Ma chère maman*, pp. 39–40.

72 *Ibid.*, p. 23.

73 *Ibid.*, p. 25.

74 Mills, 'Negotiating the Divide'.

75 NAF 22834, Succession Rostopchine.

76 Letter to André Rostopchine, c. 1830, NAF 22834.

77 D'Armaillé, *Quand on savait vivre heureux*, p. 194.

78 Letter to Eugène de Ségur from Madame Octave de Ségur, c. 1828, NAF 22830.

79 AN, Minutier Central ET/ CXVII/ 1301.

80 Letters from 1837–39, Hédouville (ed.) *Les Rostopchine*.

81 See letters from the comtesse Rostopchine, November 1854, NAF 22834.

82 Letter to Gaston de Ségur, c. November 1854.

83 Letter to Olga, 16 November 1856.

84 Letter to Templier, 6 March 1861.

85 D'Armaillé, *Quand on savait vivre heureux*, pp. 195–196.

86 See Patricia Mainardi, *Husbands, Wives and Lovers. Marriage and Its Discontents in Nineteenth-Century France* (New Haven, Yale University Press, 2003), pp. 65–66.

87 D'Armaillé, *Quand on savait vivre heureux*, pp. i–ii, v.

88 *Ibid.*, p. 195.

89 Olga de Pitray, *Mon bon Gaston*, p. 146.

90 See Chapter 4.

91 Mainardi, *Husbands, Wives and Lovers*.

92 Letter to Madeleine de Malaret, 4 August 1869.

93 Ross, *Saint-Alexandre sur-Seine*, pp. 124–125.

94 Jean de la Varende, *Lettres à Michel de Saint Pierre* (La Meyze, Editions Hervé-Anglard, 1983), preface by Michel Saint Pierre.

95 Jean de la Varende, *Les châteaux de Normandie* (Rouen, Henri Defontaine, 1937), pp. 70–71.

96 Jean de la Varende, *La centaure de Dieu* (Paris, Grasset, 1938), pp. 203–206.

97 Olga de Pitray, *Mon bon Gaston*, p. 106.

98 Mgr de Ségur, *Ma mère*, p. 89.

99 Arlette de Pitray, *Sophie Rostopchine, Comtesse de Ségur* (Paris, Albin Michel, 1939), p. 137.

100 Charles Baille, *Souvenirs sur Mgr de Ségur* (La Chapelle-Montligeon, Imprimerie de Notre Dame de Montligeon, 1901), pp. 8–9.

101 Letter from Élise Veuillot to Louis Veuillot, 26 July 1858, ICFV, Carton 18, Envelope G.

102 Olga de Pitray (ed.) *Lettres d'une grand'mère*, p. 9.

103 Baille, *Souvenirs sur Mgr de Ségur*; d'Armaillé, *Quand on savait vivre heureux*.

104 D'Armaillé, *Quand on savait vivre heureux*, preface.

105 Anatole de Ségur, *Mgr de Ségur*, 1: chapter one.

106 For more detailed discussion of the new Catholicism, see the Introduction and Chapter 4.

107 Mgr de Ségur, *Ma mère*, pp. 37–40.

108 *Ibid.*, pp. 14–18.

109 Anatole de Ségur, *Mgr de Ségur*, 1: chapter 1.

110 AN, Reserve 1018 Minutier Central ET/ CXVII/1361.

111 Dedication to Paul de Belot, in *Après la pluie, le beau temps*, Hachette, first edition, 1872. Camille was unhappy with this dedication and it was removed from later editions.

112 Letter to Gaston de Ségur, 15 March 1854.

113 Olga de Pitray, *Ma chère maman*, p. 91.

114 Letter to Louis Veuillot, 29 September 1859.

115 Letter to Templier, 5 February 1858.

116 1 October 1856, quoted in *La comtesse de Ségur au Château des Nouettes à Aube de 1821 à 1872*, Aube, Musée de la Comtesse de Ségur, exhibition catalogue 1996.

117 *Ibid.*, April 1857.

118 Michelle Perrot, *Femmes publiques* (Paris, Textuel, 1997), p. 40.

119 Jean-Pierre Chaline, 'Sociabilité féminine et "maternalisme", les sociétés de Charité Maternelle au XIXe siècle', in Corbin et al., *Femmes dans la cité*, pp. 69–74.

120 Letter to Templier, 5 February 1858.

121 Letter to Templier, 2 October 1855.

122 Hachette traités 1844–1865, IMEC.

123 Christine Planté, *La petite sœur de Balzac. Essai sur la femme auteur* (Paris, Seuil, 1989), pp. 30–31.

124 Perrot, *Femmes publiques*, p. 49.

125 Letter from Gaston de Ségur to Olga de Pitray, 17 December 1866.

126 Letter to Olga de Pitray, 21 November 1856.

127 Letter to Olga de Pitray, 13 May 1859.

128 Letter to Olga de Pitray, 30 September 1859.

129 Olga de Pitray, *Ma chère maman*, p. 44.

130 Letter to Élisabeth Fresneau, 15 November 1865.

131 Letter from Waldemar Fillipi to Olga Rostopchine, 5 March 1864, Hédouville, *Les Rostopchine*, p. 240.

132 With the notable exception of Beaussant's analysis of Dourakine, *Œuvres* 'Dictionary', 1:859–860.

133 Letter to Émile de Pitray, 11 November 1856.

134 *Œuvres*, 2:580.

135 *Œuvres*, 2:547.

136 Letter to Louis Veuillot, 21 August, 1856.

137 Letter to Templier, 5 June 1864.

138 Letter to her granddaughter, Henriette Fresneau, 4 May 1872.

139 Letter to Isaure, 9 January 1871, reproduced in *La comtessse de Ségur, née Rostopchine (1799–1874)*, Catalogue no. 29, Librairie Thierry Corcelle, Paris, 1999.
140 Mgr de Ségur, *Ma mère*, p. 90.
141 Thomas Kselman, *Death and the Afterlife in Modern France* (Princeton, Princeton University Press, 1993), p. 74.
142 *Ibid.*, p. 94.
143 Mgr de Ségur, *Ma mère*, preface.
144 Olga de Pitray, *Ma chère maman*, p. 2.
145 Cordonnier, *L'idéale grand'mère*, pp. 90–91.
146 Mgr de Ségur, *Ma mère*.

2

Nobles, saints, and delinquents:
constructions of childhood in the
collected works of Madame de Ségur

The child, as 'king' of the prosperous middle-class family, was a nineteenth-century phenomenon, a corollary of the rise of the notion of the separate spheres and the cult of motherhood. Bourgeois women increasingly stayed at home to look after fewer children.[1] There was a new respect for children, and this, along with increased prosperity, shrinking family sizes, and industrial advances which allowed manufacturers to satisfy the demands of a growing consumer society, was to have important consequences for children's books. The comtesse de Ségur wrote her works in the period that experts agree saw the first 'golden age' of children's literature in the Western world. Many use the date that Ségur signed her first contract with Hachette in 1855 to mark the dawn of this golden age in France.[2]

It is generally agreed that the Enlightenment marked the culmination of a process, begun in the early modern period, which altered perceptions of childhood, and the related concepts of pedagogy and literature designed specifically for children. In France, the publication of Rousseau's *Émile* (1762) is recognised as a turning point, in which the *philosophe* pithily summed up new medical and philosophical ideas on how children ought to be brought up.[3] In *Émile* he argued that children ought to be allowed to be 'children'; that childhood was an innocent, natural state different from that of adulthood. Children were not imperfect adults, nor were they sinful, they were simply lacking in knowledge. As such they had specific educational needs that were not being satisfied by the current state of books. Rousseau allowed his fictional pupil Émile to read only Defoe's *Robinson Crusoe* and Fénelon's *Télémaque*. Despite

Rousseau's reluctance to make young children read at all, his ideas inspired a generation of educationalists, such as Arnaud Berquin (1747–91), his pupil Nicholas Bouilly (1763–1842), and Madame de Genlis (1746–1831). Their books proved to be the best-sellers of the first half of the nineteenth century, a period which was to produce its own classics as well, notably Desnoyer's *Les aventures de Jean-Paul Choppart* (1834), and Madame Guizot's popular works. By 1840, *Les français peints par eux-mêmes* complained that the young were being turned into little consumers. In this age post Rousseau, a great industry had grown up to supply wealthy Parisian children with great numbers of books, plays, and toys.[4] Publishers were certainly not slow to exploit their market potential. In particular, the enterprising Hetzel commissioned famous names such as Charles Nodier and George Sand to turn their hand to writing for his collection *Magasin des enfants* in the 1840s.

Children's literature was flourishing, but, as it did so, there were new constraints being placed upon it. The Catholic authorities, fearing that they had lost their grip on children's education, because of the influence of the Enlightenment and the after-effects of the Revolution, were keen to reassert their authority over a domain they saw as rightfully theirs. From the 1830s onwards, bishops regularly issued urgent warnings of a 'poisonous wave' or 'torrent' of books that was threatening to engulf the nation, while Pope Gregory XVI spoke in 1841 of how 'philosophers, heretics, and adepts of modern impiety' aimed to 'attract and win over to their sect the uneducated, and particularly the young, and lead them to abandon the Catholic faith'.[5] Using tools such as distribution networks, episcopal endorsement of suitable books, and a monthly review of book production, the Church mounted an impressive campaign to regain control. Thus by the 1850s, the big Catholic publishing houses, led by Mame of Tours, dominated the children's market, bolstered by the 'good books' campaign and the growth of Catholic primary schooling. They lavished great attention on producing attractive packaging for their books, whilst ensuring the content remained as conservative as possible.[6] In Hetzel's absence (his involvement in the 1848 revolution forced him to leave the country), it was Louis Hachette who became one of the first lay editors in France to come any where near rivalling Catholic dominance in this sphere. Still, as Chapter 3 sets out, his censorship policy obeyed that set down by the Catholic publishers. He set up his children's collection in 1856, an offshoot of his *Bibliothèque des chemins de fer*, aiming to provide beautifully presented, illustrated storybooks to amuse children on train journeys. It was to become one of the company's biggest successes.[7] In

1860, when Hetzel returned from exile, he resurrected his *Magasin des enfants*, and began waging a passionate campaign to free French children from what he famously termed the 'leaden books whose weight crushes young children in our so-called frivolous country of France'.[8]

It has generally been agreed that the modernisation of children's literature in France should be attributed to the combined efforts of these two lay publishers.[9] Jean Glénisson has argued that it was Hetzel and his authors, especially Jules Verne and Jean Macé, who truly inaugurated the golden age of children's books in France. Glénisson refused to include Hachette's flagship author, the comtesse de Ségur, in this triumphant narrative, for, in his view, she was merely a skilled practitioner of the old, didactic 'governess' school of writing.[10] According to him, the important factors in the modernisation of children's literature were a freedom from Catholic morals and a return to fairy tales, such as Hetzel's re-edition of Perrault. This was part of a wider concern about stimulating the child's imagination. In his schema, religious efforts are dismissed as 'backward' and 'anti-modern' because of their recourse to censorship, their prescribed reading lists, and their emphasis on evangelisation over entertainment.

However, recent scholarship presents a more nuanced view. In 2005, Jan de Maeyer argued that scholars should see the modernisation process as an interaction between religious and secular publishers. He emphasised that religions in Europe were also modernising, even though this intellectual and technological process was often conceptualised by its actors as being a rejection of the society they lived in.[11] While it is true that the Catholic authorities sought to place restrictions on publishing for children and their reading practices, this does not imply that Catholic attitudes towards children's books remained unchanged and 'backward'. This chapter argues that it is unsatisfactory to suggest that Catholic authors like Madame de Ségur were not involved in the revaluation of the child which took place in the nineteenth century. On the contrary, children were one of the main targets of the religious revival, and so authors, publishers, and missionaries were intent upon communicating with them in the most effective way possible.

Catholic discourse on the child and children's books

Ideas on children were changing. The new, 'romantic' child became the dominant cultural construct of idealised childhood in the nineteenth century. Inspired by Rousseau's emphasis on children's innate goodness, and developed by writers such as Victor Hugo, the romantic child was a paragon of innocence; a blond-haired, blue-eyed angel, depicted as close to Heaven. This was a deeply sentimental view of children, popularised most effectively by the poetry of Hugo and Marceline Desbordes-Valmore.[12] It reflected changing attitudes towards how society ought to treat children, and the symbol of the innocent child was used to great effect by Hugo in his campaigns for legislation to protect and educate children. This new view of childhood is often contrasted with what is termed the conservative Catholic approach, based upon St Augustine's insistence on the need to discipline the child, born innately sinful.[13] The comtesse de Ségur's books, it has been argued, testify to the tenacity of the Augustinian 'evil child'.[14] Perhaps there is some evidence of this notion in her work, particularly in the famous *Malheurs de Sophie*, and yet, the divisions between the Catholic and romantic visions of childhood are not as distinct as is often suggested. Although politically they were diametrically opposed to the Republican Hugo and the romantics, Catholic sensibilities were also changing, and in some ways were evolving in a similar direction to those of the romantics, particularly where children were concerned.[15] There was a remarkable fascination for child visionaries, seen to be closer to God in their simple innocence.[16] Cholvy and Hilaire underlined the influence of romantic sensibilities on ultramontane piety,[17] while Ralph Gibson wrote of an 'infantilization' of ultramontane Catholicism in particular, which emphasised the need to make oneself as a child before God. This reached an apogee with the 'little flower' Thérèse de Lisieux (who also happened to be an avid reader of the comtesse de Ségur). According to Gibson, Thérèse de Lisieux's 'childish statement of an intense sense of the reciprocal love between God and man' encapsulated the transformation of French Catholicism from a religion of fear into a religion of love.[18] Since the son of the comtesse, Mgr Gaston de Ségur, was one of the principal authors who popularised the nineteenth-century taste for so-called 'childish piety',[19] it is no surprise to find that the comtesse conceptualised her ideas on the upbringing of children as both 'modern' and Catholic. For her it was based on the new theology centred upon love, and an explicit rejection of the old emphasis on fear.

Catholic ideas on children's literature were also changing. Despite expressing repugnance for popular reading, the Catholic Church nevertheless proved to be highly efficient at addressing the question of what new audiences ought to be reading. One of the most important consequences of the rapid growth in the Church's initiatives to distribute 'good books' was the development of a new critical discourse on books and reading. In order to create a nationwide network of libraries and good book missions, those involved needed to have a common reviewing system to decide which books were 'good' and why. The most enduring and influential publication to respond to this need was the *Bibliographie catholique*, established in 1841 by the 'Oeuvre des bons livres [Good books mission]', whose full title gives an idea of its ambitions: *Catholic Bibliography. Critical review of works of religion, philosophy, history, literature, education, etc, destined for the use of ecclesiastics, fathers and mothers, heads of institutions and boarding schools of both sexes, parish libraries, reading rooms, and all persons who wish to learn about good books and are concerned with their propagation.*[20] Similarly, Catholic magazines for children were also proliferating, and, again, they all included a book reviewing section.[21] According to Claude Savart's meticulous research, the majority of religious publishing output was books aimed at children (usually catechisms, but also prize books and more amusing stories).[22] In an article on primary education from 1863, the Republican Jules Simon observed that in France, as elsewhere in Europe, it was religious groups that had done the most to promote reading.[23]

When Glénisson argues that it was only secular authors who could be considered responsible for the progress of children's literature, what he is mainly objecting to is the smallmindedness of the 'black-garbed censors' of the reading committees in Catholic publishing houses, and at the *Bibliographie catholique*. Certainly the *Bibliographie catholique* devoted countless pages to dissecting the favourites of French children's literature – accusing their authors of Deism, or Protestantism, or worrying about the immorality of fairy tales. Reviewers readily admitted that concern for the moral purity of a book often outweighed their literary judgements when they selected volumes for recommendation. However, to argue that Catholics were alienated from all developments in children's writing is unhelpful. The 'good books' movement was essentially reactive in nature; it had been born out of a fear of the competition of cheap literature and novels from secular and Protestant sources, and so it followed that young readers were seen as being in mortal danger and needing protection. This reinforced the sense of their innocence, and led to a reconsideration of their specific needs as readers. Several members of the *Bibliographie catholique* committee in 1853 agreed that short stories and fictions were important for propagating good books for this group as 'it will never be possible to make them read more serious books'.[24] They went on to observe that one of the problems with 'good' books for children was that 'many of these books are ill-thought out, lacking in interest or badly written, and appear, in this way, not to demonstrate enough respect for the reader'.[25] It was precisely their desire to ensure that children read only 'good' books that led reviewers to promote new authors, disseminate books, consider such questions as the suitability of books for distinct age groups, and emphasise the need for illustrations. The Republican Hetzel's concern to reinvigorate the genre found his Catholic echo in the ferocious campaign of Louis Veuillot (an unlikely admirer of Hetzel)[26] against the terrible quality of writing that he felt undermined children's publishing.[27] Many of the reviews in *Bibliographie catholique* admitted that despite their alleged Deism, the works of authors such as Berquin and Bouilly, or the more recent Sophie Ulliac-Trémadeure, were well written and pleasing to children. The Catholic periodical *Semaine des familles* regularly recommended books published by Hetzel, while the staunchly pious *Journal des demoiselles* gave Jules Verne's books a positive review. What they all unanimously advocated was parental caution and the provision of support to authors who wrote explicitly Catholic books.

Similarly, it is not useful to situate the comtesse de Ségur outside the changes in attitudes towards the child. This presents a far too simplistic view of her oeuvre, and also ignores important shifts in Catholic sensibilities. While Madame de Ségur was not given to the syrupy idealisation of childhood innocence so characteristic of her contemporaries (such as Michelet, or Hugo – she could not stand his poems), neither did she adopt the didactic approach supposedly favoured by Catholic moralists concerned to discipline the 'evil child'. Jean-Noël Luc's analysis of education manuals written by Catholic authors concludes that ideas about young children were often contradictory, particularly in the Church. Was sinfulness innate or hereditary (a view gaining currency in scientific circles)? Were children primitive savages who needed socialising? Or were they angelic innocents?[28] The leading Catholic author Mathilde Bourdon commended Ségur for having struck this difficult balance: 'Madame de Ségur knows how to avoid both the mawkishness which certain authors (who are probably not mothers or fathers) lavish on *the little blond and pink angels* [her italics], and the austere and unadorned moral instruction that these same angels would find terribly dull.'[29] Further, the 'redemptive' child, whose innocence redeems adults who have been corrupted, so favoured by authors like Charles Dickens and Victor Hugo, is also to be found in evidence in Ségur's writings.

Ségur was very interested in how children read her books. This question of readership will be examined in greater detail in Chapter 5;

nevertheless it merits mention in this chapter as well, for Ségur's construction of her readership played an important role in how she wrote her books and how she wanted them to be produced. Ségur certainly went to great lengths to make her stories accessible to her readers. This meant taking care over her use of language, as well as the page layout and dialogue structure. Olga de Pitray recalled her mother's advice on how to write for children: 'I speak children's language as one speaks French, she told me one day; complicated words discourage children from reading them. They ask for an explanation for the first word, but they are put off by the second and will not reach the third.'[30] This often caused the comtesse problems: 'I am not always in agreement with *my corrector* [her italics] who would have children speak a language that is beyond their age.'[31] Ségur used theatre-style dialogue, where the characters' names clearly mark their speech, for, as she explained to her editor, 'the names give the action structure, give much more life to the dialogue, these *he said, she replied, he continued, he cried, she carried on* are tiresome and slow down the plot'.[32] The comtesse also made every effort to tailor her books to her young readers, pestering her editor to make sure the print was big and wide-spaced so that children could read them easily. This sometimes came into conflict with Hachette's luxurious packaging for the *Bibliothèque Rose*, which she felt hampered the young readers' ability to handle the book on their own. When sending her books to the Prince Imperial, she asked her editor not to give him volumes with gold edging on the pages: 'it is difficult and annoying to pull apart, the pages stick to one another and a child would not manage'.[33] (Conversely, she also objected to giving gold-edged books from her collection to 'poor apprentice' boys, this time because she was concerned it might spoil them by accustoming them to luxury consumer items).[34]

Above all, Ségur's work should not be pigeonholed. She wrote her books as part of a Catholic missionary drive, but equally she took great artistic pride in her writing, and she was very conscious of the need to please her market. When it came to constructing 'childhood', the comtesse approached her subject with a certain humour. Her donkey Cadichon commences his memoirs, 'I don't remember my childhood; it was probably unhappy like that of all little donkeys.'[35] She turned to her own childhood memories (in *Petites filles modèles*, *Les malheurs de Sophie*) or Charles Dickens (in *Un bon petit diable*) for inspiration. The comtesse did not wholly subscribe to the prescriptions of earlier authors such as Berquin and Madame de Genlis, who emphasised the pedagogic value of everyday life.[36] The comtesse often skipped over the humdrum details of children's upbringing in favour of the dramatic. Thus the heroine of *Histoire de Blondine, Bonne-Biche et Beau-Minon* falls into a deep sleep, and awakes aged fourteen, metamorphosed into a beautiful young woman. She has been educated in her sleep by her new friends, saving both Blondine, the narrator, and the reader from 'the boring early education'.[37] (What does it say about the author's attitude towards childhood if she lets her protagonist sleep through her formative years?) Similarly, in *Petites Filles modèles* she soon abandoned the rather pedestrian story-line of Camille and Madeleine educating their young charge Marguerite, in favour of the tale of Sophie and her wicked stepmother Madame Fichini – an ogress owing much to the fairy tale genre. The plot raced along from then on. Ségur's concern appeared to have been to adopt a narrative approach that would engage the interest of her young readers and amuse them; otherwise the message would never sink in. She sugared her moral pill with prodigious skill.

This survey of Madame de Ségur's works therefore looks at the vision of the child and education presented, and the ways in which she engaged with the new Catholic discourse on children's literature. It identifies, broadly speaking, three main types of children which Ségur depicted in her work: noble children, saintly children, and delinquent children. These three categories form the three phases which Ségur's writing follows, although, as noted, Ségur's oeuvre is large and varied, and any attempt to squeeze her works into neat boxes will encounter difficulties. To counter this problem, and to highlight changes in her writing, as well as the impact of the reviewers on her ideas, this survey adopts a broadly chronological approach. Finally, taking into account style, tone, content, narrative strategies, and the author's perception of her own writing, it analyses to what extent Ségur wrote as a modern, Catholic children's author.

Nobles

At the start of her writing career, Madame de Ségur produced a family health manual in 1855, followed by a collection of fairy tales in 1857. She then turned to writing novels designed for children. These works of fiction featured 'model' characters, who, she claimed, were 'not a creation, they really do exist: they are portraits; and the proof is there in their imperfections. They have faults, and these gentle shadows give the portrait its charm and demonstrate the existence of the model.'[38] Each book was dedicated to at least one grandchild, and, more often than not, the grandchild would then appear as a character in the plot. These were Ségur's 'noble' children, whose alleged basis in reality was designed to inspire readers to emulate their piety, generosity, and charity. They were noble in both blood and character. Because they were 'real', she took care to endow these 'noble' children with faults that needed correcting, designed to help the young reader to understand and imitate the model presented to them. As Mathilde Bourdon noted with approval, these were stories by a real mother, about real children.[39]

The reception of Ségur's fairy tales, *Nouveaux contes de fées* (1857), provides insight into how and why she developed her 'noble' children. Despite the continuing success of Perrault's *Contes*,[40] fairies and the fabulous were looked upon with deep suspicion by the clerical authorities. Her close friend Louis Veuillot congratulated Madame de Ségur for 'putting away her magic wand', in his first review of her books in December 1859.[41] Similarly, a review in *Bibliographie catholique* of Ségur's books in October 1859 observed that although Ségur dedicated her fairy tales to her granddaughters, they were hardly appropriate reading matter for little children.[42] The reviewer complained that her fairy tale endings taught young girls that virtuous behaviour would be rewarded with marriage to a handsome prince, rather than by recompense in the next world. He had clearly been seduced by the tales, and was concerned they would have a similar affect on children. Thus his criticism rested upon a view that was far removed from the 'evil child' – rather it was reading matter that risked corrupting infants' minds: 'their little hearts, completely innocent, impressionable like soft wax, would not receive without some danger the imprint of the deep, tender emotions that reign over all of these charming pages'. He exhorted the author to 'remain in the true and the useful'. The everyday was a far safer setting for fiction.

So the comtesse began writing her Fleurville trilogy, composed of *Les malheurs de Sophie* (1858), *Petites filles modèles* (1858) (which, confusingly, she wrote before *Sophie*), and *Les vacances* (1859). The trilogy was Ségur's first foray into realism, and it was here that she developed her 'noble' children, in the grounds of Château Fleurville, a large estate in rural Normandy. Fleurville was her idyllic vision of a world untouched by revolutions and industrialisation, where young aristocrats learned the values of religion, charity, generosity, obedience, and their roles in the gender and social hierarchy. As Françoise Mayeur points out, the comtesse de Ségur's interest in teaching Christian values to noble children could be interpreted as following the Jesuit paradigm, whereby the rechristianisation of society begins with the elite.[43] It was also part and parcel of the literary tradition she had entered. Moral tales for children generally featured upper-class protagonists. This reflected the origins of such literature in the eighteenth century, when the consumers of these books were families of the social elite, the only people who could afford to devote time and money to their children's education. By the 1850s, when Madame de Ségur began writing, the market for these books had grown considerably, but the usage remained. She drew upon the conventions of the genre. Her 'noble' children, growing up on a country estate far from the adult world, were reminiscent of the characters in the books of Madame de Genlis.[44] The name 'Ségur' was instantly recognisable as being of the aristocracy, and so further reinforced the notion that her characters really were noble children in all senses of the word.

Ségur's Fleurville trilogy was not simply a series of edifying lessons enlivened by little stories, a technique generally favoured by authors such as Madame de Genlis and Berquin. Instead she wrote her lessons as a complex narrative; itself suggestive of a certain respect for her reader, and a desire to stimulate the imagination. Reviewers such as Veuillot and the *Bibliographie Catholique* initially read her books as being composed of short episodes, to be read separately.[45] However, when they are taken as a trilogy, there emerges a narrative structure. The first book ushers in the eponymous and rather naughty heroine Sophie de Réan and her childhood friend Paul. In the second book things take a dramatic turn, as Sophie is now an orphan, and has become Sophie Fichini. Her stepmother treats her brutally, and Sophie is rescued by her aunt, Madame de Fleurville. Chateau Fleurville is also a refuge for a Madame de Rosbourg and her daughter, whose husband is presumed lost at sea. In the third book of the trilogy Sophie is reunited with Paul, who has spent the past four years marooned on an island with Madame de Rosbourg's husband. All those presumed lost are found again, and various ends tied up – including the death of Sophie's stepmother. The trilogy had much to attract the reader: shipwrecks, desert islands, and an evil stepmother.

The comtesse experimented with tone in the trilogy. In *Sophie* she adopted a more complicit tone with her readers, by focusing the narrative through the eyes of a child protagonist who was far from perfect, and with whom readers could identify. This type of strategy was becoming popular in mid-nineteenth-century Europe. As children were accorded greater respect, so authors began to try to speak to children on their level rather than dictate to them from on high.[46] The comtesse identified herself with the heroine, reassuring her readers that old ladies had been naughty little girls once upon a time: 'Grandmother has not always been good, and there are many children who have been naughty like her and who have made amends like she did.'[47] The same year Victorine Monniot's *Journal de Marguerite* adopted a similar approach, writing a diary from the point of view of a ten-year-old child preparing for her first communion.

Ségur's noble education was predicated on the importance of children, even young children, learning their responsibilities towards God. She portrayed them as capable of committing sins – childish sins, but sins nevertheless – and they therefore needed to be taught how to repent, and how to love God. In the nineteenth century a school of thought on the religious education of children had emerged, termed by historian Luc as 'partisans of early intervention.'[48] It reacted against predominant ideas on religious education, but was also concerned with the problem of dechristianisation. The austere precepts of Jansenist Catholicism of the previous century were still felt in the religious upbringing of children. Confession and communion were deferred until a person was considered to have repented their sins. Younger children were not thought capable of such sophisticated reasoning. As a result, it appears that many parents were loath to take their young children to confession, and communion was not considered appropriate until the child was almost grown up. Catholic pedagogues of the 'early intervention' school therefore exhorted parents to recognise that their children were capable of loving God, even if they could not understand everything. Most recognised the importance of teaching using 'affective piety' and advised against corporal punishment. The influential Mgr Dupanloup was the most famous advocate of these gentle methods. This was part of a growing emphasis in modern society on the importance of evangelising children early, and of adapting religious education to their specific needs. Even those on the far right of the Catholic Church could see the importance of this, for, as Mgr de Ségur wrote in 1867, such early intervention was perhaps the last hope for the Church in some parts of the country.[49] Similar changes were taking place within Protestantism, and in Britain, for example, authors like Mrs Molesworth and Charlotte Yonge argued that writing for children must change accordingly.[50] Likewise the comtesse de Ségur wrote her books according to this new approach. Four-year-old Sophie is taught to repent her sins in *Les malheurs* for example. Ségur argued that hers was a 'gentle' education, based on the ideas that young children ought to learn how to please God, and to love God according to the affective piety that was slowly coming to dominate nineteenth-century Catholicism.

Thus in *Petites filles modèles* Ségur drew a stark comparison between the pious education extolled by Madame de Fleurville and the brutal regime of Sophie's stepmother Madame Fichini, who whips her charge mercilessly, which is, she says, 'the only way to bring up children; the switch is the most efficacious of masters'.[51] Madame Fichini is a monster who keeps switches under her shawl, ready to whip them out and thrash little children, as in the episode where Sophie nearly drowns, and she beats her for having dirtied her dress. Sophie is left 'crying, running and jumping from the pain, her body striped and red'.[52] Later the child is described as looking as if she has been 'attacked by an army of cats'.[53] Rescued by Madame de Fleurville, Sophie vents her anger in wild temper. She hits, kicks, scratches, and bites the model girls, steals food, and deliberately disobeys orders. Madame de Fleurville's methods differ greatly from those of la Fichini. She locks Sophie in the 'cabinet de pénitence' to calm her down. Later, she delivers a firm lecture, and, although the child breaks down into tears and apologises, she is not permitted to leave the cabinet. Instead, Sophie must meditate on her own mortality, and the fatal consequences of her sins. This, Ségur suggests, is the only way to inculcate true contrition into the child. She learns to appreciate that, instead of beating her, Madame de Fleurville has shown her compassion. After a day and night left to her thoughts and prayers, Sophie understands the consequences of her behaviour towards her mentor, and towards God. Ségur's noble education was gentle but firm by nineteenth-century standards, at a time when parents routinely had recourse to more brutal methods.

Ségur returned to this idea of her 'gentle' education much later on, in a short play entitled *On ne prend pas les mouches avec du vinaigre* (from the collection of short stories and plays, *Comédies et Proverbes*, 1865). Here she made it explicit that her method of bringing up children was modern, and went hand in hand with the religion of love. She contrasted the new bourgeois devotion to the child, with the old aristocratic view of education, which she portrayed as cold, severe, and concerned with appearances rather than the child's spiritual wellbeing. The villainess of the piece is an ageing aristocrat, Madame d'Embrun, whose ideal children are 'docile like machines, calm and tranquil like still waters, silent like stone statues, courageous and able to endure suffering like the Lacedae-monians'.[54] In Madame d'Embrun's view, the problem with modern French families was that they no longer taught children respect: 'at present one must love everyone, even the good Lord! Children learn not to fear but to love!'[55] Ségur emphasised that in her view not only had attitudes towards childrearing altered significantly but this was also a symptom of a wider shift in religious beliefs. The eighteenth-century God of fear had become, in ultramontane rhetoric, a God of love. For Ségur, this meant a new, more loving conception of childhood. With her daughters gathered around her, the model mother of the play concludes that their 'modern' ways might be 'bourgeois and awful', but that one catches more flies with honey than vinegar.[56] Paradoxically then, Ségur's 'noble' children were being educated according to what she admitted were 'bourgeois' principles.

Ségur's understanding of childhood grappled with the idea of the child being born innately sinful. A modernising current within Catholicism, led by Mgr Dupanloup, argued that children had the capacity for evil, but that this was only the germ of evil that had not yet had the time to develop, and so they were not innately evil.[57] He even quoted from Rousseau, on how naughty boys can often, with a good education, become the most likeable and generous of men.[58] To what extent did the comtesse agree with Dupanloup and the more liberal Catholic view on the sinfulness of children? Could naughty Sophie be redeemed by the gentle Fleurville education? As discussed in Chapter 1, Sophie's education in *Malheurs* was based in part on Ségur's memories of her own upbringing based on the ideas of Rousseau. This education is seen through the child's eyes, as she struggles to satisfy her natural impulses against her mother's proscriptions. Thus, young Sophie works out ruses to make herself pretty (cutting her eyelashes to make them grow, or standing under a drain to make her hair curl like her model friends) or to satisfy her greed (by eating bread destined for horses, or stealing her mother's sweets). And yet, the narrator is not wholly sympathetic to Sophie's point of view. Sophie is constantly criticised for her inability to control herself. The title of the book does not refer to Sophie's unhappiness, rather her misdemeanours. Each episode is structured around a misdemeanour or sin, and ends with her suffering the effect caused by her naughty action – the inference being that this is the Good Lord's punishment for her disobedience. The book could be read as a Catholic critique of Rousseau's ideas on education, not least because the child's name invites the comparison, for Sophie is the girl introduced in section five of *Émile*. The child's natural impulses are invariably sinful: Sophie's urges lead her to behave in a selfish, vain, and greedy manner. Where Rousseau's Émile learns through experiencing the consequences of his actions, Sophie is told that her 'misfortunes' are divine punishment. It all feels oddly unsatisfactory, because the episodic structure of the book promises that Sophie will mend her ways by the end as the grandma did in the book's dedication. But this is not the case. The story ends instead on a cliff-hanger: readers are told to ask their mothers to buy *Petites filles modèles* and *Les vacances* to find out what happens next to Sophie. As she grows older, in *Les vacances*, the reformed Sophie is a rather sad figure. Cured of her childish enthusiasm, which provided the source for her misdemeanours, she still manages to get into scrapes, but now reflects mournfully on her fatal flaws that prevent her from being truly loved. Although Ségur professed to being a 'modern' and 'gentle' pedagogue, her books were often ambiguous on the question of children's sinfulness. In particular, her later works, discussed below, began to become more dualistic, divided between 'evil' and 'saintly' children.

In addition to learning their duties towards God, Ségur's noble children also had to learn their role in the social hierarchy. Her Fleurville trilogy emphasised the importance of simplicity. Although the stories are set in a large château, its inhabitants are taught to reject the trappings of wealth. Covetousness is the sin of the *nouveaux riches*, who invariably end up returned to their original lowly status. True 'noble' girls are dressed in plain white percaline dresses, and any hint of vanity is punished harshly. This went hand in hand with lessons on charity, which they administered to the inhabitants of the village close to their château. Noble children learn that their wealth has been given to them by God, and accordingly they must use it for the good of society.

The simplicity championed by Ségur also demonstrated a practical side to her ideas. Both Locke and Rousseau had decried the sedentary lifestyles of privileged children, and the fact that their movements were hindered by cumbersome dress. This, they argued, led to the putrefaction of children's humours, and so to disease. Such ideas were gaining currency by the nineteenth century. Clothes worn by wealthy young girls and boys became differentiated from adult fashions, to allow more movement. Girls wore pantalettes under their skirts, to allow physical activity whilst protecting their modesty.[59] Similarly, throughout the trilogy Ségur explained that little girls should play in simple dresses: 'we won't put on pretty dresses so that we can play more easily'.[60] Camille exhorts Marguerite to go for a walk, explaining, 'if you always stay sitting down, you will lose your colours and you will become ill'.[61] In *Les vacances*, when the male cousins return home for the holidays, Ségur depicted the girls happily running around with the boys. Their mothers look on with affection, and, the author notes, do not seek to stop their activities.[62] That she took care to underline this point would suggest that Ségur wanted to send a signal to parents not to prevent their daughters from taking physical exercise. She also made it clear that the girls were moving so energetically that they were sweating (although the reading committee at Hachette removed the word). It was still considered improper for girls in particular to engage in boisterous activities such as running.[63] This episode shows how important medical ideas were to Ségur's message, for the sweat indicates that their humours were circulating properly. Her concern that noble girls ought to run around outside was not unwarranted. Rousseau's arguments and the current medical vogue for the idea of girls doing gentle gymnastics and taking constitutional walks had had little impact in this respect. Throughout the nineteenth century, and with a peak between 1840 and 1860, the death rates of young girls of the upper classes were abnormally high. Doctors were mystified. The main killer was tuberculosis. The historian Yvonne Knibiehler suggests that their stultifying education, and a lack of red meat and fresh air were the main culprits.[64] Ségur was very interested in medicine. The first book that she wrote was a health manual, *La santé des enfants* (1855), and she had completed 'some studies on the physical education of children'. This manual was written with the help of her family doctor, and Ségur wanted to share her knowledge and experience with young mothers – she then continued this project in her fictions.[65]

Representations of gender in her books were therefore not always predictable, or to the taste of Hachette's correctors. Nevertheless, the Fleurville universe was ordered according to gendered boundaries. Girls learned maternal skills from their mothers, and her boys were taught to become brave and virtuous like their fathers. The overarching theme of *Petites filles modèles* is mothering: Camille and Madeleine become the 'little mothers' to Marguerite, and then together the three girls help Madame de Fleurville to look after Sophie. The premise of *Les vacances* is that the male uncles and cousins return from their work and boarding schools to spend the summer holidays at Fleurville. It was dedicated to her grandson Jacques, and she exhorted him to 'be courageous, dedicated, and Christian like Monsieur de Rosbourg'.[66] When Paul and Monsieur de Rosbourg return from their years spent shipwrecked on a tropical island, Ségur takes the opportunity to develop this notion of muscular Christianity, with tales of their bravery, and how they converted the inhabitants. The two then show the younger male characters how to apply these manly skills to being exemplary French noblemen. Still, these masculine roles were focused principally on the family – Ségur emphasized that fatherhood was the adult destiny for her noble boys. Monsieur de Rosbourg gives up his career as a sea captain, to live with his family in Normandy: 'we will cultivate our lands and we will do good while having fun, educating ourselves, and making life better for all around us'.[67] This domestic happy ending for Monsieur de Rosbourg blurred the demarcation of private and public spheres that characterised nineteenth-century rhetoric on gender.[68] Likewise, their education in her books was not always strictly separate. In *Les vacances*, and many of her later works, Ségur represented boys and girls playing together. On the one hand, her children learn in this way to differentiate their behaviour from that of the opposite sex. Sophie, for example, in *Les bons enfants* cannot join the boys shrimping by hand in a rock pool – her skirts prevent her: 'that would be a pretty sight! As if girls can do what boys can do!';[69] while in *Les vacances* Léon discovers that that he must be brave like the other boys, not 'fearful' like his female cousins. On the other hand, this mixing of the sexes also gave girls an excuse to indulge in good healthy physical exercise. Finally, the cousins and erstwhile playmates all marry one another: 'they all lived together, perfectly happy'.[70]

The comtesse's ideas on children and their upbringing were an amalgam of the concerns which dominated literature on children from the eighteenth century onwards; contemporary ideas on their welfare; modern Catholic notions on what sort of reading matter was suitable for them; and at what age they were capable of learning about contrition. Although she appeared to be criticising Rousseau in her story of Sophie's childhood, the comtesse evidently had some sympathy for his ideas on health. Her 'noble' children were dressed in plain cotton clothes for both moral and medical reasons. This same amalgam of concerns shaped the way she wrote her stories. Pressure from the Catholic reviewers may have forced Ségur to abandon writing fairy tales, but she still incorporated elements of the fairy tale into her trilogy. Madame de Fleurville's gentle methods may have won the day, but the wicked stepmother Fichini provided the drama. Ségur refused to let the moral embargo on fairy tales restrict her imagination.

Saints

When writing the Fleurville trilogy, Ségur assumed that her readers were from wealthy backgrounds, but she came under increasing pressure to change her approach. Louis Veuillot in particular argued that the comtesse must give more consideration to the question of the social class of her target readership, and their specific requirements. He worried that the luxurious world of aristocrats was not suitable for a modern readership: 'these châteaux, parks, and coaches', he said, 'could provoke too many sighs of jealousy these days; the democratic condition of readers must be taken into account'.[71] This was an odd choice of words, for Ségur's audience was far from 'democratic' in the twenty-first century sense of the word. At two francs per copy, her readership was primarily middle-class. From 1859 onwards, when Veuillot published these comments, Ségur's print runs of five to six thousand were selling out within a year. The first edition of her next book, *Mémoires d'un âne*, sold all six thousand copies in six months between 1860 and 1861.[72] This was doing well, but was not on a 'democratic' scale. As the historian Michel Manson has pointed out, Hachette's distribution in the children's market was dwarfed by that of the big Catholic publishing houses. In 1862 they had a combined output of ten million volumes per year for children and the young,[73] which was a staggering number at a time when the overall population of France was hovering around thirty-five million. Nevertheless, her books did gradually reach beyond the middle classes. By the 1850s, most French towns had a parish library, thanks to efforts of the 'good books' missions.[74] The comtesse's books by then were being endorsed by the mission's principal review, the *Bibliographie catholique*. Her works were included on reading lists for the government's new school libraries in 1862, as well as the Franklin Society's catalogues.[75] Mgr de Ségur also distributed them in his charitable work. Still, Ségur and the *Bibliothèque Rose* were not at the 'democratic' end of the scale.

What did Veuillot mean then? For him the word 'democratic' suggested revolution, bloodshed, and chaos, the rule of the people, and the corrupting influence of modern liberalism with its language of liberty, equality, and fraternity. Veuillot had made his name in the 1840s as a fierce opponent of State education. In Veuillot's view, any expansion of the reading public that was not directly under the control of the Catholic Church was 'democratic' and therefore dangerous. This was why reviewers such as Veuillot and the *Bibliographie catholique* were adamant that the old style of writing for children, designed for the social elite, also needed to change. It was under Veuillot's influence that the comtesse de Ségur began writing characters and situations designed for a middle- and lower-class, rather than 'noble' readership. As the glowing review of one of her later works, *Le mauvais génie* (1867), in the *Bibliographie catholique* explained, 'to do good works amongst families, in schools, and in boarding schools, it is necessary to choose middle-class and working-class heroes. A child from this class – and they form the immense majority – will admire the examples that are presented to him in a rarefied setting, but he will not think to imitate them; here, every situation, every piece of advice, every word is directly addressed to him and will inspire him to emulate them.'[76] These readers required different models of childhood.

The first book Ségur wrote where the protagonist was not a noble child was *Mémoires d'un âne* (1860). This was a spirited tale told by a donkey, Cadichon, which follows his misadventures as he is passed from owner to owner. It has a rebellious message, arguing that Cadichon will disabuse the world of the prejudices that donkeys suffer. The dedication is his manifesto: 'you will see eventually when you have read this book that instead of saying: *stupid like a donkey, ignorant as a donkey, stubborn as a donkey*, we will say: *witty as a donkey, clever as a donkey, docile as a donkey* [her italics]'. Cadichon took on a life of his own. Ségur called him 'my donkey' in correspondence, while her husband told the comtesse, 'you will go into posterity mounted on Cadichon's back'.[77] Cadichon was a particular favourite of Veuillot's: 'I often think that I am reading my own story. I find in it many of the things that I have thought, and a certain scorn for the human race that speaks to me at the moment. I don't know if Cadichon will go into politics. It would be a shame if he did not.'[78] At first however, Ségur did not seem to be taking her moral responsibilities towards her readers seriously. The original manuscript ended with Cadichon throwing a child into a pond to avenge the death of his friend, a hunting dog. Her editor complained that not only did the donkey behave in a vengeful manner towards a young boy, but that his new owners never condemned him for such behaviour, and therefore shared in his blame.[79] The comtesse responded that Cadichon was no Christian donkey, 'but simply a Donkey as it is understood – a Donkey and nothing more'.[80] Nevertheless, she conceded and rewrote the ending so that the naughty donkey learned to repent his sins. Perhaps unsurprisingly, *Mémoires d'un âne* was the only one of her stories selected for the school reading curriculum under the Third Republic.[81] Mgr de Ségur refused to distribute this book amongst the poor, preferring her Fleurville trilogy instead.[82] Her first attempt to write a 'good book' about a lower-class character may have been a literary success, but it had been clumsy in terms of what functions edifying books should perform.

This new phase in Ségur's writing led her to introduce another construction of childhood into her books: the 'saintly' or redemptive child. Redemptive children were often to be found in evidence in nineteenth-century literature, most famously in the work of Charles Dickens – little Nell for example, whose innate goodness led her to suffer in a wicked world, and eventually shamed adults into mending their ways. It was the sign of a growing notion of the childlike as being pure, almost superior to the corrupt state of adult society. In Ségur's version, the innate saintliness of some children led adults to convert to Catholicism. Alongside the well-known traditional Catholic view of the sinful child, there also existed the notion of the innocent child. The Church increasingly vacillated between these two contradictory views of children: the Augustinian child and the other, innocent and full of promise, ripe for evangelisation.[83] This second vision of the child had come to the fore in the Counter-Reformation, which had laid increased emphasis on Jesus' teaching that Christians ought to appear like children before God 'except ye be converted, and become as little children, ye shall not enter into the kingdom of heaven'.[84] St François de Sales wrote his classic *Introduction à la vie dévote* in 1607 using this premise. And nineteenth-century piety revived Sales's vision of a simple and innocent religion, emphasising the small, the childlike, and the humble as closer to God. Mgr de Ségur was one of its most enthusiastic devotees.[85] The *Introduction à la vie dévote* and the *Imitation of Jesus Christ* were the two most popular religious works in mid-nineteenth-century France.[86] They celebrated and compared the suffering of the lowly with that of Christ, and this was also the underlying message of Ségur's next book, *Pauvre Blaise* (whose hero, it should be noted, receives a 'superb volume of *L'Imitation . . .*').[87] This idea of childhood innocence had another connotation for ultramontanes. It was a further example of their eagerness to champion innocent piety in opposition to what they saw as the corruption of modern society. As Laura Kreyder has pointed out, Ségur's saintly children ought to be understood alongside Veuillot's portrayal of saintly, rustic shepherd boys, and the fascination for child visionaries.[88]

After her donkey's antics, the comtesse turned to the other extreme and produced *Pauvre Blaise* (1861). She announced that this was 'an eminently moral book'.[89] She was, in fact, uneasy about this pious work, and rightly so, as in comparison with Cadichon's immediate success, *Pauvre Blaise* only ever managed mediocre sales figures (see Appendix II). The story revolves around the submissive servant boy Blaise, and his struggles to make his tyrannical young master see the error of his ways. Conscious of his place in the social hierarchy, Blaise adopts a policy of passive resistance to his master's bullying – it would be unthinkable for him to disobey orders. Blaise was a saintly child: both children and adults, including the priest, are in awe of him, 'heart always filled with charity and tenderness. . . what a beautiful model to follow!'[90] He was one of several such children in her work. In *Jean qui grogne et Jean qui rit* (1865), for example, Jean (*laughing Jean*) is described as 'a soul of the elite'.[91] Everyone who meets him falls in love with him. His physiognomy expresses his piety, and adults spend hours contemplating his spiritual beauty. A farmer who meets the boys on their journey learns forgiveness from Jean, and muses 'and to think that I have been shown how to behave by a boy of fourteen years old, and me a thirty-five-year-old!'[92] Both Blaise and laughing Jean prompted adults to convert to Catholicism, through their saintly example.

Conscious that she was expected to teach children from a less fortunate position in life the need for humility, Ségur now created characters who began to speak in a much more dolourist vocabulary, which she lifted straight out of contemporary religious propaganda.[93] When 'poor Blaise' is powerless to prevent his master from bullying him, he intones dutifully, 'since I have been going to catechism classes for my first communion next year, I know that Our Lord suffered at the hands of the wicked, and it consoles me to suffer a little like he did'.[94] Her humble heroes submit to all the hard work, cruelties and injustices which they face in life, and they never question their lot. Through their saintly suffering they triumph in the end, and usually become the object of a rich benefactor. This did not mean that her lower-class characters were permitted to rise above their station in life. Blaise and his counterparts invariably live happily ever after as their benefactors' manservants. This dolourism could however also apply to the upper classes. 'Noble' children could also be saintly. One example is Roger de Grignan, in *Jean qui grogne et Jean qui rit*. Ravaged by illness, Roger is skeletal in appearance, and can hardly talk, but he accepts his plight with Christian resignation.[95] His sickbed is like that of a saint, and adults visit him to be fortified by his spiritual strength.[96] The boy's demise provides children with a sobering lesson on how to die a pious death. This gloomy tale was typical of the devotional literature of the period, and certainly Gaston de Ségur's writings were also filled with such edifying deaths. The spectacle of the innocent young lives of children cut short emphasised how brief the time on this earth is, in comparison to the afterlife.

The most striking example of Ségur exalting children's 'naive' piety is in *La sœur de Gribouille* (1862). The story centres on a young seamstress, Caroline, and her struggles to look after her simple-minded brother, Gribouille. The boy is convinced that he can talk to his mother and the angels, and predicts that he will soon join them in Heaven. And true to his word, Gribouille dies. What is particularly notable about *Gribouille* is how Madame de Ségur managed to combine to great effect ultramontane sensibility with comic frivolity. This was the comtesse's first real attempt at comedy, a genre that was to feature in many of her subsequent works. *La sœur de Gribouille* is based on a mildly bawdy *boulevard* comic opera, *La sœur de Jocrisse*,[97] 'one of the most charming and witty *trifles* [her italics] to have been set on stage'.[98] Such performances were all the rage in the nineteenth century. True to the stock vaudeville character, Jocrisse, Gribouille's lack of understanding allows for a variety of misunderstandings, play on words, and slapstick humour. Ségur removed all smut and transformed Jocrisse into a typically ultramontane romantic hero, whose simplicity allowed him to see the truth, in contrast with the hypocritical gibbering of many of the villagers. While the comtesse was writing *Gribouille*, the young Bernadette's visions at Lourdes were becoming known, with her friend Veuillot as one of the principal propagandists. *Gribouille* contained several elements reminiscent of the Lourdes story, with its small-town setting, its ignorant, gossipy village women, and of course the child visionary.[99] Ségur exploited the supernatural aspects of her tale to full effect, creating a reassuring vision of death and the afterlife, still tinged with a certain eeriness that steers the book away from becoming too maudlin. The comtesse wrote of the book, 'I sense that I have a pronounced preference for *Gribouille*; contrary to usual, I think it is very good and I am pleased with it.'[100] . . . 'I announce with ferocious pleasure the happy death of *Gribouille* . . . it is touching, but not too much, it is gay, but not too much either; in short I think it is good.'[101] This was precisely what pleased the *Bibliographie catholique* reviewer: 'if the children who read this book often find it funny in a healthy and useful way, they will also sometimes cry salutary tears.'[102]

Ségur had written *Blaise* and *Gribouille* at the zenith of the Catholic publishing boom, that is to say the years 1859–61. The great surge in publications was due largely to Catholic mobilisation in response to the threat that the Italian nationalist cause posed to the Pope as a territorial ruler in central Italy.[103] This 'Italian Question' caused political problems in France, particularly for the Ségurs and Veuillots. Should Napoleon III continue to garrison French soldiers in Rome, protecting the Pope against the Italian nationalist armies, who were increasingly gaining support internationally? In 1859, Napoleon III removed his support for the Pope, and in January 1860 he closed down Veuillot's paper, *L'univers*, for criticising this foreign policy. Pro-papal brochures written by Gaston were seized and banned in February 1860. At the same time, Persigny, minister of the interior, was attempting to curtail the power of the religious congregations, one of the largest manifestations of the religious revival. In this atmosphere of paranoia and fear of persecution, the socially engaged tone of her stories, and their obsession with suffering in a corrupt world is hardly surprising. Nevertheless, the intense dolourism of *Pauvre Blaise* and certain episodes of *Jean qui grogne* were in fact rather rare in Ségur's oeuvre, and, following what she felt was her success in *Gribouille*, Ségur began to develop her comic talents instead. She went on to write the incredibly popular *Auberge de l'ange gardien* (1863) and *Un bon petit diable* (1865), which both combined serious lessons on piety with slap-stick humour.

In these comedies more adult characters joined her 'saintly' children. For Ségur older people provided excellent comic foils, lightening the tone whilst still allowing children to take the central roles. Ségur was regularly criticised for poking fun at authority figures – paradoxically for some-body who so passionately espoused an authoritarian cause – thereby providing children with bad role models.[104] This is further evidence that she was moving away from the traditional 'didactic', authoritarian approach to writing for children.[105] The nation's grandmother was gener-ally at her most vicious and funny when mocking older people. Her first caricature of an old woman, Madame Bonbeck, appeared in *Les deux nigauds* (1862). This arthritic whirlwind kicks, hits, and shouts her way through the book, hurling the most outrageous insults at her nephew and niece. It is only through the intervention of 'noble' children that her nephew and niece discover how to behave. The comedy *Un bon petit diable* (1865) was written with schoolboys in mind. The hero Charles plays tricks on his wicked old aunt Madame Mac'Miche – including preventing her from spanking him by attaching pictures of demons to his buttocks. The book then continues to celebrate the boy's anti-authoritarian streak. Sent to an exaggeratedly horrid boarding school, Charles makes the masters look like fools, before escaping, marrying the heroine, and becoming a good Catholic.

But it was the buffoonery of General Dourakine in *L'auberge de l'ange gardien* and *Le Général Dourakine* (both 1863) that charmed readers. The highpoint of *L'auberge* is when Dourakine, a fairy godfather of Rabelai-sian appetite, arranges an enormous wedding feast for the hero and heroine. All thoughts of suffering are banished. According to the delighted reviewer of the *Bibliographie catholique*, Ségur was teaching children the values of Christian charity and the importance of a strict social hierarchy in a most attractive manner. He wrote in rapturous praise of the 'Asiatic luxury that is nevertheless quite proper'.[106] It was these books, her more light-hearted, comic works, rather than her dolourist efforts, that proved as enduringly popular as her Fleurville books and *Mémoires d'un âne* (see Appendix II). Ségur had mastered the art of 'teaching by amusing', which had become the mantra of children's authors and reviewers of all political and religious backgrounds in the nineteenth century.[107] This idea went hand in hand with the new respect for the child. Although some reviewers in the *Bibliographie catholique* remained suspicious of a concept that risked making light of the serious matter of education – 'a lesson that is difficult to learn is imprinted more profoundly on the mind than that which is learned while playing'[108] – Ségur's comedies were well received by Catholic critics.

Delinquents

Contemporary critics often designate her later works as Ségur's 'dark' phase. As the comtesse explained to Templier in 1863, personal tragedy meant she was not in the mood for writing the sort of 'stupidities' that filled her books.[109] She had just recently lost her husband, followed shortly afterwards by the death of one of her youngest granddaughters. Her daughter Sabine, 'the daughter who has chosen to bear a heavy cross',[110] was dying from tuberculosis in a nunnery. While her protestations were something of an exaggeration – for the books she had written while her husband was dying had been manic comedies – the mood of her books did become more sombre subsequently. This is also referred to as her 'social' phase, since it was at this time that the comtesse addressed more gritty issues, often drawing on the works of her sons, Gaston and Anatole. She expressed far less hope for humanity in general. Her previously exuberant happy endings became more muted. A much more overtly intransigent Catholic vision of society came to the fore. Perhaps this was because she was engaged from 1865 on in writing her Grandmother's Bible series. Correspondence suggests that she was increasingly turning to her eldest son, Mgr de Ségur, for support and advice. The mood in the Catholic Church was also hardening: in his 1864 *Syllabus of Errors* Pius IX informed believers that modern liberalism was anathema, and in 1870 he pronounced the doctrine of papal infallibility.

The comtesse's later works ought to be read in this context of gathering storm clouds for the modern Catholic Church, and in particular, Mgr Gaston de Ségur's growing concern for what he saw as the Catholic struggle with the State and secularising movements for the nation's youth. Following the Italian question, a rift had been created between the Church and Napoleon III's Empire. The government appointed the liberal Victor Duruy Minister for Education in 1863, and he attempted to inaugurate reforms aimed at broadening access to education. Needless to say, the Ségur family looked on with suspicion, and considered ways in which Catholics could respond to such changes. In 1861 Gaston wrote the tract *La révolution expliquée aux jeunes gens*. In it, he painted a lurid picture of a continent whose very existence was threatened by ruthless 'enemies' (secret societies of revolutionaries, freemasons, and Protestants) all targeting the youth in order to put their fiendish plans to destroy the Church and inaugurate the rule of Satan. His preface, dedicated to the youth of France, warned them 'it is you that that The Revolution wants to enrol against GOD'.[111] His famous denunciation of the freemasons, *Les Franc-Maçons ce qu'ils sont – ce qu'ils font – ce qu'ils veulent* (1867),[112] claimed that, along with the free press, their principal weapon was education reform. Citing the establishment of Jean Macé's ligue de l'enseignement in 1866, which aimed to promote universal, secular, and free education, Gaston argued that the masons were mounting a huge new campaign to seize control of the nation's youth,[113] a comment also directed at the policies of Victor Duruy. Gaston was convinced that Catholics must act to block liberal plans for the expansion of education: 'enemies of the Church boast loudly about their campaign plan, which is to target children to fashion them as they please. It is clear that it is on this battlefield that we must fight, we, the soldiers of Christ and the servants of his Church . . . in many parts of the country this is alas! perhaps the only way to revive the faith.'[114]

Mgr de Ségur therefore looked to the young to solve France's problems of social unrest. He was convinced that the troubles began early, as he explained in *La révolution*: 'you see that child who hits and bites his mother? There is a revolutionary in nappies.' From tantrums at home to pranks at school it was then but a small step to climbing the barricades.[115] In Gaston's works, the revolutionary spirit and liberalism are often referred to as 'young' and 'youthful'. This was not an invention of Gaston's: in Italy, Mazzini's revolutionary organisation was called 'Young Italy', for he claimed that it was only the young who were entirely untainted by old ideas (in this case, the French revolution).[116] Also, the image of the 'revolutionary' as a hot-headed youth permeated French discourse – the classic example being Delacroix's gun-toting boy alongside Liberty, in his painting *Liberty Leading the People*. In 1848, *Le charivari* featured a series of cartoons by Théodore Maurisset depicting nervous bourgeois being frightened by the cheerful games of children, who are busily building little barricades and pretending to be revolutionaries.[117] In 1862 Hugo's *Misérables* exalted the child revolutionary, with the martyrdom of the boy Gavroche on the barricades. If European societies were to prevent these little Gavroches from turning into hardened Socialists, then Gaston's advice was to get to them early, and the sole remedy was frequent confession and communion.[118] Mgr de Ségur politicised the 'early intervention' school, becoming one of the leading voices in favour of confessing the very young, working closely with them as 'spiritual guides', and preparing them for first communion early.[119]

In this climate, Madame de Ségur experienced more and more trouble in according salvation to all children. Where early characters like Sophie were naughty and rebellious, they had good hearts underneath it all. While she had always enjoyed punishing villains, Ségur now increasingly introduced protagonists who appeared to be beyond redemption. Maurice de Sibran in *François le bossu* (1864) was the first unsympathetic character to die a terrible death. In a metaphor dear to Christian exemplary literature, his death was caused by injuries sustained in a fire.[120] Ségur refused to give in to her editor's request that the boy should live, for his resurrection she explained 'would have been as laborious and difficult as that of Lazarus *by M. Renan*. I have softened his sufferings, and lessened his injuries; but it was too difficult to save him; I had to let him die [her italics].'[121] In *Jean qui grogne et Jean qui rit* Ségur offered little explanation for one cousin's good behaviour and the other's bad behaviour. Grumbling Jean's wickedness, and laughing Jean's saintliness, could be attributed only to God's will: 'I am brave, and he is weak. It was the good Lord that made us this way.'[122] Laughing Jean wins the heart of a generous aristocrat and lives happily ever after as his manservant, while grumbling Jean falls in with a bad crowd and finishes up in a penal colony. This new severity was in part due to the intervention of Mgr de Ségur. Referring to the ending of her *Mauvais génie*, he wrote, 'let us hope however that this one will not finish, like all the other rascals, his elder brothers, by converting, living happily married and having many children. Render unto Caesar that which is Caesar's and, from time to time at least, hang the rascals.'[123] The book does indeed end with the execution of Alcide, the rascal in question. Gaston also enforced a tedious rewriting of *Jean qui rit*, removing the camaraderie between servants and their masters, and the comtesse complained that she had been obliged to stay in the house until the job was done.[124]

The comtesse's grandchildren were growing older, and so accordingly were her fictitious characters. Their average age was now early to mid-teens. The adult world was encroaching upon Ségur's moral universe and destabilising it. The fire that killed Maurice de Sibran was started by his cigarette – smoking was one of the signs of entering manhood in the nineteenth century. As a devoted follower of Louis Veuillot, the comtesse was deeply suspicious of the influences of modern society. Outside the family, in the wide world, was a society dominated by capitalism, industry, and materialist values. Those whose resolve was not strengthened by religion risked perdition. Thus, in *La fortune de Gaspard* (1866) she depicted the transition from childhood to adulthood as posing serious risks for lower-class boys who might be tempted by the new promise of riches. Similarly, the main crime of Alcide in *Mauvais génie* (1867) was greed. The arrival of a wealthy industrialist in the village led to an escalation of his lust for gold. Capitalist society in her books did not just corrupt the lower orders, or indeed boys. The proud aristocrat, Félicie, in *Diloy le chemineau* (1868) was led astray by the local *nouveaux riches* who encouraged her selfish snobbery, while in *Quel amour d'enfant!* (1866), the spoiled Giselle made a disastrous marriage in her desire for wealth.

Ségur's bleakest vision of the modernisation of society and its consequences for French youth is to be found in *La fortune de Gaspard*. In this book she described with bitter cynicism her interpretation of the effects of the industrial revolution on the countryside, in which human relations and the very fabric of village society are perverted by gold lust. The anti-hero is Gaspard, a young peasant boy, with feverish ambitions: 'I will become a scholar; I will write books, make machines and lots of money, I will have workers, I will live like a prince.'[125] The most talented pupil in his village school, he is desperate to escape the grind of agricultural labour and to make his fortune in industry. Once his prowess at school has won him a job in the local factory, he flatters Monsieur Féréor, the factory owner, in order to insinuate himself into the boardroom. In the process, Gaspard cheats his father, and deserts his family. With savage irony, Ségur painted Gaspard's relationship with the factory owner using the language of a romantic novel, 'Mr. Féréor looked up at Gaspard, with an almost affectionate look in his eyes'.[126] The industrialist adopts Gaspard, and the happy adoptive son tells his new father, 'you will replace the wife that I will not love, and the factory will replace the children that I will never have, I hope'.[127] Ségur's book suggested that it was Gaspard's real father, le père Thomas, who was the true casualty of modern society. His traditional role was completely undermined. The intervention of school means that he no longer transmitted his skills to his sons, for they

both read better than their father. The comtesse was concerned that a
new family drama was playing out over the course of the nineteenth
century, as the growth of industry threatened the old certainty that sons
would do the same job as their fathers. As a conservative, she was concerned that this threatened the future of the family, and thus society.[128]

In the 1860s growing numbers of writers decried the government's
unwillingness to protect children against exploitation in industrial
labour.[129] Victor Hugo's *Misérables* (1862) and Alphonse Daudet's *Le petit
chose* (1868) denounced the abuses that were rife. On the religious right
the problem was also being considered. The question in the comtesse's
mind was not the exploitation of children, but rather the risk they ran
of being corrupted in factories. In *Diloy le chemineau* a nobleman advised
a father in desperate financial straits not to let his children work in the
local factory: 'your children will be lost; they will have no religion, no
instruction; they will become scrawny and sickly'.[130] The comtesse's main
objection was that the hours were too long to permit them to attend
catechism lessons, and that the employers were heathens who allowed
their workers to become debauched. She echoed the dominant Catholic
discourse that interpreted capitalism as a Protestant or Jewish aberra-
tion.[131] The industrialists in *Gaspard* are referred to derisively by the
locals as Jews and Arabs, and one, Frölichlein, is a foreigner, probably
Protestant. She saw the ideal solution as being healthy, agricultural labour.
However, the answer that Ségur presented in *Gaspard* was not to turn
back the clock. Instead, she introduced a female, Catholic element into
this masculine union of money and ambition. As was generally the case
in nineteenth-century businesses, expansion was achieved through
marital alliances. And so Gaspard agrees to marry the daughter of a rival
industrialist, Frölichlein. Happily, the young girl turns out to be a veritable saint. What follows is reminiscent of the domestic novels of the
period.[132] Mina works her charms, and converts them into paragons of
virtue.[133]

Ségur wrote her final book, *Après la pluie, le beau temps* (1871), in 1869,
when Garibaldi's forces were getting ever closer to seizing Rome and
dislodging the Pope from his centre of temporal power. (The publication
of the book was interrupted by the Franco-Prussian War and the Paris
Commune, which meant that it appeared in print only in 1871.) As with
several of the preceding works, the book follows the child protagonists
to a much older age, charting their growth into adults. Set against the
background of the Italian question, there was only one possible career
for her male heroes, which was to enrol as pontifical zouaves, the army

of volunteers who fought for the Pope. Jacques, who has just left school, announces, 'Rome is threatened more than ever by bandits who want to destroy the throne of our King, our father in God, the saint Pius IX . . . I have engaged in the pontifical zouaves.' To which his future wife Genevieve replies, 'oh how happy I am! My Lord, I thank you Jacques, Jacques, I too shall go to Rome'.[134] It was fitting that in her swansong the ultramontane comtesse de Ségur set her happy ending in Rome, with her children grown up and their lives dedicated to defending the Pope.

Conclusion

Catholics have wrongly been labelled 'backward' in the field of children's literature. Although Catholic discourse was essentially conservative and reactionary, they proved to be far from immobile and adapted swiftly and effectively to the problem of what should be suitable reading material for the steadily growing young audience. Reviewers for the *Bibliographie catholique* took great interest in the comtesse de Ségur, and she incorporated their new ideas on childhood into her writing. Ségur made it very clear that her views were considered by her peers to be 'modern', and this she connected with her religious beliefs, arguing that the new respect for children went hand in hand with the emergence of the 'God of love'.

This chapter and the previous one both emphasise that Ségur was conscious of new ideas concerning children and childrearing, and that concerns for their welfare as she saw it were central to her writing. We can see this in the narrative techniques that she used, even the very layout of her books. Likewise, the emphasis on the physical as well as spiritual wellbeing of children, and their agency in this, is testimony to Ségur's respect for her readers. Moreover, her early works demonstrated a great interest in the state of childhood. She wrote to her editor of 'their innocence, grace and continual development of their mind, ideas and intelligence. How is it possible not to admire and cherish this charming bundle of all that is loveable and admirable.'[135] Her little protagonists were allowed to revel in childish amusements. It was only in her later works that the comtesse began to consider their adult lives in detail.

Ségur constructed three models of childhood. Firstly, there were her 'noble' children, who dominated her work. Written from life, she wanted them to appear 'real' and so they were neither wholly innocent nor wholly evil. These aristocratic youngsters were instead 'model' children, designed to inspire readers to imitate their behaviour. They reflected the concerns of the comtesse's social class, so they learned to assume the responsibilities of *noblesse oblige*, and to respect the good Lord. This last lesson was so obvious it almost goes without saying: noble children who are identified with the Ségur family were Catholic children. Still, not all children (or indeed adults) were religious, even those from the upper classes. In this case they fell into two categories – either they would be saved by a saintly child or they would become the third type, 'delinquent' children.

The second category, 'saintly' children, represented innocence in an age many Catholics felt was impious. Ségur's saintly children tended to be from lower-class backgrounds, although not exclusively (as in the case of Roger de Grignan). They inspired religious sentiments in all those who come into contact with them. Although their self-immolation can be so extreme as to make the contemporary reader grind their teeth, it should be pointed out that such sentimentalism was not only common in ultramontane rhetoric but was also to be found in the work of Dickens or Hugo. Finally, as Ségur and her grandchildren grew older, so did her characters. The entire mood of her works grew increasingly sombre, and she peopled them with 'delinquent' children. This was in part due to the influence of her son, Mgr de Ségur, on her work. Some were innately 'evil', but most were still creations of adult society in some way.

Did this shift in Catholic sensibilities alter their approach to child protection? Their secular counterparts such as Victor Hugo not only wrote about child abuse but also campaigned vociferously on children's behalf. The 'romantic' child is credited with ushering in important reforms in work and healthcare. Certainly there were Catholic voices included in the chorus against the excesses of industrial child labour, but the comtesse de Ségur did not address the question directly, preferring rather to promote the rural way of life.[136] Moreover, did the comtesse's pleas for parents to stop beating their children, and to take care of little girls' health, make any impact? Ségur was adding her prestigious name to the list of protesters, and she was certainly daring to suggest that such abuses were taking place not just in the lower classes but also in the homes of the aristocracy and the bourgeoisie. Whether the elite took any notice is another matter. Both Yvonne Knibiehler and Eric Mension-Rigau emphasise the continued resistance to change in approaches to parenting in the upper echelons of French society.[137] If Freud's comments about her books in *A Child Is Being Beaten* are anything to go by, we might ask whether her medicine was as harmful as the illness: 'though in the higher forms at school the children were no longer being beaten, the influence of such occasions was replaced and more than replaced by the effects of reading, of which the importance was soon to be felt.' Ségur's depiction of birchings and horsewhippings haunted the imaginations of young children.[138] Was Simone de Beauvoir's mother alone in delaying giving Ségur's books to her daughter for fear of giving her nightmares?[139]

One of the most important features of the comtesse's writing was the skill with which she combined religious concerns with the art of storytelling. It was crucial to make her moral message accessible to children. To this end she employed comic episodes, fairy tale characters, and a great variety of ogres and villainesses. She explodes the myth that edifying literature is dull. The Marxist critic Marc Soriano objected to the comtesse precisely because he was such a great admirer of her literary talents.[140] The historian Margaret Lavinia Anderson suggests that ultramontane willingness to exploit the 'discovery' of the child in mission work demonstrates their 'entrepreneurial spirit'.[141] Certainly this applies to the case of the comtesse and her circle of ultramontane writers. The next chapter will now go on to dissect the comtesse's instinct of how to appeal to her market. This new interest in the child would have further implications for ultramontane culture, as we shall see in Chapter 4, which develops the notion of ultramontane 'entrepreneurialism' further. Appealing to the current 'bourgeois' conception of childhood was an important part of communicating with families.

Notes

1 Hugh Cunningham, *Children and Childhood in Western Society since 1500* (Harlow, Pearson Education, 1995, 2005) chapter 3; Colin Heywood, *A History of Childhood. Children and Childhood in the West from Medieval to Modern Times* (Oxford, Polity, 2001) chapter 2.

2 On the history of children's books in France, Penny Brown's *Critical History of French Children's Literature* is indispensable; Francis Marcoin, *La librairie de jeunesse et littérature industrielle au XIXe siècle* (Paris, Honoré Champion, 2006) offers an encyclopaedic panorama of the nineteenth century; for Europe, Ganna Ottevaere-van Praag, *La littérature pour la jeunesse* remains the best reference work to date.

3 Jennifer J. Popiel, *Rousseau's Daughters. Domesticity, Education, and Autonomy in Modern France* (Durham, University of New Hampshire Press, 2008).

4 Léon Curmer (ed.) *Les Français peints par eux-mêmes. Encyclopédie morale du XIXe siècle* (1840, this edition Paris, Omnibus, 2003), volume 4, 'Les enfants à Paris', Mathurin-Joseph Brisset, pp. 723–734.

5 Loïc Artiaga, *Des torrents de papier: catholicisme et lectures populaires au XIXe siècle* (Limoges, PULIM, 2007), introduction; *Bibliographie catholique*, Première année 1841–42.

6 Michel Manson, 'The Editorial Strategies of Provincial Catholic Publishing Houses for the Young in 19th Century France', in Jan de Maeyer et al. (eds) *Religion, Children's Literature and Modernity in Western Europe 1750–2000* (Leuven, Leuven University Press, 2005), pp. 423–444.

7 See Chapter 3.

8 Preface (under pseudonym P.-J. Stahl) to Perrault's *Contes* illustrated by Gustave Doré (Paris, Hetzel, 1862).

9 Ottevaere-van Praag, *La littérature pour la jeunesse*, pp. 186–187; Rosemary Lloyd, *The Land of Lost Content: Children and Childhood in Nineteenth-Century French Literature* (Oxford, Clarendon Press, 1992), p. 19.

10 Jean Glénisson, 'Le livre pour la jeunesse', *HEF*, 3:417–441, p. 430; Anna Green, *French Paintings of Childhood and Adolescence, 1848–86* (Aldershot, Ashgate, 2007), p. 232.

11 Jan de Maeyer, 'The Concept of Religious Modernisation' in de Maeyer et al. (eds) *Religion, Children's Literature and Modernity*; see also Brown, *French Children's Literature*, 2, introduction.

12 Heywood, *Growing up*, chapter 3; Lloyd, *The Land of Lost Content*, chapter 2.

13 Zeldin, *France 1848–1945*, 1:318; Cunningham, *Children and Childhood*, p. 58.

14 Heywood, *Growing up*, p. 48; Green, *French Paintings of Childhood and Adolescence*, p. 9.

15 Maeyer, 'The Concept of Religious Modernisation', p. 44.

16 Thomas Kselman, *Miracles and Prophecies in Nineteenth Century France* (New Brunswick, Rutgers University Press, 1983).

17 Gérard Cholvy and Yves-Marie Hilaire, *Histoire religieuse de la France contemporaine 1800/1880* (Paris, Privat, 1985), p. 153.

18 Ralph Gibson, *A Social History of French Catholicism 1789–1914* (London, Routledge, 1989), pp. 265–267.

19 *Ibid.*, pp. 182–183.

20 See Savart, *Catholiques en France*, pp. 408–411.

21 Alongside Louis Veuillot's reviews for *L'univers*, and *Bibliographie catholique* 1841–72, also consulted were Catholic magazines for children: *Journal des demoiselles*; *Semaine des familles*; *Poupée modéle*; *Journal des jeunes personnes* and *Journal des enfants de Marie*.

22 Savart, *Catholiques en France*, pp. 440–442.

23 Quoted in Savart, *Catholiques en France*, p. 423; See Noë Richter's chapter and Mollier's introduction in Jean-Yves Mollier (ed.) *Histoires de lecture XIXe–XXe siècles* (Bernay, Société d'histoire de la lecture, 2005) for the history of the Catholic Church's prominent role in promoting popular reading, from the Counter Reformation until c. 1862: pp. 7–24.

24 'Des moyens à employer pour la propagation des bons livres', *Bibliographie catholique*, 13, January 1853.

25 'Des collections de bons livres, à l'usage de la jeunesse, des familles, des bibliothèques paroissiales etc', *Bibliographie catholique*, 4, November 1847.

26 A. Parménie and C. Bonnier de la Chapelle, *Histoire d'un éditeur et de ses auteurs: P.J. Hetzel (Stahl)* (Paris, Éditions Albin Michel, 1953), pp. 489–490.

27 Pierre Pierrard, *Louis Veuillot* (Paris, Beauchesne, 1998), pp. 22–23.

28 Jean-Noël Luc, *L'invention du jeune enfant au XIXe siècle. De la salle d'asile à l'école maternelle* (Paris, Belin, 1997), p. 98.

29 Review of *Les malheurs de Sophie, Les vacances, Les petites filles modèles*, and *Nouveaux contes de fées*, by Mathilde Bourdon, *Journal des demoiselles*, 28, May 1860, 134–135.

30 Olga de Pitray, *Ma chère maman*, pp. 127–128.

31 Letter to Templier, 2 March 1858.

32 Letter to Templier, 20 February 1861.

33 Letter to Templier, 19 February 1864.

34 Letter to Templier, 23 May 1863.

35 *Œuvres*, 1:523.

36 Glénisson, 'Le livre pour la jeunesse', p. 417.

37 *Œuvres*, 1:13.

38 *Petites filles modèles*, preface, *Œuvres*, 1:119.

39 Bourdon, review of Ségur's early works, *Journal des demoiselles*, May 1860.

40 See Martyn Lyons's bestsellers lists for the nineteenth century, *HEF*, 3:369–397.

41 'Les contes de Madame de Ségur', p. 424.

42 Review of *Les malheurs de Sophie*, and *Nouveaux contes de fées*, by Maxime de Montrond, *Bibliographie catholique*, 22, October 1859.

43 Françoise Mayeur, *L'éducation des filles en France au XIXe siècle* (Paris, Hachette, 1979), p. 35.

44 Penny Brown, 'La femme enseignante: Mme de Genlis and the moral and didactic tale in France', *Bulletin of the John Rylands University Library of Manchester*, 76 (1994), 23–42.

45 Review of *Petites filles modèles*, *Bibliographie catholique*, 18, February 1859.

46 Peter Hunt, *Children's Literature* (Oxford, Blackwell, 2001), pp. 8–22.

47 *Œuvres*, 1:272.

48 This paragraph is partially indebted to Luc, *L'invention du jeune enfant*, pp. 98–100.

49 Mgr de Ségur, 'La sanctification des enfants', *Bulletin de l'Association Catholique de Saint-François de Sales pour la défense et la conservation de la foi*, February 1867.

50 M.O. Grenby, *Children's Literature* (Edinburgh, Edinburgh University Press, 2008), p. 79.

51 *Œuvres*, 1:152.

52 *Œuvres*, 1:153.

53 *Œuvres*, 1:182.

54 *Œuvres*, 1:1052–1053.

55 *Œuvres*, 2:1052.

56 *Œuvres*, 2:1058.

57 Cf. Kreyder, *L'enfance des saints*, pp. 125–204.

58 Dupanloup, *L'enfant*, chapter 1.

59 Popiel, *Rousseau's Daughters*, pp. 75–77.

60 *Œuvres*, 1:175.

61 *Œuvres*, 1:130.

62 *Œuvres*, 1:371.

63 Yvonne Knibiehler, 'Corps et cœurs', *Histoire des femmes en occident*, 4:351–387; Yvonne Knibiehler, Marcel Bernos, Elisabeth Ravoux-Rallo, *De la pucelle à la minette. Les jeunes filles de l'âge classique à nos jours* (Paris, Temps Actuels, 1983), chapter 6.

64 Knibiehler, 'Corps et cœurs', p. 360.

65 *Œuvres*, 3:1083.

66 *Œuvres*, 1:370.

67 *Œuvres*, 1:491.

68 It also had a political agenda: see chapter four pp. 142–143.

69 *Œuvres*, 2:324.

70 *Œuvres*, 1:520.

71 Veuillot, 'Les contes de Madame de Ségur', p. 425.

72 Livre de magasin B 1853–1910: Registre états des stocks en magasin, IMEC; the *Bibliographie de France* announced the first edition 21 July 1860, the second edition 15 June 1861, and a Spanish translation 6 April 1861. See Appendix II.

73 Manson, 'Editorial Strategies of Provincial Catholic Publishing Houses', p. 438.

74 Artiaga, 'Les catholiques et la littérature "industrielle au XIXe siècle', in Jacques Migozzi and Philippe Le Guern (eds) *Production(s) du populaire* (Limoges, Presses Universitaires de Limoges, 2004), pp. 221–233, p. 229.

75 See Hachette Catalogues compiled by Alphonse Langlois, 1862–66, IMEC.

76 Review of *Le mauvais génie*, *Bibliographie catholique*, 40, July 1868.

77 Quoted in Cordonnier, *Silhouettes familiales*, p. 245.

78 Letter from Louis Veuillot to the comtesse, 20 December 1860.

79 According to Olga de Pitray, *Mon bon Gaston*, p. 161.

80 Letter to Templier, 24 January 1859.

81 Yves Pincet, 'La comtesse à l'école', *Cahiers Robinson*, 9 (2001), 201–212, p. 203.

82 Letter to Templier, 16 February, 1859.

83 Luc, *L'Invention du jeune enfant*, p. 81.

84 Matthew, 18:3; see Marina Warner, *From the Beast to the Blonde: On Fairy Tales and Their Tellers* (London, Chatto & Windus, 1994), pp. 92–93.

85 Francis Marcoin, 'Petites lectures', *Revue des sciences humaines*, 1 (1992), 7–24; Gibson, *Social History of French Catholicism*, pp. 182–183.

86 Savart, *Catholiques en France*, p. 206.

87 *Œuvres*, 1:804.

88 Kreyder, *L'enfance des saints et des autres*, section four.

89 Letter to Templier, 8 November 1860.

90 *Œuvres*, 1:796.

91 *Œuvres*, 3:125.

92 *Œuvres*, 3:38.

93 Claude Savart, 'Approches de la religion populaire à travers quelques publications de la sociét de Saint Vincent de Paul', *La religion populaire* (Paris, Éditions du centre national de la recherche scientifique, 1979), p. 262.

94 *Œuvres*, 1:724.

95 *Œuvres*, 3:122.

96 *Œuvres*, 3:148.

97 Varner and Duvert, *La sœur de Jocrisse, comédie en un acte, mêlée de couplets*, first performed at the Palais Royal in 1841.

98 *Œuvres*, 2:3.

99 Harris, *Lourdes*, part one.

100 Letter to Templier, 30 May 1861.

101 Letter to Olga de Pitray, 11 May 1861.

102 Review of *La sœur de Gribouille*, *Bibliographie catholique*, by Ch. Laval, 27, April 1862.

103 On Italian unification, see Lucy Riall, *The Italian Risorgimento: State, Society and Unification* (London, Routledge, 1994).

104 Jacques Zeiller, *La comtesse de Ségur* (Paris, Bloud, 1913); Montesquiou, *Les roseaux pensants* (1897) amongst many others.

105 Hunt, *Children's Books*, pp. 8–22; Hans-Heino Ewers, 'La littérature moderne pour enfants', in Becchi, Egle and Julia, Dominique (eds) *Histoire de l'enfance en occident* (Paris, Seuil, 1998), 2:457–483.

106 Review of *L'auberge de l'ange gardien* and *Pauvre Blaise*, by Gustave Robert, *Bibliographie catholique*, 33, April 1865.

107 Jacques Chupeau, 'Instruire en amusant: théorie et pratique du récit éducatif à l'époque de la comtesse de Ségur', *Cahiers Robinson*, 9 (2001), 57–65.

108 Review of *Le journal de Marguerite* by Mlle Monniot, *Bibliographie catholique*, 19, January–June 1858.

109 Letter to Templier, 27 September 1863.

110 Letter to Olga de Pitray, 19 April 1860.

111 Mgr de Ségur, *La révolution expliquée aux jeunes gens* (Paris, Tolra et Haton, 1861), preface.

112 Published by Tolra, 1867, the edition used here is the critical edition, with essays and commentaries by Émile Poulat and J.P. Laurant, *L'antimaçonnisme catholique* (Paris, Berg International, 1994, 2nd edition 2006).

113 Ségur, *Les franc-maçons*, p. 86.

114 Mgr de Ségur, 'La sanctification des enfants'.

115 Ségur, *La révolution*, pp. 114–115.

116 Lucy Riall, *Garibaldi. Invention of a Hero* (New Haven and London, Yale University Press, 2007), p. 19.

117 Laura O'Brien, '*Une république pas pour rire:* caricature, satire and republican identity in the French Second Republic' (Unpublished PhD thesis, NUI Dublin, 2009).

118 Ségur, *La révolution*, p. 116.

119 Hédouville, *Mgr de Ségur*, chapter XII.

120 Maria Tatar, *Off with Their Heads! Fairy Tales and the Culture of Childhood* (Princeton, Princeton University Press, 1992), pp. 6–15.

121 Letter to Templier, 10 February 1864.

122 *Œuvres*, 3:15–17.

123 Letter from Mgr de Ségur to Olga de Pitray, 17 December 1866, Olga de Pitray, *Mon bon Gaston*, appendix.

124 Letter to Olga, 6 April 1865.

125 *Œuvres*, 3:201.

126 *Œuvres*, 3:294.

127 *Œuvres*, 3:333.

128 Heywood, *Growing up in France*, chapter 7.

129 Serge Chassagne, 'Le travail des enfants aux XVIIIe et XIXe siècles', in Becchi and Julia (eds) *Histoire de l'enfance en occident*, 2:239–288, especially pp. 271–273.

130 *Œuvres*, 3:810.

131 Jean Baubérot and Valentine Zuber, *Une haine oubliée: l'antiprotestanisme avant le 'pacte laïque' (1870–1905)* (Paris, Albin Michel, 2000).

132 Bonnie G. Smith, *Ladies of the Leisure Class: The Bourgeoises of Northern France in the 19th Century* (Princeton, Princeton University Press, 1981), chapter 8.

133 *Œuvres*, 3:388.

134 *Œuvres*, 3:1039.

135 Letter to Templier, 9 December 1872.

136 Chassagne, 'Le travail des enfants', pp. 271–272.

137 Knibiehler, *Histoire des mères*, p. 188; Eric Mension-Rigau, *L'enfance au château. L'éducation familiale des élites françaises au vingtième siècle* (Paris, Rivages, 1990).

138 Sigmund Freud, *A Child Is Being Beaten. A Contribution to the Study of the Origin of Sexual Perversions* (1919). Reprinted in Ethel Person (ed.) *On Freud's 'A Child Is Being Beaten'* (New Haven, Yale University Press, 1997), p. 180.

139 Beauvoir, *Mémoires d'une jeune fille rangée*, p. 29.

140 Marc Soriano, *Guide de littérature pour la jeunesse: courants, problèmes, choix* (Paris, Flammarion, 1975), pp. 473–485.

141 Margaret Lavinia Anderson, 'The Divisions of the Pope: The Catholic Revival and Europe's Transition to Democracy', in Ivereigh, Austen (ed.) *The Politics of Religion in an Age of Revival* (London, Institute of Latin American Studies, 2000), pp. 22–42, p. 31.

3

The tribulations of an author:
writing, censorship, and the reading
public under the Second Empire

Under Louis-Napoleon's authoritarian rule, even fifty-six-year-old grandmothers came under suspicion. When the comtesse de Ségur signed her contract with the publisher Hachette, on 1 September 1855, she was immediately subject to the tight strictures that were placed upon the public sphere in this period. Excessive as it may seem, Ségur's tales of talking donkeys and model little girls were rigorously scrutinised; her manuscripts were read by a series of censors, culminating in the colportage commission of the Ministry of Police, before they were allowed to go into print.[1] Entire sections were amputated from the comtesse's books without her prior consent or knowledge. One happy ending where the hero and heroine married prompted her editors to reach for the scissors, sternly condemning the work as 'hardly suitable reading material for little girls'.[2] Ségur's turbulent relationship with her publisher provides a window on to the concerns and difficulties an author faced in Second Empire France.

She wrote her stories in exciting times in the history of print culture. The 1850s proved a period of great economic and industrial dynamism, and the print trade was booming. Even little girls were officially encouraged to read, as, thanks to the Falloux Law of 1850, communes were obliged to provide schools specifically for girls. The size and nature of the public sphere were undergoing a drastic transformation. Contemporaries were only too aware of this phenomenon. All sides were keen to exploit the new possibilities for communication, but were also fearful of the enormity and potential threat to the established order that new readerships represented. This was compounded by the political situation, which was far from conducive to a liberal public sphere. The collapse of the July Monarchy and the bloody aftermath of the 1848 Revolution had provoked a sharp swing to the right. The Second Republic, now dominated by the Party of Order, promoted a return to the traditional values of family, order, property, and religion. President Louis-Napoleon Bonaparte took advantage of the unstable atmosphere to seize power through the *coup d'état* of 2 December 1851. To protect his position, he swiftly instigated a repressive authoritarian regime. This regime was particularly keen to regulate the burgeoning publishing industry, seen as one of the primary culprits in the spread of radical ideas.[3] The restrictions on freedom of speech were not simply government-imposed however. Fear of the pernicious effects of 'bad' reading on society was one of the all-pervading neuroses of the period. Publishers, libraries, writers, the Church, and social reformers all had their view of what the general public ought to be reading. Ségur was part of a wave of authors and publishers conscious that they could access a larger-scale audience. The problems she encountered, and ambitions she had for her readers, illustrate well the ambivalence with which contemporaries viewed the dynamic new phase of the reading revolution they had entered.

The question of what was to be culture for the masses, of new opportunities coupled with paranoia and censorship, lies at the heart of this chapter, which explores the extent to which the comtesse clashed with the censor and her publisher Hachette over the suitability of her works for a new, young (and especially female) reading public. The censorship of the comtesse de Ségur has occupied many scholars, as it has had serious implications for how Ségur is perceived as an author today. Jean-Yves Mollier, leading historian of the publishing industry, has written a series of articles on the comtesse.[4] According to Mollier, Madame de Ségur's reputation as a reactionary is not wholly deserved, as she had no choice but to comply with the norms of the period. He characterises the whole publishing process as an ordeal, and casts Ségur as a victim of the excesses of Napoleon III's regime. Similarly, Ségur's most recent editor, Claudine Beaussant, refers to the moral 'straitjacket' placed upon the comtesse.[5] However, these arguments risk glossing over the deeply conservative views the comtesse de Ségur expressed freely in her private correspondence. In contrast, Rémi Saudray has shown how the comtesse de Ségur's editor at Hachette also doctored her work to dilute her conservatism, and make it conform instead to the publishing house's emphasis on popular education.[6] This took place later in her career, in 1866. By this date, Napoleon III's regime was no longer concerned to support the

Catholic Church's agenda, and had appointed the liberal Victor Duruy to the Ministry of Education. As Ségur's work more or less spans the Second Empire, this problem of ideological shifting sands is perhaps not surprising. Moreover, Madame de Ségur did not always humbly submit to censorship. While it is possible to argue that the comtesse was to a certain extent a victim of her editor's zeal to conform to government diktat, in other respects she managed to capitalise on her elevated position in society. Her aristocratic status had market appeal, which gave Ségur a certain amount of leverage with an editor concerned above all with revenue. The moral pressures of the 'public sphere' placed upon the comtesse de Ségur and her colleagues were multiform. In light of these apparent contradictions, this chapter considers the excellent work by historians on the publishing history of the period,[7] but also takes Madame de Ségur's oeuvre as a whole, to try to tease out the complexities of the comtesse's relationship with Hachette.

The principal source that has been used to study their relationship is the letters Ségur sent to her editor, preserved in the publisher's archives.[8] They detail her objections to being censored and discussions concerning his suggested modifications, as well as her suggestions for the marketing of her books, and financial negotiations. Some scholars, notably Beaussant and Strich, make the case for a kind of feminism, while many have underlined Ségur's skill in dealings with her editor.[9] Using the Hachette correspondence, they trace Ségur's efforts to establish herself as a modern, professional author, keenly involved in all stages of the publishing process. Mollier however has pointed out that the comtesse's negotiations were less successful when it came to remuneration. Certainly, there is no contesting that it was her publisher, rather than the comtesse who enjoyed the bulk of the profits. But was it Ségur's gender, or rather the fact that she wrote for children that led to this? Were businesses more interested in profit than the abstract problem of gender? The question of to what extent issues concerning gender – the gender of her readership, and her status as a woman author in the masculine public sphere – had an impact on her professional life is incorporated into the analysis within this chapter.

Literary studies of Ségur have neglected the reception of her books under the Second Empire, and yet, contemporary perceptions of her constructed image were crucial, as press endorsement formed the core advertising strategy of the book trade at this time.[10] They have also hitherto overlooked the observations on the popularity of the comtesse de Ségur and the children's collection, written in 1868 by Alphonse Langlois, an employee at Hachette. Hidden inside a series of old Hachette catalogues is the weird and wonderful work of Monsieur Langlois. Langlois had worked all of his life as an accounts clerk at Hachette, and in the late 1860s he undertook the task of writing a history of the company. It was never published. Instead Langlois bound up his work inside old copies of trade catalogues, along with tables of sales, statistics, relevant newspaper clippings and other Hachette ephemera.[11] This source has provided a useful source for studies on Hachette by historians Mollier and Jean Mistler. Langlois also wrote on the comtesse. In order to trace how the comtesse negotiated the difficult task of writing children's books in an age of nascent democracy, censorship, and politico-religious culture wars in the masculine public sphere, all aspects of the production process need to be examined.

M.M.L. Hachette & Co.: the construction of an empire

The story of the comtesse de Ségur in the public sphere is in many ways the story of her relationship with her publishers, M.M.L. Hachette & Co.[12] They published all of her storybooks in the Hachette *Bibliothèque Rose* children's collection, and it is to this series that she owes her enduring fame. The comtesse de Ségur and the *Bibliothèque Rose* are virtually synonymous in the French imagination. Ségur's books enjoyed almost immediate success, and by the twentieth century were a publishing phenomenon. The *Bibliothèque Rose* was one of Hachette's most successful ventures, owing in no small measure to the popularity of Madame de Ségur.[13] Theirs was to be a highly lucrative association for M.M.L. Hachette & Co., while providing the comtesse with the financial independence she craved. It was also to prove a highly tense collaboration. Hachette was commercially minded, with one eye on the censor, and the comtesse often found that her artistic and religious agenda came into conflict with her publisher's interests. M.M.L. Hachette & Co. was to play a significant role in shaping the final product.

The comtesse de Ségur was one of the new authors recruited by Louis Hachette as he was just beginning to construct his publishing empire. Louis Hachette had originally trained as a teacher, but when he graduated in 1822 he was barred from the profession by the Grand Maître de l'Université, under the stipulations of the Restoration monarchy. His passion for education led him to publishing. He made his fortune under the July Monarchy, after securing a contract with the education ministry to supply the new state schools with textbooks. With the advent of Louis-Napoleon's prosperous and rapidly industrialising France, he saw the opportunity for his business to grow. Inspired by W.H. Smith's success in England, Hachette began to prepare his bid for a monopoly on trading in railway stations. As well as entering into negotiations in 1852–54 with the heads of the respective rail companies, he also began to construct an entire new catalogue of books destined to be sold in these new kiosks. Hachette needed a new and exciting 'leisure' catalogue to sell to passengers to amuse them on their journeys. With this aim in mind he bought out publishers specialising in novels, travel guides, and advice manuals, as well as re-editing authors whose works were already in the public domain. He also set up new collections, designed to exploit profitable developing markets, including children's literature. It was during these negotiations that he met the president of the Eastern Rail Company, the comte Eugène de Ségur, who suggested his wife as a possible author for their new children's collection.

Money and morality: the Hachette editorial policy

The tense circumstances surrounding Hachette's railway station monopoly were to have important implications for the company's subsequent editorial policy. His bold move ruffled the feathers of competitors. They accused Hachette of trying to secure an illegal monopoly, and, worse still, of contravening the existing legislation on bookselling, which stated that booksellers were permitted only one premises (which the initiative flagrantly flouted). The Chief of Police rectified the situation by decreeing that Hachette railway station kiosks were not technically bookshops; rather they were to be considered to have the same legal status as book hawkers (*colporteurs*). In this case, all publications destined for sale in these spaces would be required to obtain the notorious 'blue stamp' of approval from the Commission de Colportage before being allowed to go to the presses. The law was designed ostensibly to try to regulate pamphlets sold by itinerant book hawkers who had proved to be the most effective method for the dissemination of political ideas during the revolutions of 1830 and 1848. However, as Mollier points out, the new legislation regulating booksellers clamped down hard on anyone who attempted to sell publications on a large scale. This was the paranoid response of the authorities to the dramatic new opportunities offered by the ever-growing rail network for diffusion of books, and general expansion of the book trade beyond its traditional bounds.

The implications for Hachette and his authors were clear. In 1853, an editor explained to Alphonse de Lamartine, 'the production of the

Bibliothèque des Chemins de fer [railway station collection] might be held up by the government; it could even fail owing to their ill will – we know that they have already looked into it – we must therefore take extreme care not to provoke them in any way and we would be grateful if you would kindly give your permission for the removal from the edition that we are going to publish of your book, of two passages that are not essential to the plot and that could become for us a source of difficulties'.[14] The offending passage concerned a discussion of Bonaparte, which could well have upset his nephew. It was not just political references that were considered sensitive. In the moral backlash of the Second Empire, Hachette's new collections promised that 'all publications that could excite or sustain political passions, as well as immoral writings, will be banned'.[15] Even the slightest deviation from the holy trinity of property, family, and religion was considered a danger to public decency. In this atmosphere, writing books for children was a delicate business. As it came under the umbrella of education, the ecclesiastical authorities, notably via the organ *Bibliographie catholique*, watched this book production like hawks. The big Catholic publishers dominated children's literature until the 1880s, when school reforms began to squeeze them out. Their grip only really loosened following the 1905 separation of Church and State, which lost them all their valuable schools custom.[16] Thus, for most of the nineteenth century, the Catholic publishers set the tone for the market. In practice, this meant that Hachette's team of correctors had to ensure they followed the type of editorial policy found at Mame, who was currently the market leader: 'a censorship committee takes in hand all the manuscripts sent to Monsieur Mame and subjects them to a long critical examination, where the author's doctrines and the form of his work are the object of delicate attention and severe judgement. Two contradictory reports are produced about every manuscript.'[17] Competitors had little choice but to comply. Hachette often imported authors for the *Bibliothèque Rose* from Catholic publishers.[18]

In addition, the comtesse wrote books that would be read by little girls, the most delicate reading public of all. Nineteenth-century fears of the moral dangers young women ran by reading provided Flaubert with rich material for *Madame Bovary*.[19] If women were at risk of corruption from books, then in the eyes of moralists girls' reading matter could be a matter of life and death. Take for example the dire warnings issued by *La semaine des familles*, which described the dangers that could befall such vulnerable readers exposed to the iniquities of the modern novel. One young victim commits suicide, while Eugène Sue's *Mystères de Paris* drives another mad.[20] Parents were advised to ensure that the faculties of reasoning of their sons were developed enough to withstand the temptations of literature, but their daughters were not considered capable of such sophistication. Exposure to novels could therefore be fatal.[21] Cautionary tales like these were commonplace. The Second Empire proved the high watermark of the restrictive education model for well-to-do young girls that consisted of keeping them in absolute ignorance to preserve their purity.[22] This had an important impact upon book production. Editorial policy was also dictated to a certain extent by readers, who apparently complained when marriage or 'sentiments' were portrayed in books for their children, as will be seen in this analysis of the censorship of the comtesse's books.

Unlike Lamartine, the comtesse was not a famous author but a novice. She therefore did not receive a polite request for her permission. Her editor despatched a letter concerning the conditions for the publication of *Petites filles modèles*, informing the comtesse that M.M.L. Hachette & Co. reserved the right to make any changes or adjustments as they saw fit. This evidently piqued her aristocratic pride, for her response expressed shock at the authoritarian tone she felt she detected in the letter: 'in spite of the modesty that ought to have prevented me from having such an expectation, I had hoped to reserve for myself the role of making changes, additions, or removing sections. But, since you think it so important that you hold absolute and unique power over my *Petites filles modèles*, may your wish be granted over my own.'[23] She discovered the true meaning of these conditions when she received the printer's proofs of *Petites filles modèles*. Words had been changed or removed, and several lines, in some places whole episodes, had been mysteriously deleted without her consent.

Ségur wrote a passionate complaint to her editor that rendered her evident fury in colourful, witty prose:

> Sir, I am no doubt blinded by Authorial pride; I was outraged first by the fact that two *entirely true* episodes were judged impossible, and then by the unheard of and cavalier manner by which your corrector proceeded. The Author being human, may err; the right to reprimand is of course accorded to the Editor, who reins as a despot over his Authors, but the right to remove passages without consulting the Author seems to me to be quite new, and not yet common practice. This is the opinion shared by the half dozen Authors that I know personally. However, the Good Lord having not marked me with the sin of obstinacy, I shall give in to your demand . . . I am therefore sending back the proofs for publication having been revised, damaged and diminished, and I await the next set in the humble attitude of a deflated balloon.[24]

In this letter Ségur underlined that she may have been a newcomer to the profession, but that she knew several old hands, and would not stand to be made a fool of. By fashioning herself as the 'Author', Madame de Ségur was also assuming a professional, masculine persona. She had won her contract thanks to her husband's position, but Ségur did not want her editor to imagine that she was therefore simply writing for pin money, and would care little if he doctored her work to suit Hachette's needs. This glittering display of literary prowess was a serious challenge to any such misunderstandings: Ségur was daring her editor not to take her seriously as an 'Author'.

It would be interesting to know how her editor reacted to this outburst. The letter's recipient, Émile Templier, was a partner in the Hachette business, a contract sealed by his marriage to Louis Hachette's daughter. Templier was in charge of the railway collections, and in this capacity he was to act as the comtesse de Ségur's editor throughout her career at Hachette. Described by one obituary as having an almost military air, Templier was a serious, quiet man, known for his traditionalism and piety. He was also an astute businessman, which was the perfect combination in the moral, and prosperous, Second Empire. 'All those who met him will remember him as a representative of the old French bourgeoisie, respectful of tradition, yet at the same time open to new ideas.'[25] Their correspondence provides an insight into the relations between an author working in what was considered a minor literary genre and a publishing house concerned with running an industrial production line to compete within a dynamic market. This was also the first time that the comtesse entered into the professional, public sphere. She was assuming her new role of businesswoman. Only the comtesse's letters remain, but they often contain references to his missives. They are usually in the form of indignant complaints from the comtesse, although a friendship developed, and later on they clearly enjoyed discussing the progress of Templier's young grandson. The original manuscript copies of Ségur's letters also show that Templier sometimes annotated her letters with his initial response. Theirs was a lively dialogue, with the comtesse acting the part of the 'Author', keen to defend her precious work from the scissors of the correctors, while the more reserved Templier worked to rein her in, to keep the spirit of the collection strictly within the bounds of his keen sense of moral decency and that of the government. His letters were no doubt often brief and presumably a little curt, judging from the defensive tone the comtesse's replies often adopted. The obituary which appeared in the magazine he directed for several decades noted that Templier was a man who disliked fuss in such matters, 'in business dealings he got straight to the point; taking a moment to reflect, and then deciding with a singular precision'.[26]

Given the readership for which it was destined, were Hachette's correctors not right to detect something troublesome in the book? *Petites filles modèles* promises an education story for girls. But, three chapters into the story, a terrifyingly evil stepmother rips her way into the pages, and upsets the genteel education manual structure by snatching her young stepdaughter and giving her a good thrashing. The reader, along with the model little girls of the tale, is shocked (but also, as the comtesse no doubt intended, instantly hooked). Needless to say, Hachette's correctors were also less than pleased. From her letter on this censorship, quoted above, with its alternating indignation and humility, it seems likely that she was responding to a letter from Templier upbraiding her for providing her vulnerable young readership with a bad example. She mentions that two episodes had been 'judged impossible', which could well be quoting from Templier's letter. She goes on to concede that she will remove everything that shocked the corrector, but insists, 'and I repeat', that 'the two episodes that shocked your corrector *really took place*, with the only difference that it was not a step-mother, but a mother who brought her child up in this manner, and I could have used other, even more cruel, examples'.[27] Clearly then, the two scenes featured Madame Fichini, the evil stepmother, inflicting cruel punishments on her stepdaughter Sophie, and the complaint arose from her portrayal of a brutal mother figure. Her defence rested on the notion that this wicked woman was based on true life: she had not invented this immoral behaviour. Such arguments proved futile. Madame Fichini was the polar opposite of the femininty exalted by the nineteenth-century cult of the loving mother. Moreover, the book's sequel, *Les vacances*, takes the reader further into Madame Fichini's psyche, and, oddly enough, made it into the bookshops more or less untouched by the censor. The reader learns that she beats her stepdaughter with such malignant force in revenge for the horse-whipping she had received from the girl's dead father. Mathilde Bourdon, in her review for the *Journal des demoiselles*, was one of the rare critics to pick up on this aspect of the trilogy, which in Bourdon's opinion risked undermining the message of Ségur's works:

> We only have one reason to reproach two of these excellent books, and that is to have portrayed, completely unnecessarily, a woman; a stepmother both evil and ridiculous; and to have placed before the eyes of children a scene of conjugal brutality (*les Vacances*), which, in spoiling such a

charming tableau, could well trouble in no small way the notions of justice
and morality which flow so naturally from this author's pen.[28]

This episode calls into question the comtesse de Ségur's reputation as an
author with solely didactic aims. As discussed in Chapter 1, the impulse
to revisit her childhood led the comtesse to abandon the strict education
manual structure. Memory was also the excuse she used to justify her
inclusion of scenes of brutality in *Petites filles modèles*. That she continued
to depict Madame Fichini in *Les vacances* suggests that Ségur preferred
to risk her moral reputation and profits rather than compromise the
character she had created.

The comtesse appears to have got away with it. Mathilde Bourdon's
concerns were not universally shared. Where twentieth-century critics
delighted in analysing the dark psychological issues being played out in
this book, not all contemporaries picked up on the violence in *Petites
filles modèles* as being out of the ordinary or sadistic. The idea that children's books ought to protect their young readers from the realities of
violence and death is a twentieth-century invention. Maria Tatar, for
example, notes the levels of excessive punishment meted out in 'improving' literature: 'the numbers of children who go up in flames in nineteenth-
century story books is nothing short of extraordinary'.[29] Indeed, when
the Catholic journalist Louis Veuillot objected to the portrayal of violence
in the comtesse's book, it was because he felt she was arguing against
corporal punishment, in contradiction to teachings in Scriptures.[30]
Meanwhile the glowing review in *Bibliographie catholique* did not make
any mention of impropriety. Rather, the reviewer read the book as the
comtesse suggested they should: 'the author announces, in her short
preface, that the principal characters in her book, *Camille and Madeleine*,
are portraits. We have only one wish, and that is that these portraits
inspire many copies.'[31]

It was not only Madame de Ségur's stories for girls that attracted
moral censure, as demonstrated by the forced revisions to the ending
of her *Mémoires d'un âne*, discussed in the previous chapter. Nevertheless,
the most violent objections to Ségur's work were raised over the
question of the suitability of her books for a female audience. They
illustrate just how onerous the task of writing books for girls under the
Second Empire could be. Templier received complaints about *Les
malheurs de Sophie*, although what his correspondents objected to
remains a mystery. The comtesse told him to ignore them.[32] The problem
resurfaced when she centred *L'auberge de l'ange gardien* on the theme of
marriage. The General Dourakine's views on marriage were far from

complimentary. Worse still, the heroine, the beautiful young Elfy, jokes that she would have proposed to her suitor if he had not got there first. Such scenes were bound to cause trouble. The most vehement reaction had been from the fortnightly children's magazine, *La semaine des enfants*. Hachette collaborated with this journal as a publicity exercise, for it pre-serialised *Bibliothèque Rose* books. Its editors adhered to an even more strict editorial policy, no doubt owing to the strict political conservatism of the owner of the review, Charles Lahure.[33] The magazine's editor, Théodore Barrau, a long-time Hachette collaborator and author of many official school manuals, wrote to the comtesse directly. He asked her to tone down her love story, explaining that readers regularly asked him to avoid any mention of what he rather prudishly called sentiments that 'lead to marriage'.[34] Incensed, Ségur accused him of having a dirty mind, saying that several of her entourage that she had consulted were in agreement with her.[35] The underlying message of her response was that she was the comtesse de Ségur, an author whose books they had hitherto been happy to publish, and, moreover, mother of a highly respected priest. How could she possibly be capable of writing anything untoward? Again, she used her wider circle of influence as a bargaining tool with Templier. By this time, 1863, the comtesse had produced a string of bestselling books for the *Bibliothèque Rose*, and she was in a much better position to bargain. The situation reached a stalemate, as the comtesse steadfastly refused to give in to what she felt were ridiculous demands. Privately, Barrau complained in a memo to Lahure that he was exasperated by Ségur's behaviour: 'she has neither modified, nor changed anything; she has not removed one single passionate outburst [*joyeuseté*] . . . I persist in the belief that this is hardly suitable reading material for little girls.'[36] Despite these serious misgivings, in the memo Barrau went on to explain that he would give in and publish the story, noting that Lahure's common business interests with Hachette meant that he felt obliged to concede. This was a none too subtle hint that he felt the venal interests at Hachette led the publishers to forget their duty, and simply let the public be duped by their faith in the comtesse's name.

Her story therefore made it into the collection intact. Paradoxically the notoriously gimlet-eyed *Bibliographie catholique* missed any suggestion of immorality in the book. Its review was even filled with praise for 'the piquant and virtuous Elfy'.[37] The comtesse advised Templier: 'if Mr. Barrau listened to all the people who offered him their opinion on his *Semaine des enfans* [*sic*], he would risk making nobody happy, like in the fable of the miller, his son and the donkey'. In other words, she implied that Barrau took the complaints of a few busybodies far too seriously, rather than considering his wider audience, and so he risked making his product tiresome and losing its readership.[38] Ségur clearly understood the market better than Barrau, and it appears that some at Hachette secretly recognised this. In 1868, Alphonse Langlois wrote that *La semaine des enfants* had enjoyed immense success at the beginning, but had not managed to live up to its promise. He estimated that the publication 'owed in large part its great success to their collaboration with the very moral and well-loved Madame la comtesse de Ségur', but that the project was mismanaged, as the editors failed to capitalise on the New Year peak-time sales, and over-expanded too quickly. (Traditionally New Year, not Christmas, was the time in France when presents were exchanged.) He predicted that the business would fail soon.[39] The publication folded immediately after the comtesse's death. Madame de Ségur's moral reputation served her well. The perceived morality of the name on her books for girls mattered more than the inexact science of determining what was suitable for them.

As a *Bibliothèque Rose* author, the comtesse had to walk a tightrope between money and morals. She was very conscious of the importance of writing what she called 'Hachette' books, or 'infantile' books [*niaiseries*].[40] What did Ségur mean by that? What indeed was a 'Hachette' book? Editorial policy was clear – to follow government directives as closely as possible. Most importantly for the comtesse however, was that the *Bibliothèque Rose* was aimed at the middle-class, leisured market. Its children's books were beautifully packaged in red and pink, inlaid with gold lettering, and sold for two francs each. In this sense, Ségur had to satisfy two potentially conflicting briefs. She was paid to write fun books for children, but also to ensure that the moral tone of the collection was maintained. This she accomplished with prodigious skill. While her publishers had to be seen to preserve public decency, or risk losing their licence, Émile Templier soon recognised that the comtesse de Ségur was fast becoming a trusted brand name. Her exuberant and sometimes excessive fictions may have risked offending the sense of decency of their correctors, but they sold well. Moreover, venerable Catholic critics did not always share the opinions of her editors and correctors. Thus, in 1868, when Alphonse Langlois delivered his assessment of the *Bibliothèque Rose*'s success, he attributed it above all to the comtesse de Ségur's books, 'which gave this charming collection the distinction of publishing works that were in good taste, of excellent morals, and that were above all extremely cheap'.[41] Langlois, whom Mollier describes as an intransigent Catholic and committed royalist,[42] was perhaps predisposed to find Madame de Ségur 'very moral', as she espoused his politico-religious beliefs. Nevertheless, his comment encapsulates all that was ambiguous in the Hachette house morality.

Ségur certainly, in the eyes of the public, had excellent moral credentials. For a start, she was the mother of a leading prelate. Mgr de Ségur's celebrity as the so-called blind apostle gave an added lustre of piety to her product. The concerns that motivated the discerning bourgeois mother when she selected a book for her precious infant were overwhelmingly religious in mid-nineteenth-century France. Women were encouraged by the clergy to act as 'priests in the home', charged with reviving their husband's all too often flagging piety, and bringing up their children to be good Catholics.[43] A mother who bought the comtesse de Ségur's fictions could feel reassured that she was fulfilling her duty of teaching her children Catholic values. Ségur's books had received endorsement from the clerical establishment via the *Bibliographie catholique* and the influential Veuillot in *L'univers*. This was important for any editor with his eye on sales figures, as Catholic editors dominated the children's market. Second, her aristocratic pedigree was central to the comtesse's appeal. Unlike many other women authors of the nineteenth century she did not mask her identity or create her own independent public identity by using a pseudonym.[44] Thus she – and more to the point, her publishers – were able to exploit the appeal of the Ségur name. For her readers, the gold lettering on her book covers that spelled out LA COMTESSE DE SÉGUR evoked the impossibly exclusive upper echelons of the French nobility, the proud vestiges of *ancien régime* France. Her books promised the genuine aristocratic education, at a price affordable to the middle classes. Langlois had noted that her books gave the collection a cachet of class, that they could then sell cheaply, and at great profit. Théodore Barrau had also noticed the reluctance at Hachette to rein in their golden goose, remarking cynically during the *Auberge de l'ange gardien* debacle, 'in any case, this book has in the eyes of our public, sufficient guarantee in the name of the author'.[45] Developing this 'name' was absolutely crucial to the comtesse's sales, which helped prevent the further doctoring of her work by the correctors.

Moreover, the recognition of Ségur's reputation with her public did not mean that Ségur and her editor saw eye to eye over the nature of the image she ought to cultivate. M.M.L. Hachette & Co. also had a strong house ethos, stemming from Hachette's background in education. Mistler notes how Louis Hachette had not forgotten his dismissal from the teaching profession under the Restoration for political reasons. When the same thing happened to a new generation of student teachers under Louis-Napoleon, his publishing house became a refuge for them.[46] Education remained a central concern. Furthermore, Hachette maintained a neutral stance over religion and politics. This meant that any references to the sort of combative religion of the comtesse's milieu was anathema. The *Bibliothèque Rose* book should not be confused with the ultramontane product. As we shall see below, her politico-religious agenda sometimes led to potentially destructive tensions between author and editor. The following section highlights how the situation was compounded by the production process of *Bibliothèque Rose* books, which followed Hachette's entrepreneurial approach to publishing.

The author in the 'age of the publisher'

Writing for Hachette meant the comtesse was from a distinct stable. As an editor, publisher, and bookseller all at once, Hachette exercised a great deal of control over his authors. This was the 'age of the publisher',[47] who came to the fore as the expanding publishing industry looked to create new markets, and entice new readers. One important innovation was the 'collection'. Books were sold together under a theme, which was the ideal way to create a recognisable brand that could sell in bulk. Hachette contracts therefore often specified the style, content, tone, and even length of the commissioned work. This was culture as standardised product. However, the Comtesse de Ségur also had very definite ideas about the production and marketing of children's books. Her forceful personality and creativity likewise defined the collection. Through her success she became the first flagship author of the *Bibliothèque Rose,* and contributed to its distinctive reputation. This was not a creation process that was easy – the strong personalities, differing political agendas, and business interests involved ensured that it could often involve much wrangling.

Mollier explains how Hachette created what he calls the 'logic of supply'. More than simply responding to demand, the publisher sought to create products that would seduce the customer. He commissioned books, and made many stipulations about their content.[48] There are several indications which suggest that the comtesse de Ségur's books could have been designed to conform to the *Bibliothèque Rose* collection. Although (as far as we know) Templier only once asked her to write on a subject of his choosing, he regularly demanded cuts and extensive rewrites of her books. The length of Ségur's books and their illustrations were also prescribed by her editor. In the first letter to her editor she informs him she is sending the first half of the 'long-awaited' manuscript, which she promises will be 'at least 300 pages'.[49] Ségur had been instructed to write a book of a specified length. This process was applied to all of her subsequent works. Letters to her daughter often referred to her writing in terms of page numbers, and only having a certain number of pages to go before the work is completed: 'yesterday I wrote 20 pages of *Pauvre Blaise*; I am at 275 and am approaching the ending. I hope to have finished it this week' . . . 'I have made such advances with my *Blaise* that I am at 296 and I will finish it today.'[50] If he considered that a book was too short, Monsieur Templier would complain.[51] Ségur warned him this insistence on length hampered her abilities as a writer: '*Jean qui rit* bores me as well, but it will read more or less the same. And there I was thinking I was doing you a service by lengthening my books by several dozen pages!'[52] She was expected to produce several books for the collection in the year. As Alphonse Langlois explained, the success of the children's collection placed even more pressure on authors to produce enough books to satisfy demand: 'the immense success and turnover, especially at the time of the new year, means that authors and publishers must write and publish a great number of volumes. Many of these charming works were reissued several times as well, up to four to six times, particularly those by the comtesse de Ségur.'[53] As their prize author, the comtesse certainly felt under pressure. She responded to Templier's request for more books with a certain weary frustration: 'you appear to suggest in your letter that I do not provide enough manuscripts for your *Bibliothèque Rose*. It would be difficult for me to write more, but if you need a third volume in the year, I will try to manufacture one for you.'[54] Such pressure on authors was common. They were expected to respond to the new thirst for books at an industrial rate. The Catholic houses could be just as demanding as their secular counterparts, who were supposedly more commercial-minded. The novelist Zénaïde Fleuriot lamented the fact that she could never get the endings of books quite right, because her editors were always 'harassing her' to hand in manuscripts before they were ready.[55]

In spite of her complaints about Hachette's insatiable thirst for more books, Ségur was more than willing to produce material. There was definitely a mercenary aspect to her vocation as a writer. In addition to her storybooks, it has been suggested that the comtesse also sold Hachette unfinished manuscripts or stories she did not intend for publication under her name. They were allegedly then published under a pseudonym in the *Semaine des enfants*.[56] Mgr de Ségur observed: 'the game is worth the candle. Ten francs per page, one hundred or one hundred and fifty francs per day: I wish all sorts of blessings for this *mauvais génie*' (the title of the book she was working on).[57] Mistler suggests that the comtesse 'naively' counted her work by the page.[58] A second intepretation would be that she received payment by the page or line for some of the work that she did. While ten francs per page corresponds with the price Hachette paid for her manuscripts in the 1860s, it is possible that the comtesse also earned money when her books were pre-published in the *Semaine des enfants*. This was part of the package that Zénaïde Fleuriot was offered when she joined the *Bibliothèque Rose* in 1873.[59] Earlier, in 1866, Ségur had tried to negotiate a similar arrangement for her daughter, but it would appear the *Semaine des enfants* was not interested in Olga's works.[60] These transactions were not usually recorded, and the comtesse did not have any contract with the publication. However, Marielle Mouranche notes that this was common procedure. Ségur may have received between ten and fifteen centimes per line, in addition to the payment for the manuscript. She received 500 francs each for her first three manuscripts, a similar sum to the payment Flaubert received for *Madame Bovary*. Both were novices. However, while most authors who achieved recognition could then expect a substantial pay rise – Flaubert earned 10,000 francs for *Salammbô* – the comtesse's requests for increased payment fell on deaf ears. She managed, through regular threats to move to other publishers, and no doubt her solid reputation, to raise her price to 2,000 francs for *Gribouille* and then to 3,000 francs for *Les deux nigauds*. So, by 1862, Madame de Ségur's earnings, depending on how many books she wrote in a year, could vary from 3,000 francs if she only wrote one to 6,000 francs if she wrote two, which was her average. If the *Semaine des enfants* did pay her for the pre-publication of her stories, she could expect to double this sum. Thus, she might well have earned between 6,000 and 12,000 francs per year, and this not including her extra, anonymous work. According to Ségur's own calculations in her books, 10,000 francs per year provided comfortable revenue for a bourgeois family.[61] It was, of course, not enough to maintain an aristocratic estate, and the Ségur family was experiencing difficulties. Les Nouettes would be sold in 1872. Nevertheless, such a tidy sum was presumably stimulus enough to keep on the production line, and manufacture the requisite number of pages.

The question of gender is an interesting one in their dealings. Did the comtesse receive lower payments than Flaubert because she was a woman author? Mollier has argued forcefully that this was not the case; that in business, it was the iron law of capital that ruled. Fierce competition forced publishers to keep the prices they charged as low as possible, which placed pressure on profit margins. Authors were paid accordingly.[62] The deciding factor in the case of the comtesse, according to him, was that she wrote in a new, minor genre, that of children's books, and so she never received the remuneration that other authors (of both genders) writing education manuals or novels were paid. Ségur's reputation earned her more pay than most in her field. Mistler argues that Ségur was not so canny when it came to the business side – she raised her manuscript prices, but was more interested in up-front payments than in earning royalties.[63] Hachette granted her fellow 'governess' author, Julie Gouraud, a percentage of the profits of her *Lettres de deux poupées* in 1863.[64] Looking at the evolution of Ségur's contracts with Hachette suggests that she appears to have cared more about preventing alterations to her manuscripts than about negotiating for a percentage of the profits. Still, gender remained a deciding factor. As Mollier concedes, young children's literature itself was designated 'minor' partly because it was perceived to be feminine. The first section of this chapter has demonstrated that editors and reviewers frequently used the fact that her readership included girls to justify criticisms of her work, and indeed censorship of them. As Chapter 5 makes clear, the reputation that Ségur established, which eventually gave her more leverage in negotiations and allowed her to charge more for her books, was clearly determined by the strict gender codes of the nineteenth century.

Although she was willing to profit from the Hachette production line, the comtesse was determined not to let the industrial nature of the enterprise spoil the creations that bore her name. Madame de Ségur did not have the sort of personality suited to being treated in the 'modern' way, as she told Templier right away when his correctors modified her *Petites filles modèles*. Similarly, when she felt that the product was being compromised, she was quick to respond. For example, typographical errors sent Ségur into fits of rage. Her daughter Olga detailed how the comtesse would go to the printing factory herself. If true, this testifies to the intensity of her feeling, as Hachette printers Lahure and Crété had both decamped to the suburbs where land was cheap – hardly the sort of place a *grande dame* like the comtesse would normally deign to visit.

My mother attached great importance to the corrections of the *proofs*[65] [her italics] of her books and would make a terrible drama out of the mistakes that the typesetters [*protes*] sometimes made. In this case, when she was in Paris, she would go in person to give them a piece of her mind, and would address one poor invalid who could do nothing and who was apparently terrified of her! He said, 'that lady has eyes like pistols!', after one visit to the printing factory from the indignant descendant of Genghis Khan [i.e. the comtesse].[66]

Judging from the tone of her letters on the subject to Templier, the description of her eyes flashing with fury was no exaggeration. She became so exasperated by the inferior quality of Monsieur Crété's printing of her Bible series that she took to referring to him as 'that awful Monsieur Crété', or in one missive, 'Monsieur Crétin'. Templier's response must have been sharp, as she soon apologised for her 'error'.[67]

The real bone of contention proved to be the illustrations. This was the area where she had to struggle the hardest, caught between her concerns as an author, her publisher's commercial interests, and her milieu's religious ideals. She was frustrated at every turn. The main selling point of the *Bibliothèque Rose* collection was that it was illustrated. The catalogue announcing the launch of the collection emphasised its artist, rather than its authors: 'children have their own books: amusing books where they will find lots of pictures. These pictures will please them all the more, as in the future they will be drawn by the crayon of Bertall, our talented artist. It is good to keep these little travellers quietly occupied.'[68] Templier was also something of an art enthusiast, and he specialised in editing illustrated albums.[69] Ségur's first book, *Nouveaux contes de fées*, was accompanied by drawings by Gustave Doré. This was an honour for a first book by an unknown author, as Doré had already established quite a reputation by 1855.[70] The Comtesse however was not pleased with the results.[71] This was understandable, as it was fairly obvious that Doré had not read her tales very attentively. He produced the illustrations with his studio of artists, and there was significant variation in the plates by the different artists. One protagonist, 'little Henri', described in the text as a 'poor child of seven years', appears in some of the plates to be an attractive, muscular youth, which completely undermines the pathos of her narrative. She was even less impressed with the in-house artist, Bertall. Following the illustrations Bertall produced for *Petites filles modèles*, she asked Templier not to use him again.[72] Looking through the book it becomes clear that Bertall took very little interest in the young heroines of the book: out of twenty plates, the girls feature in only five. Instead, the artist exercised his talents in drawing snooty local dignitaries, doctors,

1   Bertall, 'Elle s'élança sur Sophie et la fouetta à bras redoublés',
published in comtesse de Ségur, *Petites filles modèles*

sailors, and servants, despite the fact that many of these characters are
only mentioned fleetingly. Furthermore, the incongruity of using an
artist who had been heavily involved in revolution – producing political
cartoons in 1848 – to draw Ségur's model little girls did not escape Veuillot's attention. He felt that they ran contrary to the ethos of Ségur's text:
'Monsieur Bertall has taken it upon himself to introduce into the purity
of these pages, particularly in *Petites filles modèles*, certain figures that
have all the coarseness and often all the venom of satirical cartoons. Truly
these are serpents nestling amongst flowers and fruits.'[73] Bertall may have
offended the comtesse's and Veuillot's sensibilities, but it is precisely one
of his drawings for *Petites filles modèles* that has come to symbolise her
work – a particularly dramatic rendering of the scene where the evil
Madame Fichini whips little Sophie (Figure 1). This striking image of a
tiny, knickerless Sophie, trapped in the grip of this monster in huge
crinolines, probably contributed to the accusations of sadism and perver-
sion Ségur has faced over the years.[74]

Ségur never managed to gain control over the images accompanying
her books. This was not for lack of trying. For example, when it came to
Les malheurs de Sophie, Ségur asked, 'may I choose the subjects for the
engravings?'[75] It appears that the request was ignored, as she continued

to write to complain about specific plates whenever a book came out, suggesting that she did not get to preview the illustrations. Fortunately for the sanity of all involved, her new illustrator Horace Castelli proved to be much more to the comtesse's taste. Once their friendship was established, he would come and visit her, to discuss the next book that they would work on together.[76] Still, since the collection's main selling point was its illustrations, the comtesse was not permitted to choose her illustrator. Castelli was not always selected by Templier for the task.

The problem flared up once more over the question of the illustrations for her *Évangile*. Nowhere did the clash of interests become so bitter as over her Bible series. This was a battle she was never going to win. Templier considered the publication in 1873 of 'the *Évangiles*, with the simple and noble engravings by Bida' to be one of his major achievements.[77] This was an immensely ambitious project begun in 1860 by Louis Hachette, which Templier had taken over following Hachette's death in 1864. The house had invested vast sums of money in Bida, even sending him to Palestine to draw inspiration from the Holy Land.[78] Templier had very clear ideas on the subject, and considered himself to be a specialist. This was a relatively new area for Hachette. Although they had always published religious education manuals, the publishers had refused to consider printing the type of religious works that the comtesse and her milieu wanted to produce. However, in the early 1860s, when religious publishing was experiencing a boom, the proposition began to look attractive to the company. Templier agreed to take her Grandmother's Bible project on.

It got off to a bad start. Templier reacted angrily when her son, Anatole de Ségur, an adept of new ideas on ultramontane art, suggested that Templier's choice of illustrations for the first edition of the comtesse's *Évangile* were 'anti-Christian', and disfigured the book. The original illustrations were a workshop production by a number of artists, and were rather workaday. They differed little from the images that usually accompanied her storybooks (Figure 2). By contrast, French ultramontane theory held that stiff, hieratic art best expressed divinity.[79] The publication in 1863 of Renan's *Vie de Jésus*, in which the author had portrayed Jesus as human rather than divine, had heightened tensions. In its otherwise glowing review of Segur's *Évangiles*, the *Bibliographie catholique* presented a fierce criticism of the illustrations, fearing that they undermined the book's pious intentions. Why, the reviewer asked, was the Virgin depicted suffering 'like an ordinary mother: was it not in fact she who presented her divine son to those first called by grace?'[80] The

2 J. Huyat 'Jésus est enseveli', published in comtesse de Ségur,
Évangile d'une grand'mère

comtesse became concerned that the bishops would threaten to withdraw their patronage unless the illustrations were changed.[81] The cardinal Donnet's endorsement of her *Évangile* had indeed specified that her book would 'speak to the child's eyes with these engravings or images that will represent events and which will be indelibly imprinted in his memory.'[82] The comtesse therefore demanded to have the final say for the rest of her Bible series, because 'the illustrations badly affected the sales of the *Évangile*'.[83] She went on to explain to him that 'a religious book cannot be treated in the same way as *Jean qui rit* or an infantile book of the same type; the image must be in harmony with the text. In order to judge this one has to be inspired by a religious sensibility that not everybody is fortunate enough to possess, and without which one risks offending the beliefs of fervent Catholics.'[84] Her implication that his choice of illustrations showed his lack of religious sentiment went too far, for Templier was a pious man, and, as we have seen above, already involved in a highly ambitious illustrated Bible project. The letter is covered with his indignant annotations, indicating that he would not concede. He had been deeply insulted. Her next few letters tried humbly to make up for her mistake: 'my good Monsieur Templier, I am deeply upset to learn that I have caused the sadness to which you refer'. When she received a reply not from Templier but from another Hachette employee, this further heightened her concern.[85] A compromise was eventually reached. The second edition in 1867 was illustrated with woodcuts copied from the German artist Julius von Carolsfeld Schnorr (1794–1872), one of the 'Nazarenes' who specialised in religious art.[86] Importantly, Jesus and the apostles all have haloes, and their poses are more static and dignified (Figure 3). Although this proved to be the worst argument that they had, it shows just how tense things could get when her sons and the ecclesiastical authorities became involved.

In fact, the whole *Évangile d'une grand'mère* episode was a mess. Madame de Ségur and her editor had two conflicting ideas of what she was going to produce. Templier evidently had it in mind to produce a children's version of the Bida project, as this was a new area of business that the publisher was hoping to enter.[87] He therefore marketed the final product in the luxury 'illustrated albums' section. Ségur on the other hand had hoped to produce a religious book for the masses. The comtesse was not happy with the price of ten francs that Hachette was charging for the book. She told Templier that her follow-ups would be published elsewhere, with the 'modest aim of being distributed in the countryside, in schools for the people; this is what I had dreamed of for the *Évangile*;

3 After Schnorr, 'Jésus est enseveli', published in comtesse de Ségur,
Évangile d'une grand'mère

this dream has faded; it is not selling well; it is too expensive for those of modest means'.[88] After more negotiations, she got her way on the question of price, and a cheaper version, at one franc fifty centimes a copy, shorn of its engravings, was also produced.[89] However, it was still advertised in the luxury albums section.[90]

Finally, the question of the ecclesiastical approbations, which she felt were so important to the books' sales, also proved complicated. Her *Évangile* appeared complete with the endorsement of seven bishops and archbishops, and a cardinal. Although such endorsement was standard practice at Hachette as with all publishers, their comments were far removed from Hachette's policy of neutrality in matters of religion and politics. Cardinal Donnet's letter of approval commended the comtesse for providing religious instruction when the government's education system was failing children. As discussed below, this was precisely the type of sentiment that would be systematically removed from the comtesse's *Bibliothèque Rose* volumes. In 1865, when the liberal Victor Duruy was in charge of education policy, it was also a pointed remark about the direction the government was taking in general, and insulting to her publisher, as Duruy was a prized contributor to Hachette's collections. Subsequent books in Ségur's Bible series were published without such troublesome endorsement, despite her best efforts. The publisher claimed to have mislaid the approbations for her *Bible d'une grand'mère*, which were from Mgr Pie, Bishop of Poitiers, Mgr de La Tour d'Auvergne, Archbishop of Bourges, and Mgr Rousselet, Bishop of Séez, 'those with whom I am closely linked'.[91] She protested that the lack of ecclesiastical support meant that her Bible was not selling well, but – unsurprisingly – the letters never materialised. Despite her struggle to control the illustrations and distribution of her books, so crucial to the spread of her religious message, the comtesse did not succeed. The conflict was particularly fierce over the Bible series as the comtesse was conscious that she was writing books to satisfy her religious brief. These were not 'infantile' Hachette books. In this way the tension between money and morals became too great.

This was taking place in the mid-1860s, as the Empire was liberalising, and her publishers were under far less pressure to enforce the moral tone of their collections. In particular the fall-out between Catholics and the Emperor over the Italian wars meant that religious morality was not the primary concern it once had been. In this freer atmosphere, Templier suggested in 1865 to the comtesse that she should write a book on 'the benefit of education for the people'.[92] This had always been a subject close to the heart of Louis Hachette, who wanted to reduce gently the influence of the 'clericals' who had nearly ruined his career.[93] His resolution on being forced to leave the teaching profession was *Sic quoque docebo* (I too shall teach), which became the house motto. The result of Templier's commission was *La fortune de Gaspard*, which, as noted in the previous chapter, was an odd, dark book, because the comtesse was suspicious of the notion of extending education for the people beyond religious instruction, and evidently found it difficult to answer her editor's brief. Rémi Saudray's article on the production of *Gaspard*[94] shows how Hachette handed over her manuscript to the *Semaine des enfants* without even reading it. No doubt they were keen to hurry the serialisation along. This would suggest just how much more relaxed the censorship process had become. The version published in *Semaine des enfants* appeared several months before there is any evidence that Templier had consulted the manuscript. The differences between the text serialised in the *Semaine des enfants* and the book which appeared in the *Bibliothèque Rose* reveal the exact episodes that Templier objected to. Saudray notes how it would appear that Templier went so far as to rewrite several passages of the book, in which Gaspard uses his intellectual superiority over his ignorant father to swindle him. The version published in the *Bibliothèque Rose* diluted the underhand behaviour of Gaspard.[95]

This was not the first time that the comtesse and her editor had disagreed over their ideas on education, and how it should be portrayed in her books. Earlier, in 1862, correctors had edited out sectarian religious references in *Les deux nigauds*. The offending passages are placed in italics: 'his friends took the opportunity of his confession to offer him good advice; *they were very religious* they made him see how wrong his behaviour had been . . . I will become as studious as I was once lazy *and as religious as I was once indifferent*.'[96] Similarly, her 1865 boarding school comedy, *Un bon petit diable*, which depicted a young boy making fools of his evil masters, before escaping and finding true enlightenment in religion, got a hostile reception from Templier. He objected fiercely to Ségur's critique of such an important national institution, and told her the book contravened the Civil Code. Her wry response explained that she had transferred the action to Scotland, 'where', she said, 'they allow everything'.[97] Both cases illustrate the clash between the beliefs of the comtesse and the politics of her publishers.

Tellingly, the comtesse's criticism of schools received the endorsement of her family. Mgr de Ségur had given the manuscript of *Un bon petit diable* his wholehearted approval, and said it would be 'a great comic success, *particularly in schools*' (her italics).[98] In spite of Gaston de Ségur's role as chaplain at the major Catholic school in Paris, the Collège Stanislas, he, his mother, and his brother remained ambivalent towards the education system as it stood in the Duruy era. Correspondence indicates his disapproval of the 'liberal' ideas he perceived in some of the priests and tutors in the Collège Stanislas.[99] Gaston de Ségur's biographer concluded her chapter on his work at Stanislas, and notably his lack of enthusiasm for the post, with his quotation 'charity [is] the education method par excellence'.[100] His brother Anatole's thoughts on the education minister, Victor Duruy, ran in the same vein: 'Lord give us a few more cloisters and fewer lycées; a few more capuchins and far fewer teachers; give us prefects who do not destroy cities and ministers who do not destroy souls.'[101] Anatole de Ségur also withdrew his two sons from the Jesuit school at Vaugirard, confiding to his diary that their harsh discipline was not necessary in the schooling of such obedient children.[102] He appears to have secretly shared his mother's views on corporal punishment. It appears that, like their good friend Louis Veuillot, the Ségurs were unable to be wholly reconciled to schools still subject to the authority of the University.[103]

In short, religion invariably lay at the heart of these later problems. Hachette did not publish her children's *Livre de messe* (1858), as she noted, 'it is not in your area of specialism'.[104] Later Ségur was nervous that they would not publish her *Pauvre Blaise* (1860) – 'Mr Hachette will probably think that he is too pious and he prays too much' – although her worries proved unfounded.[105] Her Bible project with them had proven a tense affair, to say the least. Her final, and most overtly militant fictional work, *Après la pluie, le beau temps*, also caused a few difficulties. This was mainly because she wrote the book with an ultramontane bias against the revolutionary armies in Italy, referring to them variously as Garibaldi's 'brigands', or his 'vermin', and 'the bandits who want to destroy the throne of our King, our father in God, the holy pope Pius IX'.[106] The language in the version that made it into print was toned down, as the comtesse explained: 'I removed all appellations and epithets that might have shocked the virtuous Garibaldi and his no less virtuous henchmen.'[107] Despite the changes that Templier had demanded, the whole thrust of the book remains deeply pro-papal. The happy ending was played out close to the battlefield of Mentana, site of a Catholic victory. The comtesse continued to press her agenda to the last, and Hachette continued to profit happily from her works.

In her last letter to her editor the amicable tone indicated the strong friendship that had developed between editor and author; this was in spite of the often confrontational nature of their dealings over the past fifteen years. By 1870 Madame de Ségur was seventy-one years of age and had retired, while Monsieur Templier had become a grandfather. Their relations were now friendly as well as professional. She concluded the letter, 'if you have a moment to waste, one day or another, come visit'. Several references indicate that she had met Templier for business, but she now also spoke of her friendship with Madame Templier. She enjoyed asking for news about his family, and giving her opinion on his grandson's latest misdemeanours.

Such was the comtesse's centrality to the *Bibliothèque Rose* collection that once she had stopped writing Templier began looking for her replacement. He approached Zénaïde Fleuriot, by then an already well-established author, who recorded, 'I have been asked to replace the comtesse de Ségur, who entranced an entire generation with her lively books.'[108] Fleuriot initially had reservations about working for 'the king of booksellers'.[109] Fleuriot's Catholic disdain for modern capitalism meant that she rejected the society his mighty book empire symbolised. However, like Ségur, she was not immune to the temptation of Hachette's money and power, and agreed to take on the role. She also approached her new job with trepidation, as she was being asked to emulate the style of her famous predecessor. Émile Templier greatly admired the comtesse's dynamic writing style, which, he apparently once remarked to Olga de Pitray, combined a sense of freedom and energy with a talent for narrative that ensured readers were gripped.[110] Following a discussion with her new editor on what sort of books he wanted her to write for the *Bibliothèque Rose*, Fleuriot worried that her version would not please audiences in the same way as the comtesse de Ségur's books had: 'I am worried that I will seem dull next to her. Her uninhibited writing style did not shy away from anything.'[111] Fleuriot's remark was ambiguous, because her private intention in writing for Hachette was to try to 'purify' French childhood. As this chapter has shown, the comtesse struggled hard against the idea that children could not read about violent mothers, or marriage, and one senses that Fleuriot was not keen to follow Ségur's lead. Templier warned Fleuriot not to choose serious subjects, or to speak over children's heads. Evidently he hoped to maintain the energy of the collection created by the comtesse de Ségur. Nevertheless, in choosing the militant Fleuriot, Templier had also ensured that Ségur's combative Catholic agenda would continue, and develop further in Fleuriot's hands. Their correspondence has not been preserved, but it would be interesting to speculate as to whether she faced a similar struggle to her predecessor.

Conclusion

When Madame de Ségur became an author, she entered into the masculine professional sphere of the publishing industry. She was immediately confronted with the problems that faced all who wished to produce printed material for the public in this period. At the same time as there were new opportunities for publishers and writers to reach a larger readership in the 1850s, there were also the harsh restrictions placed by Napoleon III's regime upon any organisation that dared to seek new audiences, or expand the distribution of the printed word in any way. Her indignant letters to Émile Templier at Hachette illustrate just how invasive the censorship could be, even in the case of innocuous-sounding books about educating little aristocratic girls. However, it was precisely because her subjects and her projected readership included little girls that Ségur's manuscripts were scrutinised in such surprising detail. The comtesse's approach to writing was, as Zénaïde Fleuriot put it, rather free, and she did not shy away from portraying scenes of a violent or disturbing nature. Little girls were considered to be the most vulnerable readership, and so Ségur's books regularly fell foul of the censors.

Ségur proved adept at negotiating such structures. She fashioned an imposing professional persona for herself in her letters to Templier, referring to herself in the third person, as 'the Author'. The tone of her letters was by turn sarcastic, playful, or humble, but they were always carefully composed, and designed to impress upon her editor that he was dealing with a skilled writer; not an amateur. Templier was a serious, upright man, and did not hesitate to rebuke the comtesse when he felt her manuscripts contained passages that were inappropriate for her readers. But he was also a businessman. Following the success of her first few books, their relations became a little easier. Although various correctors and editorial committees continued to find problems with her works, their concerns about questions of morality were often outweighed by her positive reception, coupled with the public's faith in Ségur as a trusted name and eagerness to buy her books. The comtesse used her reputation to effect in wrangles with Templier and associates. Internal memos at Hachette indicate that many were aware of what was happening, and not all were happy that her stories were often making it to press without important amendment.

The problems did not end here, however. There were to be further issues concerning the increasingly ultramontane tone of her writings. Her growing militantcy was in part a response to the liberalisation of the regime, which circumstance in fact made matters worse, for in this new climate publishers were no longer under such pressure to censor their authors. Ségur often found herself in conflict with Templier's idea of the direction the children's collection should take, and her own desire to spread the militant Catholic message to her young readers. These tensions came to a head over the comtesse's Bible series. Still, overall their collaboration proved to be very fruitful. Ségur was a prolific author, who was more than willing to respond to the demands placed upon her as the star author of the *Bibliothèque Rose*. She managed to accomplish successfully the unenviable task of creating books that appealed to children but that did not offend the sensibilities of the State, a whole series of editorial boards, and, finally, parents. That this delicate balance finally began to wobble slightly when she tried to satisfy her own Catholic agenda and that of her milieu is hardly surprising.

The tribulations of the comtesse de Ségur as an author illustrate the efforts of an author to respond to the new, ever-growing market of young readers. Her struggles with her editor reveal she had a keen sense of her public, and tried to be closely involved in the publishing process. Although Ségur's efforts to maintain control over her creations were often frustrated, her books soon came to define the Hachette children's collection. Mollier is correct to argue that it is unsatisfactory to label the comtesse a 'reactionary', if by using this label we accept the attendant connotations of backwardness, and alienation from modernity. However, this does not mean that we ought to brush aside her religious agenda in the process. Recent scholars of religion have argued convincingly against the rigid association of secularism with modernity.[112] The case of the comtesse should in turn make us reassess the burgeoning children's market, dominated by women, and their contribution to Catholic culture in an age of nascent democracy. The next two chapters will develop this question in more detail.

Notes

1 Jean-Yves Mollier, 'Éditer la comtesse de Ségur ou les ruses de la raison policière', *Cahiers Robinson*, 9 (2001), 14–22; Marcoin, *Librairie de jeunesse et littérature industrielle*, p. 430.

2 Internal memo, undated circa March/April 1863, *Œuvres*, 1:lxxxvii.

3 Roger Price, *The French Second Empire. An Anatomy of Political Power* (Cambridge, Cambridge University Press, 2001), chapter 6.

4 'La comtesse de Ségur et la Bibliothèque Rose', *L'auteur et son éditeur, à travers les collections de l'institut mémoires de l'édition contemporaine* (Caen, IMEC, 1998), pp. 15–26; 'Éditer la comtesse de Ségur ou les ruses de la raison policière'; *Louis Hachette (1800–1864) Le fondateur d'un empire* (Paris, Fayard, 1999), pp. 374–376.

5 See Beaussant's annotations to the Hachette correspondence in *Œuvres*, 1, and comments 1:829–831; Marie-France Doray, *La revue des livres pour enfants*, pp. 131–132 (1990).

6 Rémi Saudray, 'La fortune du texte', *Cahiers Séguriens*, 3 (2002), 97–104.

7 Along with Mollier's articles on the comtesse and biography of Louis Hachette, see volume 3 of Martin, Chartier, and Vivet's *HEF*; Élisabeth Parinet, *Une histoire de l'édition à l'époque contemporaine XIXe–XXe siècles* (Paris, Seuil, 2004); Jean Mistler, *La librairie Hachette de 1826 à nos jours* (Paris, Hachette, 1964); Marielle Mouranche, *Les livres pour l'enfance et la jeunesse de 1870 à 1914*, École Nationale des Chartes, thesis, unpublished, 1986.

8 166 letters, IMEC. They have been reprinted (with only the occasional omission of the editor's annotations) in Ségur, *Œuvres*, 1:lxi–cxlvi.

9 Kreyder, *L'enfance des saints et des autres*, pp. 40–49; Beaussant's annotations, *Œuvres*, 1; Marie-José Strich, 'Critique génétique d'un manuscrit: La Bible d'une grand-mère (1869)', *Cahiers Robinson*, 9 (2001), 183–192; Cécile Petit, *La comtesse de Ségur et l'édition: Étude de sa correspondance avec Émile Templier, son éditeur* (Mémoire de DEA, Université Paris IV-Sorbonne, 2004, Unpublished).

10 Frédéric Barbier, 'Libraires et colporteurs', *HEF*, 3:231; Colette Becker on Émile Zola's job in the Hachette advertising department provides valuable insights, *Les apprentissages de Zola, du poète romantique au romancier naturaliste 1840–1867* (Paris, PUF, 1993), pp. 97–100.

11 The full set of catalogues can be consulted at the IMEC. Volumes 15, 17, 28, and 30 contain Langlois's work. Volume 15, 1868 catalogue, is the most interesting for research on the comtesse de Ségur, as it contains Langlois's *Notice historique et statistique sur l'origine, la formation et le développement de la librairie de MM. Hachette 1828–1868*.

12 This section on Hachette is chiefly indebted to Mollier, *Louis Hachette*; Mistler, *La librairie Hachette*.

13 Mistler, *La librairie Hachette*, p. 136; 150th Anniversary of Bibliothèque Rose press pack, Hachette 2006.

14 Letter from Templier to Lamartine, 18 August 1853, quoted in Mistler, *La librairie Hachette*, p. 143.

15 Brochure from 1 April 1852. Quoted in Mollier, *Louis Hachette*, p. 305.

16 Parinet, *Une histoire de l'édition*, pp. 88–91.

17 *La Maison Mame, le passé, le présent, l'œuvre* (Tours, Mame, 1878), p. 28.

18 Francis Marcoin, 'Autour de la comtesse', *Cahiers Robinson*, 9 (2001), 32–33.

19 Lyons, *Readers and Society*, pp. 86–91.

20 'La lecture des romans', *Semaine des familles*, 4 December 1858, p. 154.

21 *Semaine des familles*, 29 December 1860, p. 194.

22 Knibiehler et al., *De la pucelle à la minette*, p. 91.

23 Letter to Templier, 12 October 1857.

24 Letter to Templier, 16 March 1858.

25 *Monsieur Émile Templier 1821–1891* (Paris, Imprimerie D. Dumoulin et Cie, 1892), pp. 20–22.

26 Extrait du *Tour du Monde*, by Fr Schrader, quoted in *Monsieur Émile Templier*, pp. 33–34.

27 Letter to Templier, 16 March 1858.

28 Bourdon, Review of Ségur's early works, *Journal des demoiselles*, May 1860.

29 Tatar, *Off with Their Heads!*, pp. 6–15.

30 Veuillot, 'Les contes de Madame de Ségur'; pp. 23–24 above.

31 Review of *Petites filles modèles*, *Bibliographie catholique*, 18, February 1859.

32 Letter to Templier, 2 January 1859.

33 According to Mollier, *Louis Hachette*, p. 374.

34 Letter from Barrau to the comtesse, March 1863.

35 Letter to Templier, 7 March 1863.

36 Internal memo to Charles Lahure, undated, anonymous – but it can be inferred from its discussion of editorial policy of *La semaine des enfants* that it was written by Barrau, or certainly another member of the publication's editorial board, *Œuvres*, 1:lxxxvii.

37 Review of *L'auberge de l'ange gardien* and *Pauvre Blaise*, by Gustave Robert, *Bibliographie catholique*, 33, April 1865.

38 Letter to Templier, 16 December 1863.

39 Langlois, *Notice historique*, ff. 152–153.

40 See letters to Templier dated 27 September 1863, and 22 March 1864.

41 Langlois, *Notice historique*, f. 73.

42 Mollier, *Louis Hachette*, p. 440.

43 See di Giorgio, 'La Bonne Catholique'.

44 Planté, *La petite sœur de Balzac*, pp. 30–31.

45 Internal memo to Charles Lahure, undated, *Œuvres*, 1:lxxxvii.

46 Mistler, *Librairie Hachette*, pp. 183–184.

47 This is the title of the volume of *HEF* on the nineteenth century.

48 Mollier, *Louis Hachette*, chapter xiii.

49 Letter to Templier, 2 October 1855.

50 Letters to Olga de Pitray, 23 and 26 November 1860.

51 E.g. letter to Templier, 24 January 1859.

52 Letter to Templier, 8 December 1865.

53 Langlois, *Notice historique*, f. 73.

54 Letter to Templier, 11 May 1863.

55 Letter from the Princess de Sayn-Wittgenstein to Zénaïde Fleuriot, 25 August 1873, quoted in Francis Fleuriot-Kerinou, *Zénaïde Fleuriot: sa vie, ses œuvres, sa correspondance* (Paris, Hachette, 1897), pp. 405–406.

56 Letter to Templier, 4 April 1859. See Beaussant's research, *Œuvres*, 1:976–977.

57 Letter from Gaston de Ségur to Olga de Pitray, 17 December 1866, published in Pitray, *Mon bon Gaston*.

58 Mistler, *Librairie Hachette*, p. 215.

59 Mouranche, *Livres pour l'enfance et la jeunesse*, p. 274.

60 Letter to Templier, 25 April 1866, *Œuvres*, 1:cxiv.

61 Pierre Bleton, *La vie sociale sous le Second Empire. Un étonnant témoignage de la comtesse de Ségur* (Paris, Éditions Ouvrières, 1963), chapter VI, annex F.

62 Jean-Yves Mollier, 'Les femmes auteurs et leurs éditeurs au XIXe siècle: un long combat pour la reconnaissance de leurs droits d'écrivains', *Revue historique* (2006), pp. 313–333.

63 Mistler, *Librairie Hachette*, p. 215.

54 Contract, 13 December 1863, Traités 1844–1865, IMEC, f. 413.

65 The French *épreuves* means both proofs and ordeals.

66 Olga de Pitray, *Ma chère maman*, p. 128.

67 See letters to Templier, May–October 1869.

68 Hachette Catalogue May 1855–March 1856.

69 *Monsieur Émile Templier 1821–1891.*

70 Isabelle Nières-Chevrel (ed.) *La comtesse de Ségur et ses illustrateurs*, Catalogue (Rennes, Bibliothèque Municipale, 1999), p. 40.

71 Letter to Templier, 24 June 1859.

72 *Ibid.*

73 'Les contes de Madame de Ségur'.

74 It appears on the front cover of the first volume of Laffont's collected works of the comtesse de Ségur.

75 Letter to Templier, 29 April 1858.

76 Letter to Olga de Pitray, 2 January 1861.

77 *Monsieur Émile Templier 1821–1891*, p. 27.

78 Mollier, *Louis Hachette*, pp. 426–428.

79 Michael Driskel, *Representing Belief: Religion, Art and Society in Nineteenth-Century France* (University Park, Pennsylvania State University Press, 1992).

80 Review of *Évangile d'une grand'mère* by V. Postel, *Bibliographie catholique*, 35, April 1866.

81 Letter to Templier, 18 May 1866.

82 Letter from Cardinal Donnet, 5 November 1865, published in Ségur, *Évangile d'une grand'mère.*

83 Letter to Templier, 20 July 1866.

84 Letter to Templier, 27 July 1866.

85 Letter to unknown recipient, 7 August 1866.

86 Cf. *La comtesse de Ségur et ses illustrateurs*, which suggests (p. 56) that Schnorr was 'imposed' on Ségur in 1865, and that she did not like his 'realistic' and 'cold' drawings. This interpretation seems unlikely, given that copies of his pictures do not feature in the 1866 edition, which Ségur objected to, but later, in the second edition in 1867.

87 Mollier, *Louis Hachette*, pp. 424–429.

88 Letter to Templier, 8 September 1866.

89 Hachette Contracts 1866, f. 165, IMEC.

90 Hachette Catalogues, IMEC.

91 Letter to Templier, 2 December 1871.

92 Letter to Templier, 3 December 1865.

93 For example he was involved in popular library initiatives. See leaflets c. 1865–66 inside *Catalogues: Notices et Prospectus 1852–1863*, IMEC.

94 *Cahiers Séguriens*, 3 (2002), 97–104.

95 *Ibid.*, p. 101.

96 Gabriel Aymé, 'Sophie conforme', *Grand Album Comtesse de Ségur* (Paris, Hachette, 1983), pp. 237–245.

97 Letter to Templier, 30 June 1864.

98 Letter to Templier, 12 May 1864.

99 Georges Sauvé, *Le collège Stanislas deux siècles d'éducation* (Paris, Éditions patrimoines et médias, 1994), p. 261.

100 Hédouville, *Mgr de Ségur*, pp. 376–383.

101 Anatole de Ségur, *Souvenirs à mes enfants*, NAF 11401, 16 April 1866.

102 *Ibid.*, 22 June 1866.

103 Robert D. Anderson, 'The Conflict in Education. Catholic Secondary Schools (1850–70): A Reappraisal', Zeldin Theodore (ed.), *Conflicts in French Society: Anticlericalism, Education & Morals in the 19th Century*, (George Allen & Unwin, London, 1970).

104 Letter to Templier, 29 October 1857.

105 See letters to Olga de Pitray, 26 November 1860, 30 November 1860, and 6 December 1860.

106 See *Œuvres*, 3:1039, 1078 footnotes.

107 Ségur wrote 'suppôts': the direct translation would be 'minion of Satan'; see her letter to Templier, 28 January 1870.

108 Letter from Zénaïde Fleuriot to the Princess de Sayn-Wittgenstein, 26 December 1873, Fleuriot-Kerinou, *Fleuriot*, pp. 419–420.

109 Letter from Émile Templier to Zénaïde Fleuriot, 28 January 1873, Fleuriot-Kerinou, *Fleuriot*, p. 395.

110 Olga de Pitray, *Mon bon Gaston*, p. 160.

111 Letter from Zénaïde Fleuriot to the Princess de Sayn-Wittgenstein, 26 December 1873; Fleuriot-Kerinou, *Fleuriot*, p. 420.

112 In particular Clark, 'The New Catholicism'.

4

The comtesse
and the culture wars

> The comtesse de Ségur is quite simply one of the most innovative literary talents of our time . . . She has become the grandmother storyteller to all French children, and amongst them I can testify that there are a good number of greybeards, listening with equal wonder and enjoyment. Finally, her two sons, Monseigneur de Ségur and the comte Anatole de Ségur, each one devoted to public service, have also played an important role in the work of this apostolate that can be so usefully exercised with the pen.
>
> Louis Veuillot, 'Les Fables, par Anatole de Ségur',
> 10 December 1865, *Revue du monde catholique*

Louis Veuillot was a fervent supporter of the literary efforts of the Ségur family. A great admirer of the comtesse, in the review quoted above he added his heavy, gout-ridden figure to the children sitting at grandma's feet, listening to her telling stories. 'Maman Ségur', as Veuillot called her, was matriarch of a literary dynasty in Second Empire France. Her eldest son, the prelate Mgr Gaston de Ségur, was the best-selling contemporary religious author of the period; this at the time when religious publishing peaked at 20 per cent of the market. His *Réponses courtes et familières aux objections les plus répandues contre la religion* proved to be the runaway success of the period. Published in 1851, it immediately ran to multiple editions per year, reaching 211 editions by 1891.[1] The second son, Anatole de Ségur, was also a prolific author and journalist, as well as a politician. 'Frère Louis', as the Ségurs called Louis Veuillot, was a journalist, author, and international Catholic celebrity. Together they formed a literary group, all dedicated to the 'apostolate of the pen', with Veuillot also playing the crucial role of publicist. All members of the 'family' had been converted to Catholicism as adults. This shared discovery of religious faith bound them together, and gave them a common mission: to revive the faith in modern France.

In order to understand the specific pressures that helped shape the comtesse's work, both as a mother and an author, we must read her in the religious context of the period, in which her family and intimate circle were so involved. The nineteenth century witnessed heated conflicts between Catholics and anti-clericals over the place of religion in society, and the comtesse was positioned in close proximity to some of the key players in the particular turn the drama took mid-century. The Revolution of 1789 had tried, and failed, to reconcile the Catholic Church to the revolutionary project. Bloody civil war had ensued, between monarchists and Catholics ranged on one side, and anti-clerical Republicans on the other. This 'war of the two Frances' simmered over the century, flaring into violence sporadically over the course of the century that followed, but a sense of embattlement persisted on both sides throughout. Furthermore, this was a time of great spiritual renewal. Under Napoleon and even more so under the restored monarchy, the French Catholic Church had set about repairing the damage done by the Revolution. By the 1840s, the religious revival had gathered momentum, becoming a movement of great missionary zeal and renewed piety.[2] An important innovation of the Catholic revival was the intensity of devotion to the Pope. Increasingly, Catholics in Europe looked 'over the mountains' to the Pope. He was championed by intellectuals such as Joseph de Maistre and Lamennais (in his early years) as the divinely ordained authority that would restore order in this revolutionary age.[3] This question became acute following the two revolutions of 1830 and 1848. Mid-century, the comtesse's close circle, notably her eldest son Mgr de Ségur and her friend Louis Veuillot, emerged as two of the leading lights of a new, more aggressive form of ultramontanism that was beginning to take shape.

The 1850s proved a turbulent time for the Catholic Church in France.[4] The ultramontanes were engaged in a fratricidal war of words. The liberal branch, headed by men like the comte de Falloux, and the comte de Montalembert, wanted to reconcile the Church with parliamentary politics. But for the more intransigent, 1848 simply proved that any compromise with liberalism was the first step on a slippery slope towards revolution. The intransigents' vision, as expounded by Louis Veuillot and Mgr Gaston de Ségur, argued against any compromise with a system they saw as having sprung out of the Revolution, and therefore stemming from the diabolic lineage of rebellion that could be traced back to Satan's refusal to serve. Concurrent with this quarrel was the ongoing struggle between the ecclesiastical hierarchy of the French Catholic Church and the centralising efforts from Rome. Pope Pius IX launched a vigorous campaign to strengthen the Papacy, which he perceived to be threatened by the growth of liberal nation states. After 1848, when the revolutionary armies had succeeded in capturing Rome and forced the Pope into exile, his views on the dangers of liberalism were confirmed. Pius IX's centralising reforms once more set the Papacy on a collision course with the French ecclesiastical hierarchy. The impetus for the French Catholic Church to retain a large degree of national authority, known as gallicanism, has a long history. In the period that concerns this book, the gallicans were a large force to be contended with. A series of strong-willed archbishops of Paris, along with other outspoken bishops such as Dupanloup of Orléans, proved a bulwark of fierce resistance to papal initiatives. These men became engaged in a series of heated polemics with Louis Veuillot, whose newspaper had become the unofficial mouthpiece of the pro-papal camp. Meanwhile, from Rome, Gaston de Ségur wrote secret letters encouraging Veuillot, telling him that the Pope was firmly on his side. Gaston de Ségur was closely involved in the power struggle between Paris and Rome; as between the crucial years of 1852 and 1856 he held the high-level diplomatic post of auditor of the rote. This essentially meant that he acted as go-between for the Emperor Napoleon III and Pope Pius IX. The Ségur/Veuillot 'family' was animated by a sense of embattlement.

For the Ségur family, the relationship of religion to the State and society was absolutely central to their identity. Like many aristocratic families of the nineteenth century, they felt the lax morals of their ancestors in the previous century had been partially to blame for the Revolution of 1789. This new generation embraced the religious revival, and set to repenting for their predecessors' sins. What was needed was a reformulation of the aristocracy, according to the principles of the revival, and in response to the new challenges to social order that were posed by modern, industrial society. As they saw it, if the old hierarchies that were fundamental to Christian society were to be preserved, then they had to be regenerated. The Ségur family, under the aegis of Gaston de Ségur, assumed an important representative function: to incarnate the new, militantly Catholic aristocracy that would one day regain the reins of power and bring France back into the fold. This idea permeated their books, which is not surprising, as they often worked together, referring to each other in their books, borrowing phrases, ideas, and subject matter from one another. 'Frère Louis' then championed their books, as well as this idea of the new era of the Ségur family, in the pages of his newspaper. The comtesse de Ségur assumed the role of matriarch. Much of their action was centred upon education, and children were specifically targeted by the revival. Thus, the comtesse's ability to captivate the interest of children was of no small importance when the ultramontane propaganda campaign was desperate to appeal to these 'little missionaries in the home', as Gaston called them.[5]

This chapter looks at the religious ferment of the Second Empire through the optic of the relationship between the Ségurs and the Veuillots. Such an approach risks being reductive. Both Louis Veuillot and Gaston de Ségur were engaged in vast activities. For men who were engaged in a fight for ideological supremacy, mobilising wide support was imperative.[6] Both worked hard to develop channels through which they could spread their vision. In light of this, choosing to isolate only a few actors risks distorting their relative importance. However, a narrow focus allows us to gain an insight into the workings of such ideological networks, and how their development influenced the thought and production of those involved. Owing to her sex, the comtesse de Ségur was relegated to the peripheries of the action for most of the time. Biographies of Veuillot either underline her role as a charming hostess or refer to her only in her capacity as the mother of young Olga, with whom Veuillot was allegedly in love.[7] However, through the examination of letters, articles, and memoirs, her involvement in the culture wars of the time can be traced, particularly in the more informal sociable forms of action to which ultramontanes were often forced to have recourse. While she lacked formal access to the masculine domain of politics, the comtesse was nevertheless engaged in the 'combat', firstly as matriarch of the Ségur family, and then slowly gaining their respect as a fellow writer. So, looking at the comtesse de Ségur in the context of her relationship to the Ségur/ Veuillot literary powerhouse offers insights into such women's interaction with the masculine Catholic establishment. Finally, this narrow focus can be justified by the fact that the 'Ségur family' was a concept developed together by Mgr de Ségur and Louis Veuillot, ably helped by the comtesse and her son Anatole, and her daughter Olga de Pitray. By isolating this one idea, and looking at how and why the group went about developing this notion of the 'family', we have a case study of how the family could play an important role in the politics of identity in Second Empire France.

The new Catholic era of the Ségur family

A striking theme that emerges from the Ségur family papers is the militant design of Gaston de Ségur, aided by his grandmother Catherine Rostopchine, to convert the family into a Catholic dynasty.[8] Gaston envisaged a new 'Catholic era' for the noble house of Ségur, symbolised by the baptism of the first male in the next generation: 'the name Peter would mark the Catholic era of our family, which this child would be charged with continuing and developing'.[9] He had his sights set on the creation of an ultramontane dynasty, which would have an important cultural and political role to play in the religious revival.

Madame de Ségur had an incredibly close relationship with her eldest son, Mgr Gaston de Ségur. He occupies a central role in the family biographies, while her husband is relegated to a very minor role. Olga de Pitray, Ségur's youngest daughter, produced two biographies of her mother and eldest brother, *Ma chère maman* and *Mon bon Gaston*. She claimed their lives were so closely enmeshed, that each book contains biographical details pertaining to the other subject, as if a biography of one could not exclude the life of the other: 'mother was Gaston and Gaston was mother'.[10] She hinted that, because of the strained relations with her husband, the comtesse found solace in her son. Gaston and his father could not stand each other. Gaston had been an effete young boy: 'as a small child my brother greatly enjoyed dressing up and his favourite activity was to solemnly parade in my mother's bedroom, decked out in one of her court dresses with an immense train that swept the floorboards behind him'.[11] Olga related how the comtesse was distraught when Eugène de Ségur sent his son off to boarding school at the tender of six. There were further arguments over Gaston's evident lack of talent for riding and hunting.[12] His talents lay elsewhere. It became apparent that Gaston was a gifted artist, and a glittering future beckoned when the renowned artist Paul Delaroche took him on in his studio. Highly displeased, Eugène de Ségur wanted Gaston to abandon this career path for a far more respectable diplomatic post. Gaston expressed his frustrations in a self-portrait dated 15 June 1836, his hair gathered in a chignon and adorned with a garland of roses, wearing a large pair of earrings and gaudy women's clothing, staring angrily at the pompous red face of the Maréchal Philippe Henri de Ségur (1724–1801).[13] This famous warrior had been Minister of War under Louis XVI, and represented the pinnacle of masculinity and Ségur family glory.

Gaston de Ségur discovered the faith which was to become his life's work, in September 1838, aged eighteen.[14] Following a visit from his grandmother Rostopchine, and intense discussions with his cousin, Augustin Galitzin, he embraced Roman Catholicism wholeheartedly. His brother Anatole recounted how Gaston embarked on a strict regime of fasting and violent self-flagellation. According to Anatole, this was because he was so ashamed of his previous impiety (and transvestism?) that he had to purify himself while he prepared to take Holy Communion as a true Catholic for the first time. The family looked on with 'a sort of respect mixed with fear'.[15] The romantic Catholicism of the 1830s, a religion of ruined catacombs, and naive rustic piety, appealed to his artistic sensibilities. Gaston's diary, produced during his visit to his grandmother in Russia in the summer of 1841, bears the imprint of the generation inspired by Chateaubriand and Lamennais. He painted beautiful, delicate watercolours of Russian peasants praying, and recorded that 'the people are good, fundamentally good. Their faith is so strong that it even borders on superstition; all they need are to be enlightened.'[16] Horrified by what he was told of the ignorance and drunkenness of the Russian priests (and of course their refusal to accept the truths of Roman Catholicism), he concluded that the people were being betrayed by the sophistry of their leaders. This was an idea typical of the new current of thought in young French clergy regarding France, and was to inform his interpretation of the social responsibilities of Catholicism as well.[17] A large part of the visit was spent engrossed in discussions on religion with his grandmother, whom he called 'my good and saintly mother, a living book where I would like to read often my duties and seek counsel'.[18] She was a respected religious scholar, and devotee of the salon of Joseph de Maistre in St Petersburg at the beginning of the century.[19] Gaston de Ségur returned to France with his religious convictions strengthened. In December 1842, he made a vow of chastity in Rome, and then announced to his family his intention to take orders. His mother was distraught, sending him reams of 'tear-stained' letters, imploring her son to renounce his plans.[20] This was not the destiny his parents had planned for their eldest son.

But once he became a priest, Gaston de Ségur's relationship with his mother altered significantly. A family friend recorded how he became for his mother 'a father, a guide, her greatest honour, and her most intimate confidante'.[21] It was now the son who exercised the moral authority over the mother. He was seconded in this by the comtesse's mother, Catherine Rostopchine. Gaston wrote reports to her on his mother's inattention to Christian morality, shocking the comtesse Rostopchine with tales of Anatole and Edgar being allowed to attend their grandmother Ségur's *comédies*, or their sisters going to balls.[22] Meanwhile, 'grand-mère Rostopchine' reinforced Gaston's efforts in her letters to her daughter, and reported to him, 'your mother wrote to me that if she was feeling better she would come see me this summer. In my reply I advised her to strengthen her body with frequent and very frequent communion . . . I think in so doing I have followed your wish.'[23] Their concerted efforts were eventually rewarded, and the comtesse began to take communion more frequently. It was not just Gaston's relationship with his mother that changed. In his capacity as a man of the Church, Gaston de Ségur assumed the spiritual headship of the family.

A family friend records how at family gatherings Gaston appeared strangely aloof from their worldly concerns. It was as if he was on a higher spiritual plane. His religious charisma worked its charms: along with his mother, most of his brothers and sisters wholeheartedly embraced his faith. The comtesse Rostopchine received news of their conversions with delight.[24] The family papers even contain letters from the adulterous comtesse Octave de Ségur, promising Gaston that she would engage in charitable acts. He convinced her to see the Jesuit Father Ravignan and repent for fifty years' worth of sins and rejection of the Church.[25] As already mentioned, the first grandson, Pierre, symbolised the hope Gaston placed in the family. In 1860, aged seven, Pierre de Ségur wrote to the Pope a letter which offers insight into the nature of the education the Ségur children received: 'my name is Pierre, because Saint Peter was the first Pope, and on my birth I received a gold medal that you had blessed; so you see I must love you a lot.'[26] Gaston cherished hopes that at least one of his nephews would continue his work and join the priesthood. However, his chosen favourite, Louis de Pitray, died young.[27] Only Madeleine de Malaret fulfilled his wish, by entering a convent.

The main member of the family who resisted Gaston was his father. Charles Baille, who worked briefly as Gaston's secretary and remained a friend of the family, described a family disagreement he had witnessed:

> The old comte saw in the opposition of his sons a sort of ingratitude towards the Emperor who, he said, had been responsible for their advancement, and would say 'regarding Anatole words fail me, he is a fanatic; but that you, Gaston, a priest; that you Edgar, a politician, that you should behave with such excesses of passion disgusts me!' Monsignor tried to make his father understand that he could not allow his debt to the Emperor to shackle his conscience, nor could it free him from what he considered to be his duty to the Church; furious his father interrupted him: 'Gaston I forbid you to continue! – the respect that I owe to you father

forces me to hold my tongue, but this respect will not cause me to sacrifice my convictions.'[28]

The comte watched on, powerless, as his progeny were turned one by one into religious 'fanatics'. They were transforming his name into something very different. In 1866, Anatole wrote to his sons, 'until now, our family had been distinguished in the military profession, diplomacy, literature, in all the glories of this world, but my brother is the first to have given it the only glory it had not achieved and the one true glory, which is saintliness!'[29] The conception of family honour passed on to the next generation had been altered.

As Baille's anecdote made explicit, this new religious direction was inseparable from politics. Gaston's convictions led him to remodel the family, and this new version involved rejecting the family's current Bonapartist sympathies. The Ségurs in the early nineteenth century had distinguished themselves in their military service to Napoleon I. Eugène de Ségur had even rejected his right to the title of Marquis, in favour of that of comte, which had been awarded his family by Napoleon. By contrast, Gaston had embraced the regime of his nephew, Napoleon III, only because in the aftermath of 1848 he was convinced that France needed to be governed by a strong hand. He wrote to Veuillot in December 1851:

> Continue to fight *steadfastly* for the President. He is the salvation of France and the Papacy, no more, no less – I cannot understand the accusations that I know the legitimists are levelling at you. I am a legitimist like you; and that is precisely why I am voting for Napoleon – he is *tarmacking* the road for Henri V, if that is we will ever be capable of having a real king; which does not seem likely to me. [his italics][30]

While he ardently wished to see monarchy restored to France, Gaston de Ségur lamented, 'France is not Christian; how could she accept a Christian government?[31]

Gaston's lukewarm support soon transformed into outward hostility, as he grew concerned that Napoleon III's foreign policy would withdraw French support for the Pope's temporal powers in the Vatican States. Between 1855 and 1856 a group of French and Roman prelates met regularly at Mgr de Ségur's apartments in Rome to discuss such matters, and the mood was apparently far from moderate.[32] After the fall of the Second Empire, he became openly legitimist. In a letter to Chambord, from 1871,[33] Gaston explained not only that his book *Vive le Roi!*, a declaration of adherence to throne and altar, was expedient politically but 'this act of faith is at the same time an act of justice and reparation'. In his view, the Ségur family had fallen victim to Voltaire and the errors of the eighteenth century. Consequently, not only had they lost their faith, but they had also lost their way politically. The Ségurs had been cut adrift from centuries of tradition, and so they vacillated between Bonapartism, Orleanism, and once more Bonapartism. Gaston felt that his declaration of faith in public went some way to restoring his family to its former glory, and setting an important example. 'As head of this family, I had the good fortune to have found, in religious faith, the old monarchist traditions of my ancestors, and . . . I come to ask [your] forgiveness for this long apostasy . . . I have the good fortune of seeing my two brothers, the comte de Ségur conseiller d'État, and the comte de Ségur-Lamoignon, former diplomat and ex-député, fully sharing in my sentiments.' This concept of the family's place in society was very far from the 'liberal milieu' in which Gaston de Ségur had been raised by his father.

By converting family members, Gaston was not only saving their souls from eternal damnation; he was also creating a formidable political force. There were Ségurs at court, in parliament, in diplomatic circles, and in the Emperor's household. When government policy ran counter to Catholic interests, the family mobilised its channels of influence.[34] For example, when Veuillot's *L'univers* was threatened with closure, letters of support from Edgar de Ségur, posted in Constantinople, were sent to Veuillot via the family network. He and Gaston advised Veuillot on the appropriate diplomatic line to take in his articles on the subject.[35] However, Mgr de Ségur's militant agenda could also prove a hindrance for the advancement of his siblings' careers. His younger brother Edgar lost his diplomatic post when Napoleon III altered his policy towards the papacy.[36] Similarly, gossips whispered that the family of Edgar's wife could not stand him. They regarded the new husband and his ostentatious piety as something of an embarrassment.[37] Laura Kreyder has suggested that Anatole de Ségur's failure to get elected to the Académie Française in 1869 should also be attributed to the violent dislike generated by Gaston's campaign for the Pope's infallibility.[38]

The picture that emerges of Gaston de Ségur is of a deeply divisive figure. Though he was considered by many Catholics to be a saint, his ardent desire to spread the word of God (as the intransigents saw it) as widely as possible led him to dispense with subtleties: 'it was important to be simple'.[39] In the eyes of those who viewed him from a more dispassionate perspective, he appeared a troublesome figure. The French ambassador to Rome, Alphonse de Rayneval, remarked, 'he is one of those souls who doubt nothing and know nothing'.[40] For freethinkers and liberals of all hues – liberal Catholics included – he was the enemy incarnate, a dangerous fanatic who personified of all that was ridiculous and terrifying in their time. While Pierre Larousse's *Grand dictionnaire universel du XIXe siècle* described the comtesse as a charming, cultivated woman of letters, the entry for her son Gaston unleashed a torrent of invectives. His vast oeuvre is dismissed as 'completely insignificant . . . grotesque . . . reason is replaced with insult'.[41] Similarly, Flaubert saw in Mgr Gaston de Ségur the pinnacle of the stupidity of his age. He drew upon Gaston's books in his research for *Bouvard et Pécuchet*, and in his correspondence he spoke of reading, 'stupid or rather stupefying things . . . modern religion verges on the ridiculous . . . these people think they are living in the twelfth century'.[42] Modern historians agree that Mgr de Ségur's influence on the French religious imagination should not be underestimated. According to Jacques-Olivier Boudon, Gaston de Ségur played a pivotal role in establishing an ultramontane political party in France.[43] In Jean-Baptiste Duroselle's view, he was vital in the construction of social Catholicism.[44] Guillaume Cuchet's thesis underlines the important role played by Gaston de Ségur's opuscules in disseminating new devotions nationwide.[45] Émile Poulat calls him 'this sort of bishop without a diocese whose popular ministry covered the whole of France'.[46]

In the early stages of the Second Empire Gaston had obtained an influential position as auditor of the rote in Rome. In practical terms, his role was to act as the Emperor's spiritual ambassador to the Pope. However, Gaston de Ségur's heart really lay in mission work amongst soldiers, and urban working-class men and boys. The cheaply produced pamphlets, which made him famous, were designed to teach the public about Catholicism and so formed the complement to this work. Once ordained, Gaston became a military chaplain in 1848, and so began a long fascination with converting soldiers and young working-class boys and men. In fact, this mission work was the start of his lifelong commitment to social Catholicism, which focused on helping the casualties of modern industrial society.[47] Industrialisation had created new forms of poverty, which traditional Christian charity was ineffectual at combating. Catholics responded by developing new 'social' initiatives, designed to alleviate, if not to eliminate, the flagrant inequalities within society. Most successful under the Second Empire was the St Vincent de Paul Society (successful in terms of numbers that is, not eradicating social inequalities), whose members visited deprived families. There were also 'patronages': groups which offered food, sociability, and religious education to young men and boys, and workers' circles, for adult men. Gaston became one of the important voices of the authoritarian, conservative current within this social Catholicism, which argued that these charitable measures were needed in order to win workers back to the Church and prevent them from turning to Socialism. This cause remained his real passion, for he felt that it lay at the heart of the re-ordering of France as a Christian monarchy. In private correspondence, Gaston dismissed any ambition to scale the Church hierarchy.[48] Later he referred to his diplomatic responsibilities as 'insipid', and complained that they prevented him from engaging in his pastoral work amongst the soldiers posted in Rome.[49] He preferred to play down his high birth, and live a simple existence, 'in order to preach the word of JESUS-CHRIST to the working-classes, one of the first conditions is not to live like a fat bourgeois or a great seigneur'.[50] Gaston strove to embody the ethos of social Catholicism, which fulminated against the worship of individual glory and wealth in this bourgeois century.[51]

In all his various incarnations, Mgr de Ségur was always positioned on the frontline of the culture wars. As Émile Poulat explains, Gaston de Ségur was a 'maximalist', whose simplistic approach was entirely suited to a situation of ideological warfare. Either you loved Jesus, or you were a revolutionary.[52] He styled himself on St François de Sales, the seventeenth-century Genevan prelate, who penned many polemics denouncing the Protestant Reformation. Gaston became enthusiastically embroiled in the struggles between liberal and intransigent ultramontane Catholics, between liberal Catholics and intransigent Catholics, between Catholics and anti-clericals, and finally he proved extremely adroit at fanning the flames of hatred between Catholics and Protestants, Freemasons and all freethinkers. Needless to say, by converting his family, Gaston ensured that they too became embroiled in the culture wars, and the comtesse became a most enthusiastic soldier for this cause.

Frère Louis

The Ségur 'family' was an extended one, based as much on religious values as on blood ties. Mgr de Ségur related how a visit to Rome in the winter of 1852–53 had contributed greatly to his mother's increasing piety.[53] Gaston emphasised the role played by the 'Christian atmosphere' of the holy city. He failed to mention a far more important detail however, namely that it was during this trip that the comtesse met Louis Veuillot. The journalist was to have a profound influence upon her religious beliefs, almost equal to that of Gaston. Madame de Ségur embraced vehemently the intransigent politico-religious creed known as *Veuillotisme*. This was the vision of a rigidly hierarchical society, whereby France, and eventually Christendom, would become a theocracy totally subservient to the authority of the Pope, which Louis Veuillot expounded tirelessly in his newspaper *L'univers*. Veuillot had been friends with Gaston de Ségur for a while previously, through their activities in the promotion of Rome's cause over the interests of gallicanism. In the mid-1850s, the two families became very close. Veuillot and his sister Élise were also included in the new Catholic era of the Ségur family. In keeping with the ideals of social Catholicism, the Ségurs and the Veuillots brushed aside class considerations and called each other brother and sister (the Veuillots were of solid working-class origins – their father had been a barrel-maker). 'Frère Louis' addressed Madame la comtesse de Ségur, née Rostopchine, as 'maman Ségur'. The comtesse, naturally, assumed the role of matriarch.

Their meeting in Rome was the beginning of a long friendship and correspondence between the comtesse and Veuillot.[54] By this time he was already a well-known journalist, feted in Rome and the Catholic world. The comtesse was not only his friend but also a great admirer of his work. According to Olga, 'my mother considered Louis Veuillot to be a sort of Christian genius whom she loved and admired with an enthusiasm and a perseverance that were touching to watch'.[55] Ségur read *L'univers* avidly, and asked family members to save copies she had not managed to obtain. She was particularly interested in Veuillot's articles, and appreciated his choice of subjects: 'in two or three days *L'univers* will contain an article by him [Veuillot] on Voltaire. He is undertaking the arduous task of proving that Voltaire was *stupid*; keep these *Univers* for me, there are some articles I would like to read [her italics].'[56] She did not want to miss a single utterance of the great man.

Veuillot, even more so than Gaston de Ségur, was a notorious figure. His pugilistic stance had earned him the respect of many clerics, and provincial nobles. He was a self-styled *condottiere* of the pen. At the point when the two families met, Veuillot was embroiled in a particularly heated dispute with his fellow Catholics Falloux and Montalembert, as well as gallican Bishops such as Dupanloup and Sibour, who wanted to prevent the distribution of *L'univers* in their dioceses. The falling out with Falloux and the more liberal branch of the ultramontanes was over the question of whether to compromise with the State, in order to push through education legislation favourable to Catholics. For Veuillot this was unacceptable. This argument was also played out in the Ségur household, as the comtesse's son in law, Armand Fresneau, was a close associate of the comte de Falloux, and had been involved in drafting the law. Ségur often referred to Veuillot as a 'lion' in her correspondence, and she admired his combative spirit. Opposition to all those who attacked *L'univers* animates the correspondence between Veuillot and the comtesse. In one colourful letter, following a recent warning issued to the paper, she imagined Dupanloup, Falloux, and various members of the government attacking Veuillot with their horns, cloven hoofs, and forks.[57] To which Veuillot replied, 'Madame, and very dear friend, if the valiant and triumphant La Guéronnière [government minister] could read your letter, I would be truly avenged.'[58] In their correspondence the comtesse revealed herself to be a passionate *Veuillotiste*, who, like her hero, relished a good fight.

Their correspondence is unique among the examples of her writing available in the public domain. These are carefully crafted pieces of writing, in which she revealed a defiantly intellectual side that did not appear in her letters to her family or (overtly) in her published books. Writing to the journalist provided her with a soundboard for her political ideas. The tone she adopted in her letters to Veuillot was ironic, caustic even. The first letter in particular played upon her acceptance of the role of admirer writing to the great man: 'Ah! you think, tiresome tyrant that you will be obeyed, that we will hold our tongues at your command, that we will allow you to gripe without saying shush! I will speak, I want to speak!' The comtesse then backed down, admitting she was challenging the writer whose words she venerated: 'me, a pygmy against the giant'.[59] She adopted a figurative religious and military vocabulary in homage to Veuillot's style, which she greatly admired. Thus, in one letter, in which she apologised profusely for her slow response to a missive from him, Ségur beat her chest and intonated a litany of reproaches.[60] Her prose was peppered with metaphorical gunshots, and impregnated with the odours of sulphur and incense. Similarly, Veuillot was a past master at wordplay, a skill the comtesse appreciated (her father had also been a great comic wordsmith). Falloux's name for example provided a great source of amusement. Veuillot played with 'Falloux–Fallax' (*fallax* in Latin meaning deceitful), and used the adjective *Fallouxieux*, *Fallouxienne*, or even *à la Falloute* to express disdain for something. The comtesse de Ségur denied ferociously any suggestion that she was a 'falloutine' for example. At one stage she even considered writing a children's version of one of Veuillot's books, *Ça et là*.[61] Veuillot would have considerable influence not only on her political ideas and religious beliefs but also over the development of her works.

Their interaction was not one-sided. Veuillot evidently appreciated her letters: 'they are so good and charming, and I am grateful to be one of your correspondents!'[62] He accorded her the great honour of reviewing her work in his newspaper *L'univers* – a particularly proud moment for the comtesse.[63] While Pierrard points out that this article was not without ambiguities,[64] notably on the subject of her views on corporal punishment, we should not conclude as Pierrard does that Veuillot remained suspicious of his friend's talents. Rather, he appears to have grown to appreciate the comtesse's work more and more as her oeuvre progressed. In 1866, a good few years after his article on the comtesse had been published, Veuillot wrote, 'it is now that I can appreciate the prodigious talents of maman Ségur, and I can see what masterpieces are her *Mémoires d'un âne*, *Les malheurs de Sophie*, *Le Général Dourakine* and the others'.[65] The praise he lavished on her work, in an article ostensibly dedicated to her son Anatole's *Fables*, cited at beginning of this chapter, made his admiration absolutely clear.

'Les Bacquois': an ultramontane network

Every Thursday evening, the comte Eugène de Ségur attended his weekly business dinner in his capacity as director of the Eastern Railway Company. The comtesse took this opportunity to hold a dinner for the Veuillots and their circle. According to Charles Baille, the 'very authoritarian' Eugène de Ségur detested Veuillot, and could not stand having him in the house. The comtesse could only usher the journalist in once her husband was out.[66] Once they were free to talk, these dinners swiftly turned into loud, clamorous affairs, where they hotly debated the latest issues of the day. The role such social gatherings played should not be underestimated. From 1856 onwards, Eugène Veuillot notes, they became one of the principal channels of political action for Louis Veuillot: 'these conversations at table, where abandon reigns, where trust is forged, generally cause those who are neutral to take a stand, and often change the undecided into men of action. I have seen it happen.'[67] Dinners at the Veuillot household were established as a regular meeting place for Catholics from all over France, and indeed the world, both for conversation but also as 'war councils'.[68] In 1869, Louis Veuillot noted, 'this evening, dinner at Gaston de Ségur's house with [the bishop of] Poitiers. High politics.'[69] Informal network structures were crucial in the transmission of ultramontane ideas, as many bishops were hostile to the new emphasis on the Pope, and Roman piety. Moreover, as the Italian question became heated, they also faced the increasing hostility of the State. Not only were the Ségurs and the Veuillots spiritually and politically close, but they also lived in proximity to one another. Veuillot dubbed them the 'Bacquois', after the rue du Bac in the heart of aristocratic Paris, around which they all lived.[70] Theirs was a tight-knit little community of writers and campaigners.

It was not just a Parisian network, however. Both Mgr de Ségur and the Veuillots covered a vast amount of ground across France, generating support for their cause. Eugène Veuillot describes the working holidays of Veuillot, where he visited friends. On these visits, priests from each diocese would come to meet the great Veuillot, so they often proved to be mini publicity tours for him. The comtesse encouraged their visits to her estate Les Nouettes, as her husband never went there. Often the whole Veuillot family, brother, sister, and two little daughters, would decamp to Normandy for the summer. Pierrard however, suggests that Louis Veuillot's personal friendship with the women in the Ségur family was really due in large part to his secret love for the youngest daughter, Olga de Pitray.[71] Their correspondence does indeed show there was a real affection between the two; an infatuation of some sort should not be ruled out. However Veuillot increasingly referred to Olga in private family correspondence in more ambivalent terms, especially concerning her temper tantrums.[72] It seems likely that their visits to Les Nouettes, and the family apartments in Paris, were motivated by professional concerns as well as by friendship. Eugène Veuillot laid the emphasis on the Ségurs as loyal allies, 'the noble, lively, charming Ségur family, passionate supporters of the Church, passionate writers, politically influential'.[73] The family provided not only moral support but also a useful network of contacts. And, as will be seen from the example of summer 1856 below, in this rather less formal context the female members were very much involved.

The summer of 1856 Louis Veuillot paid a visit to Les Nouettes that became an occasion for roused political passions. The year 1856 had seen particularly violent arguments between Veuillot and the liberal Catholics. In July, Veuillot had packed his bag and left Paris for the Normandy countryside to visit the Ségur family. He was relaxing, but also taking the chance to collect his thoughts, and gather his ammunition. He was about to publish his first series of collected works, *Mélanges*, which would trace his version of the recent ructions with his fellow Catholics: 'we will correct the proofs at Les Nouettes, where I will write my preface'.[74] Theirs was a community of writers and so he took his work with him. However, on 22 July, the newspaper was alerted to the publication of a new gallican book, *L'univers jugé par lui-même*. An anonymous volume, believed by the Veuillots to be written by his gallican enemies,[75] it used quotations from *L'univers* to denounce the newspaper. As Eugène Veuillot wrote, the Ségurs provided stout moral support in these 'stormy days'. The invitation extended by the comtesse to Eugène Veuillot, for example, had assured him, 'come to Les Nouettes to hear your friends exalted and your enemies ridiculed'.[76] On 25 July, as the gravity of the attack became clearer, Louis Veuillot noted that her energetic support meant that 'Mme de Ségur is good to see'.[77] The journalist was obliged to return to Paris, 'sabre in hand',[78] but Élise Veuillot and his daughters remained, soon joined by brother Eugène to replace him at Les Nouettes.

Over the next few weeks, the château was in a state of great agitation, with flurries of letters communicating news. It was decided at the beginning of August that the newspaper would take the book's publisher to court. The Ségurs and Veuillots at Les Nouettes had been on tenterhooks. 'When I read out to maman Ségur: Mlle Veuillot wants us to plead or will plead, she threw her arms around my neck and kissed me with even more tenderness than usual. She said 'oh how I thank you, oh how I am consoled! Those scoundrels will be punished, ah Dupanloup!''[79] The Ségurs tried to use their influence to help their friends. The journalist learned from Gaston de Ségur that in his correspondence Falloux had been suggesting that Louis Veuillot was in the pay of the Emperor. Élise wrote, 'maman Ségur has finally laid her hands on the letter from Falloux, and it is effectively very clear. Mgr authorises it to be given to Mgr Sacconi [the papal nuncio] and also to tell him that it was addressed [*sic*] he prefers to be named even though he would rather that Falloux did not know that he has almost betrayed him. You would have been touched Lou, if you had seen the zeal and tenderness with which maman Ségur and sister Olga tried to find a way to bring poor Gaston to hand over the letter.'[80] Madame de Ségur's enthusiastic desire to help her friend and to engage in the thrill of a fight meant that she was willing to coax her eldest son to act as well. She was a useful ally for Veuillot.

Although a friend of Veuillot, Gaston did not necessarily encourage the comtesse's involvement with the journalist. It led her to intervene in Gaston's affairs, and he was wary of the passions it roused in his mother, because she was not always as discreet as her son wished. For example, a letter he wrote just following this visit indicates that he was unhappy with their relationship. Veuillot and the comtesse had been exchanging an excited correspondence on the struggle between the ultramontanes and the gallicans. One of her letters (now lost) had touched upon the adoption of the Roman liturgy by the French Churches. This question of the liturgy was one of the central sites of conflict in this struggle, as the gallicans fought to protect the regional particularities of the French Church, while the ultramontanes sought to impose the Roman liturgical style, and cause embarrassment to the gallican bishops.[81] The question had stirred the comtesse enough to put her lucrative work for Hachette to one side, and set to writing a Roman missal for children in 1857.[82] In the summer of 1856 Gaston was successfully concluding negotiations with the principal seminary in France and gallican nerve-centre, Saint-Sulpice (where he himself had trained as a priest), getting them to adopt the Roman liturgy. However, Gaston was worried that Veuillot's crowing over this victory risked destroying any possibility of goodwill between Rome and the seminary. The comtesse's letter to Veuillot had been written in this triumphant vein. Unfortunately for Gaston de Ségur, his mother's letter had made it into the hands of the seminary, and had caused outrage. Gaston had to write an apologetic letter:

> Mr Icard has concluded from this letter that the opinion of my mother must reflect my own, and that I am in consequence secretly an enemy of Saint-Sulpice, all the more dangerous because I appear to be its friend. By the grace of God, Monsieur le supérieur, this is not the case. My mother has known Louis Veuillot and his sister personally for several years, and has developed a great affection for them; and, as so often happens with women, she measures only with her emotions all that concerns Mr. Veuillot and his works. A short visit that he has just paid to her in the country has not contributed to calming this great ardour.[83]

The description of the comtesse's letter as not reflecting his own opinions on the matter was more than a little disingenuous, coming from Gaston de Ségur, whose own letters to Veuillot on this very subject had been no less partisan. In fact, two years previously he had sent information from Rome to Veuillot asking him to publish it in *L'univers*. This concerned the Papal brief on the adoption of the Roman liturgy by Saint-Sulpice. The fear was that the head of the seminary, and leading gallican agitator, Carrière,[84] would bury the matter. The Pope hoped to use *L'univers* to force his hand, and so the letter related the main content of the document. Gaston pleaded, 'for the love of God, do not reveal where this information comes from'.[85] This particular episode illustrates the importance of keeping their communication clandestine. Letters which fell into the wrong hands could cause embarrassment back in Rome, as Gaston was widely seen to be the Pope's bishop in Paris. Gaston's comments on his mother and Veuillot are telling, however, as they indicate that he had little control over his mother's fascination with intransigent ultramontanism.

The ultramontane community became aware from 1859 onwards that their names were also on government blacklists. Following Veuillot's vehement criticism of Napoleon III's withdrawal of his support for the papacy against the Italian nationalists, the comtesse warned the Veuillots that at the Imperial court '*L'univers* is in complete disgrace and they are simply waiting for an opportunity to close it down'.[86] Agents of the State were certainly monitoring Louis Veuillot and Mgr de Ségur. The suppression of *L'univers* on 29 January 1860 led to the seizure of Veuillot's papers. This was at exactly the same moment that Gaston de Ségur found his pamphlet *Le Pape* banned by the State. Even the comtesse was convinced that family correspondence was being intercepted. This was one of the principal methods of censorship under the authoritarian regime. Postmasters regularly read mail, and in particular foreign newspapers, confiscating seditious material.[87] After receiving a rather heated missive from her daughter, in which Olga vented her spleen over the closure of their beloved *L'univers*, the comtesse warned 'take care what you write, family secrets or otherwise; letters are regularly read and you know that with maliciously interpreted words, one can be prosecuted and charged'.[88] An anti-English pamphlet that the comtesse sent to Olga during the Italian question was also confiscated, and she was concerned that other, anti-government pamphlets (which she had hidden inside a package of children's books) had been seized.[89] She waged a veritable war with the local postmaster in Normandy, 'our old enemy',[90] accusing him of all kinds of misdemeanours, real and imagined. The issue became something of a joke, as in this letter from Louis Veuillot to Olga, 'Shh! It's me. Hide, and check that no one is listening. I cannot be sure that what I am writing will not bring down the empire. . . . You must love the Emperor; you must obey him and love him. He is great, he is wise, he is pious, and no other sovereign has such an attentive police force. Long live the Emperor Madame.'[91] Their persecution by the State really served to confirm the Ségurs' and Veuillot's view of modern society, and the community celebrated their 'outlaw' status, as this dinner invitation from Gaston suggests: 'the honourable Louis Veuillot, infamous public offender, is summonsed on pain of death, to reserve his evening on Friday 8 of this month, to come dine at precisely six o'clock, at the residence of Mgr de Ségur, the exalted ultramontane, and dangerous man'.[92]

Despite the privately expressed reservations on the part of Gaston about Veuillot, this notion of being a 'family' had important functions for its members. The Ségurs formed part of a much wider network of vocal support that Veuillot so badly needed in this time of conflict. Also, thanks to their connections they acted as a useful source of information. But the relationship was also important for the comtesse. It provided her with the opportunity to engage in the political fray, and a chance to discuss her ideas with the journalist she greatly admired. The Ségurs found in Veuillot an important mouthpiece for their ideas, and a publicist for their work. 'Frère Louis' was crucial to the Ségur family, as it was he who championed the notion of a reformulated, ultramontane house of Ségur in the pages of *L'univers*. The Veuillot/Ségur 'family' was also an ideological construct.

'The love of the small': the family literary mission

Louis Veuillot shared Gaston de Ségur's view of the importance of the very public return of the Ségur family to Catholicism. He promoted their new image in the pages of his newspaper,[93] and in his correspondence. They developed the idea in their books, which he then reviewed, and made it clear that the works by individual members of the Ségurs needed to be read as part of a whole family literary production. This section therefore looks at the ways in which the Ségur/Veuillot family worked together as writers.

In 1865, Veuillot wrote in praise of the Ségur family, portraying them as a united force: 'here we have, I think, a family of aristocrats that are beyond the reproach of democracy. It would be hard to find many bourgeois or lower-class households in which there burns more ardently a love for the small (*les petits*), and a zeal to help them join the divine aristocracy. Long live the Ségurs!'[94] The role of the divine aristocracy was to help the 'small', which, according to Anatole de Ségur, meant either 'the small in age or social situation'.[95] Catholic rhetoric often conflated the lower classes and children, as they were both vaunted as being free from the corrupting taint of power and money, and in need of paternalistic guidance. Veuillot's eulogy plays with the idea of the small and mighty. The great, noble Ségurs, who hold power thanks to God's ordained social hierarchy, take the greatest care over the welfare of the small. He argues that divine order is the true democracy, a far superior beast to the secular parliamentarianism peddled by politicians. This was a typical Veuillotism, and it goes some way to explaining why he took such great interest in the Ségur family.

Together, the Ségur family produced some of the best-selling religious education material in this period. The very act of publishing religious books was a political gesture of no small importance. Veuillot praised Anatole for having the courage to write, as a politician, a book as overtly religious as *Témoignages et souvenirs*. The book was a provocative profession of ultramontane faith, filled with descriptions of stigmata and visionaries.[96] The Ségur family presented their writing project as an extension of the conversion process. They were devoted to educating their children and grandchildren, and in so doing they provided a model for their readers to emulate. Both the comtesse and her son Gaston began writing in earnest around 1855, when he returned from Rome.[97] In her dedications, the comtesse created an image of the young generation of Ségur children as pious models. She rendered tribute in her *Livre de messe des petits enfants* (1857) to Pierre de Ségur, 'so gentle, so good, so charitable, and already so pious in spite of your youth' (he was four years old!).[98] Around the same time, Gaston published *La religion enseignée aux petits enfants* (1857), a similar book, with the same publisher.[99] It was designed, according to the preface, to help Gaston's sisters introduce their young children to the rudiments of the Catholic faith. Between 1864 and 1872, Gaston wrote a whole series of booklets on the religious instruction of children. Anatole de Ségur also took great interest in writing for children. As well as writing several books for children, in the 1860s he became a regular contributor to the two main journals for teenage girls, *Journal des demoiselles* and *Journal des jeunes personnes*. Both publications shared a militant Catholic agenda. When his sons went away to boarding school, he began writing a diary of his life and thoughts, in order to continue contributing to their moral education.[100] The family mission therefore translated into a shared writing project, to provide the instruments for teaching their children.

Above all, the Ségurs wrote for children. As John Sharp and Bernard Aspinwall have shown for the case of the British Catholic revival, missionaries became very interested in targeting children.[101] The same was true of the French Catholic revival. In the first half of the nineteenth century, this was led by the missions, and then consolidated within elementary schools.[102] The 1850 Falloux Law allowed the Church to regain its footing in secondary schools. More often than not, social Catholic initiatives were directed towards children and the young.[103] Furthermore, when missions entered a new industrial phase, and large quantities of books, pamphlets, newspapers, and magazines were produced for the 'oeuvre des bons livres' and Catholic schools, much of this religiously inspired publishing was aimed at children.[104] Children also formed the principal target of Gaston de Ségur's propaganda campaigns. Distribution networks used children to try to get through to their families, as Gaston explained: 'many conversions have taken place and take place each day thanks to the influence of these little missionaries in the home, who do not realise that they are preaching when they innocently relate how good *monsieur le curé* is to them'.[105] For example, in 1860 during the Italian Wars, priests handed out over two hundred thousand copies of Mgr de Ségur's brochure *Le Pape* in schools and catechism classes up and down the country. The children were instructed to take them home and read them to their families.[106] The aim was not only to attract volunteers for the Papal zouaves but also to convince their parents of the urgency of the situation. Children, in Gaston's view, represented the last hope for the Church.

Louis Veuillot was also greatly concerned about the need to write for children. For Catholics the destruction of the Church's infrastructure and the persecution of its personnel during the late stages of the Revolution had meant that several generations of French children had grown up without any religious education. Veuillot, whose father had been one such child, attacked the villainy of the bourgeoisie, who exploited the worker, and whose intellectuals then 'deprived him of the religion which might have given his life some meaning'.[107] Veuillot had twice set up children's magazines with his brother Eugène; both were shortlived. Many of his works were published by Mame in his *Bibliothèque de la jeunesse chrétienne*.[108] The *Journal des enfants de Marie* along with *La semaine des familles* republished his articles, while he reviewed other children's authors. He also therefore took great pleasure in promoting the efforts of the Ségurs to reconstruct religious childhood.

> My mother, filled with confidence in my brother's judgement, liked to seek his opinion on the manuscripts of her books for children. It was a touching sight, mother and son, alternately serious and smiling, carefully examining the heroic deeds of Cadichon, the mischievous antics of *Sophie* (in other words, my mother as a child), the ordeals of *Blaise* . . . Three books were the object of particular scrutiny: the *Bible d'une grand'mère*, *L'évangile d'une grand'mère*, and *Les actes des apôtres*, three masterpieces that it is absolutely necessary to read to children, particularly in these times.[109]

As this quotation from Olga de Pitray's biography of her brother shows, the notion that they were a family of writers, who worked together to edify the nation's children, formed an important part of the image the

Ségur family projected to their public. A photograph from 1872, taken by family friend Louis Samson, represents the comtesse de Ségur reading a book to her blind son. This is the only photograph in the public domain of the comtesse in her capacity as a woman of letters. Rather surprisingly, there is not a grandchild in sight. Instead she is portrayed as a mother with her son, meditating over a religious book together. Her role is subservient; she is reading to Mgr de Ségur. Gaston used this image to form the frontispiece to his biography of his mother. The picture, coupled with the quote from Olga de Pitray above, suggests the input Mgr Gaston de Ségur is supposed to have had on her writing process. Gaston was not the only judge to whom she submitted her work. When facing difficulties over the title of one of her books, the comtesse referred to having held a 'family council' to discuss the problem.[110] She asked her children and grandchildren to give their opinion on her stories, and, when she finally sent her manuscripts to her editor, it was usually with the recommendation that he should ask the opinion of his two daughters before making his final decision. She also then sent her first editions to Veuillot, ostensibly for his daughters to read, but this often coincided with the run-up to Christmas and New Year's Eve, that is to say the perfect time for a favourable review which might influence the buying public looking for gifts.

Her son's contribution to Ségur's works, as discussed in Chapter 2, was generally to enforce a more rigid and hierarchical view of society. Nevertheless, Gaston de Ségur often proved far less rigorous than her editor in his treatment of his mother's books. Where Gaston judged that *Un bon petit diable* was a fine comedy that would go down especially well in schools,[111] her editor found it highly offensive, and demanded that she cut it down by fifty pages.[112] Similarly, her son never objected to the violence in her books. Nor did he see anything wrong in the occasional love story that ended in Christian marriage, as compared to the storm caused at Hachette headquarters by the romance in *L'auberge de l'ange gardien*. It was Templier who ordered the rewrite of *Mémoires d'un âne*, not Gaston, even though he had also deemed the book's moral to be objectionable. Although the frustrated tone of letters to her editor suggests that Gaston's opinion was not always welcome to his mother, she did sometimes use his endorsement of a manuscript to counter Templier's objections. On handing in the manuscript of *Un bon petit diable*, she told Templier, 'I admit that I have no concerns about your approval of the manuscript, it having already received that of my son Mgr de Ségur to whom I have read it from one end to the other.'[113] When

Templier did indeed have some serious objections, her subsequent refusal to comply added, 'I will let you know on my son's return what we decide.'[114] It was really her Biblical works that interested Gaston, and this caused the most friction between mother and son. 'I will not be able to send you my *Évangile* until it has passed through the grindstone of my son Mgr de Ségur, who is of a rigidity that makes one despair, but is reassuring for the orthodoxy of the work.'[115] The only other time she used the word 'grindstone' in this sense was to describe the censure of her work by the hated Barrau at the *Semaine des enfants*, which is a clue to the strain she was put under by Gaston's scrutiny of her Bible series. In this case Gaston made it perfectly clear to his mother that she was not to give in to her editor. She wrote to Templier in 1866: 'if you have any observations to make, I cannot change anything without first consulting my son, who corrected it with great care and who recommended to me that I make no further corrections, each word having its value in a work of this type.'[116]

It is difficult to gauge the extent to which Mgr de Ségur intervened in his mother's writing process. There is more detailed evidence of Gaston's initial involvement in his brother Anatole's writing, thanks to the letters preserved by the younger brother in the family papers.[117] Their correspondence shows how Mgr de Ségur took a keen interest in his brother's work, even to the point of commissioning books for his mission work. Gaston encouraged Anatole to carry on writing books for apprentices and soldiers, when he could no longer do it, when his time was taken up by his duties as auditor of the rote. These early works by Anatole, written so that Gaston could distribute them amongst the French soldiers garrisoned in Rome (and thus help prevent these men being 'corrupted' by the Italian revolutionaries), clearly bear the mark of Gaston's influence. Many of the amusing stories and anecdotes are based on Gaston's experiences as a military chaplain, upon which Gaston also drew for much of his 'edifying' material for boys and young men.

In fact, the whole family shared not only anecdotes but also themes and ideas. The comtesse did not shy from adapting sections of Gaston's writings and inserting them in her works, in the same manner as Anatole had done. This is most clear in the case of her *Mauvais génie*. The book features an episode set during the Algerian war, concerning a soldiers' rebellion. It was Mgr de Ségur who insisted that the rebel leader, Alcide, be executed. A very similar story can be found in Anatole's *Dimanche des soldats* (1850).[118] Anatole's biography of Mgr de Ségur shows that these were anecdotes from Gaston's days as a military chaplain during the 1848 revolution.[119] It appears that Gaston collected a bank of moral tales, which his family then drew upon. Gaston often suggested anecdotes that Anatole should use. He also told Anatole which sections in his books moved the soldiers in Rome to tears.[120] He was convinced of the utility of stories concerning the masculine subjects of war, soldiers, and militarism in his missionary work amongst young boys and soldiers. Both of these were groups of men whom Catholics like Veuillot and the Ségurs were keen to emphasise were not irretrievably lost to the Church.[121] This conviction influenced his brother Anatole's choice of subjects. Similarly, the comtesse portrayed Christian soldiers in her storybooks several times: for example, Moutier the zouave in *L'auberge de l'ange gardien*, and Jacques the pontifical zouave in *Apres la pluie, le beau temps*.[122]

Occasionally, the whole Ségur/Veuillot family could be moved to write on the same subject. Laura Kreyder has written an insightful article on the comtesse's Bible series, in which she asserts that the books were part of a concerted literary offensive by the '*Bacquois*' community, designed to refute the heresy of Renan's *Vie de Jésus* (1863).[123] This notorious publication, in which Renan wrote the life of Christ as a human being, rather than the divine Son of God, had sent shockwaves throughout the Catholic establishment. The Ségurs and the Veuillots were of course outraged. They all then proceeded to publish their own responses to the question of Christ's divinity. Ségur's *Évangile d'une grand'mère* (1865) dealt with this question decisively. The manuscript is covered with notes in several hands, working out how best to answer the conundrum of emphasising the orthodoxy on Christ's divinity in a way that made it simple for children.[124] The Cardinal Donnet's approbation, published at the front of the book, praised her effort: 'this *Évangile d'une grand'mère* is well-timed, following the refutations of this modern Arianism published by bishops and learned and conscientious publicists. The latter were addressing an erudite audience; but you speak to the young.'[125]

Louis Veuillot also exercised a decisive influence over the subject matter the comtesse chose for her writing. In a review of her works he urged the comtesse to portray children from all classes of society. Both *Pauvre Blaise* and *La sœur de Gribouille* then featured lower-class protagonists. She often developed with the idea of the small and mighty in her books, particularly through making use of the figure of a redemptive child. Take, for example, the central idea of *Pauvre Blaise* of the contrast between the corruption of the high and mighty and the piety of the humble. The book seems to bear the imprint of conversations with Veuillot. The young hero, a poor gardener's son, managed to convert the inhabitants of the château.[126] Several of her happy endings follow this schema, as in *La fortune de Gaspard*. As the holidays draw to a close in *Les vacances*, Monsieur de Rosbourg and his adopted son Paul conclude that they will stay in the countryside, together, and 'we will show them what a good, a true Christian can do with the wealth that God has given to them'.[127] She echoed a refrain that can be found in Veuillot's writings, namely the idea that France would be saved if its nobility gave up its frivolous ambitions and returned to their real, feudal, duties: 'stay on your lands, gentlemen; spend your revenues there . . . stay on your lands, bring your children up there, the plough and the gun in your hand, amongst those who they will one day have to defend'.[128]

Finally, they worked together to promote one another's books. The comtesse took an active interest in the writings of her sons. She published Gaston de Ségur's first book, *Réponses*, at her own expense after the St Vincent de Paul Society had rejected it.[129] When Veuillot visited her château in 1857, she placed a copy of Anatole's latest work by his bed. A laudatory review duly appeared in *L'univers* a few moths later.[130] Gaston also used the opportunity of his mother's connection with Hachette to try to negotiate publishing contracts for his own works.[131] The first time, in 1857, her editor declined. Later, in 1861, Templier did approach Mgr de Ségur with a proposal concerning publishing a Bible with Hachette.[132] This Bible never materialised. However, his mother eventually realised this project instead, and Gaston ended up playing an important role in the ideas behind the book. In 1869, bursting with maternal pride, she sent her editor a copy of Gaston's latest book, *La liberté*: 'it is irrefutable in my opinion'.[133] She also used her own books to advertise books written by her sons. For example, in *Les vacances*, the hero Monsieur de Rosbourg fortifies his courage by singing Anatole's canticles for soldiers. The brave zouave Moutier in *L'auberge de l'ange gardien* picks up a copy of Anatole's *Mémoires d'un troupier*, and immediately becomes absorbed in the volume: 'I would never have believed that a book could be so interesting and amusing.'[134] Moutier's description of the Crimean War that follows is an almost word for word copy of that found in Anatole's *Troupier*, so she is also slyly signalling her sources to the reader. Her *Jean qui grogne et Jean qui rit* opens with an advert for Mgr de Ségur's books, as the good mother packs two books into her son's bag, the *Manuel du chrétien*, and *Conseils pratiques aux enfants*. 'He must be good, you can tell from his books. And he loves children, you can see that as well.'[135] And so the list goes on.[136] Gaston also returned the favour. He was so pleased with her moral tale *Le forçat ou à tout péché miséricorde* (in the collection *Comédies et Proverbes*) that he serialised it in a publication he was involved with,

L'ouvrier. The comtesse explained to Templier, 'my son thinks that the *Forçat* could be useful to the poor ignorant public in the countryside'.[137]

The literary members of the family worked hard to present their work as part of a unified front to the public. There is a fair amount of intertextuality between her work and that of her sons, Gaston and Anatole. They worked together, read one another's manuscripts, made suggestions, borrowed from each other's writings, and publicised their respective books. Their corporate identity had initially frustrated the young Anatole, who was obliged to subsume his literary ambitions to Gaston's vision of the greater good. He was keen to establish his own reputation, distinct from that of his famous brother: 'if I wanted to establish my individual reputation, I would have to write a very impious book; maybe then I would no longer be confused with you. All in all, we will end up by becoming together a great religious [word illegible: possibly 'author'] who will go down in posterity under your name.'[138] It is interesting that the comtesse only very rarely wrote for Catholic publishers, preferring instead to stay with Hachette who was not always sympathetic to her militant agenda. It was her husband, rather than Gaston, who helped her find a publisher. Perhaps she too wanted to ensure that she also established her own reputation as a writer, independent of the family identity.

The Ségurs and the Veuillots shared a common cause: educating children, as part of a greater mission, the Catholic revival in France. Together they formed part of a network of militant writers and propagandists, working hard to reinvigorate the faith and save the nation's soul. Their shared mission expressed in writing was part of a wider Catholic mobilisation. The comtesse emerged as the children's favourite, however, so it is no surprise that Veuillot's article on the Ségur family in 1865 reserved the warmest praise for the matriarch, the 'grandmother storyteller to all French children'.

Conclusion

> Look at what God is doing . . . This saintly abbé de Ségur and his seven brothers and sisters, perfect Christians and perfect Romans, are the grandchildren of the Catholic Voltairean Ségur and the Greek Voltairean Rostopchine.[139]

Veuillot's eyes glistened as he watched maman Ségur, frère Gaston, frère Anatole, frère Edgar, sœur Sabine, and sœur Olga transform their family into the ideal aristocracy he had so often eulogised in his writings.[140]

Instead of the glories of profane war, they were active in the holy war against the forces of secularism, which he conceived as a delicious affront to the corrupt old order the noble house of Ségur had once incarnated. Veuillot and the Ségurs were not simply reactionaries who hoped to simply turn the clock back to the *ancien régime*. Their divine aristocracy was a new creation, an invented tradition, formulated as a rejection of older models of comportment. They would be leaders of a counter-revolutionary vanguard. As militant Catholics they would realise Joseph de Maistre's vision of a regenerated Christendom. For Veuillot the nobility would be the natural leaders of such a movement, as he wrote in the aftermath of 1848: 'I pay tribute to the hereditary aristocracy; I would like them to hold together and rise up, because revolutions congratulate themselves on abolishing them. I would like to see the revolution flattened by a gentleman: it would be one more slap in the face for the unbearable arrogance of democracy.'[141] In typical provocative fashion, he had styled the aristocratic hero of this book, *Le lendemain de la victoire* (1850), Valentin de Lavaur, 'the people's representative'.[142] In the same vein as his comments on the Ségur family, he suggested that Lavour was the only representative who truly understood the needs of the people. Veuillot felt the people needed their rulers to set an example. He was therefore delighted when he met the Ségur family in the 1850s. This was the motivation underpinning his generous praise for the Ségurs as a corporate entity. Together, their new conception of aristocracy was united in particular by their loathing of the old order, execrated by men like Veuillot and Mgr de Ségur for their alleged dissipation, and resultant failure to provide a strong moral authority for the people.

Historians have recognised the significance of all these men in Second Empire politics, but have hitherto overlooked their collaboration, and in particular the close, familial nature of their network. The family writing project was central to their vision, for it acted on two levels: as a defiantly public declaration of faith on the part of the new, divine aristocracy, and as a method for diffusing their new Catholicism. Together they wrote books designed to encourage a return to the faith in France. Hence, we find an important level of intertextuality in their books, and similar concerns reflected in their choice of subjects. Through their correspondence their reliance upon each other for support can be traced.

The role of the comtesse, as a woman, was not easily defined. Her political opinions were dismissed by Gaston as being led by the 'passions' to which her sex were prey, and even as a hostess she was not necessarily invited to the all-important 'war councils' to which Eugène Veuillot referred. Nevertheless, she won Veuillot's great admiration on the strength of her literary talent: 'now Maman Ségur is decorating this old political and military name with a completely new glory', he wrote, 'she will gracefully defeat the grandfather and the great-uncle who has written so many stories, and even the academician still alive today'.[143] Veuillot's prediction that the comtesse's fame would outshine that of her husband's ancestors came true. In addition, if the cherished dream of Mgr de Ségur and Louis Veuillot was to champion the new Catholic era of the Ségur family as an example to the nation, then the comtesse de Ségur was the most successful of them all. While over the course of the twentieth century the writings of her sons and Veuillot fell out of favour, the comtesse's books continued to sell and sell. This chapter has shown how the comtesse found her political voice. The next chapter will now further develop this notion of how women as writers could be 'soldiers' for the ultramontane cause, by setting the comtesse in her literary context, examining how these women constructed their militant identities and what their legacy was for feminine culture.

Notes

1 Originally published Paris, Lecoffre, 1851. Information on editions from the BN-Opale online catalogue.
2 Cholvy and Hilaire, *Histoire religieuse de la France contemporaine*; Gibson, *Social History of French Catholicism*; Clark, 'New Catholicism'.
3 Horaist, *Dévotion au pape*.
4 Gough, *Paris and Rome*; Jacques-Olivier Boudon, *Paris capitale religieuse sous le Second Empire* (Paris, Les Éditions du Cerf, 2001).
5 Quoted in Abbé Henri Chaumont, *Monseigneur de Ségur Directeur des âmes* (Paris, René Haton, 1884), p. 407.
6 McMillan, 'Louis Veuillot, *L'univers* and the ultramontane network'; Boudon's chapter 'L'archevêché de Paris face au Saint-Siège', *Paris capitale religieuse*.
7 For the former interpretation, see Eugène Veuillot, *Louis Veuillot*, and for the latter, Pierrard, *Louis Veuillot*, p. 14.
8 Their correspondence is in NAF 22834, and Anatole de Ségur, *Mgr de Ségur*, volume 1; cf. Hélène Jaulmes, 'Les lettres de Catherine Rostopchine à Gaston de Ségur (1840–55)', *Cahiers Séguriens*, 2 (2001), 17–22.
9 Letters from Gaston de Ségur to Anatole de Ségur, 31 October 1852, NAF 22830, f. 158, and 4 December 1852, f. 159.
10 *Ma chère maman*, p. 169.
11 Olga de Pitray, *Mon bon Gaston*, p. 2.

12 Olga de Pitray, *Mon bon Gaston*, chapter 1.

13 Loyrette and Strich, *Sur les pas de la comtesse de Ségur*, p. 55.

14 Anatole de Ségur, *Mgr de Ségur*, 1:15–18.

15 *Ibid.*, 1:17–18.

16 Gaston de Ségur, Diary and sketchbook 1841, Loyrette and Strich, *Sur les pas de la comtesse de Ségur*, p. 115.

17 Gough, *Paris and Rome*, chapter 4.

18 Gaston de Ségur, Diary and sketchbook 1841, p. 132.

19 Narichkine, *1812*, pp. 227–228.

20 Anatole de Ségur, *Mgr de Ségur*, 1:52–53, Mgr de Ségur, *Ma mère*, p. 31.

21 Anatole de Ségur, *Mgr de Ségur*, 2: appendix I.

22 Letter, undated, to the comtesse Rostopchine, NAF 22834.

23 Letter from the comtesse Rostopchine to Gaston de Ségur, February c. 1848, NAF 22834.

24 Letter from the comtesse Rostopchine to Gaston de Ségur, 1845, NAF 22834.

25 Declaration of faith, Paris, 5 September 1848, NAF 22833, f. 168; Anatole de Ségur, *Mgr de Ségur*, 1:143.

26 Letter, 6 February 1860, in Horaist, *Dévotion au pape*, p. 366.

27 Olga de Pitray, *Mon bon Gaston*, p. 115.

28 Baille, *Souvenirs sur Mgr de Ségur*, pp. 33–34.

29 Anatole de Ségur, *Souvenirs à mes enfants*, 15 April 1866, NAF 11401.

30 Letter from abbé Gaston de Ségur to Louis Veuillot, 15 December 1851, NAF 24633, f. 248.

31 Letter from abbé Gaston de Ségur to Anatole de Ségur, 19 December 1851, NAF 22830, f. 153.

32 Roger Aubert, 'Mgr de Mérode, ministre de la guerre', *Revue générale belge*, 15 May 1956, p. 1109.

33 Letter from Mgr de Ségur to the comte de Chambord, 29 June 1871, reproduced in M. le marquis de Moussac, *Mgr de Ségur* (Paris, Librairie des Saints-Pères, 1906), pp. 102–105.

34 Jean Maurain, *La politique ecclésiastique du Second Empire de 1852 à 1869* (Paris, Librairie Félix Alcan, 1930), p. 114.

35 See letters in NAF 24226, ff. 657, 669–671.

36 Maurain, *Politique ecclésiastique*, p. 114.

37 Horace de Viel Castel, *Mémoires sur le règne de Napoleon III* (Paris, Berne, 1883–84), 6 volumes, 4:280–281.

38 Kreyder, *L'enfance des saints et des autres*, p. 232.

39 Quoted in Anatole de Ségur, *Mgr de Ségur*, 1: appendix I.

40 Letter from Rayneval to Thouvenel, 4 February 1853, quoted in Maurain, *Politique ecclésiastique*, p. 47.

41 Pierre Larousse, *Grand dictionnaire universel du XIXe siècle, français, historique, géographique, mythologique, bibliographique* (Paris, Administration du grand Dictionnaire universel, 1866–77), vol. 14 (1876), p. 487.

42 Letter to Madame Roger des Genettes, October 1879, in Gustave Flaubert, *Œuvres completes*, 13–16, *Correspondance*, volume 5, 1877–1880 (Paris, Club de l'honette homme, 1974–76), p. 258.

43 Boudon, *Paris capitale religieuse*, pp. 457–465.

44 Jean-Baptiste Duroselle, *Les débuts du catholicisme social en France (1822–1870)* (Paris, PUF, 1951), p. 611.

45 Guillaume Cuchet, *Le crépuscule du purgatoire* (Paris, Armand Colin, 2005), p. 111.

46 Poulat and Laurant, *L'antimaçonnisme catholique*, p. 113.

47 Duroselle, *Les débuts du catholicisme social en France 1822–1870*, chapter 2; Boudon, *Paris capitale religieuse*, chapter iv.

48 Letter from Gaston de Ségur to Anatole de Ségur, 19 December 1851 NAF 22830, f. 153.

49 Letter from Gaston de Ségur to Louis Veuillot, 11 September 1854, ICFV Carton 16, Envelope S.

50 Anatole de Ségur, *Mgr de Ségur*, 1:70.

51 Jean-Marie Mayeur, 'Catholicisme intransigeant, catholicisme social, démocratie chrétienne', *Annales ESC* (1972), 483–499, p. 486.

52 Poulat and Laurant, *L'antimaçonnisme catholique*, p. 106.

53 Mgr de Ségur, *Ma mère*, p. 38.

54 Olga de Pitray published a selection of the comtesse's letters to Veuillot in the biography of her mother, reprinted in Strich's collection. There are also letters from the comtesse to the Veuillot brothers in the catalogued collection at the Institut Catholique, Fonds Veuillot, Carton 16, Envelope S. The cartons yet to be catalogued undoubtedly contain more letters – and possibly the comtesse's correspondence with Élise Veuillot. Veuillot's replies are in his *Correspondance*, 4–9.

55 Olga de Pitray, *Ma mère*, p. 65.

56 This, dated 21 August 1858, is one of several letters to Olga asking her to save *L'univers* for her.

57 Letter to Louis Veuillot, 13 July 1859.

58 Letter from Louis Veuillot, July 1859.

59 Letter to Louis Veuillot, 21 August 1856.

60 Letter to Louis Veuillot, 15 October 1866.

61 Letter to Olga de Pitray, 2 January 1861.

62 Letter from Louis Veuillot, 1 October 1859.

63 Olga de Pitray, *Mon bon Gaston*, p. 174.

64 Pierrard, *Louis Veuillot*, p. 22.

65 Letter from Louis Veuillot to Olga de Pitray, 23 November 1866, Veuillot, *Correspondance*, 9:104.

66 Baille, *Mes souvenirs sur Mgr de Ségur*, p. 7.

67 Eugène Veuillot, *Louis Veuillot*, 3:196.

68 Eugène Veuillot, *Louis Veuillot*, 3:454.

69 Letter from Louis Veuillot to Élise Veuillot, 29 June 1869, *Correspondance*, 10.

70 Laura Kreyder, L'évangile selon Sophie de Ségur, *Revue des Sciences Humaines*, 1, (1992) pp. 61–80, p. 61.

71 Pierrard, *Louis Veuillot*, p. 14.

72 See letter from Louis Veuillot to Élise Veuillot, 19 April 1853, NAF 24220, f. 290; his letter to Eugène Veuillot, September 1866, NAF 24221, f. 512.

73 Eugène Veuillot, *Louis Veuillot*, 3:199–200, 457.

74 Letter from Louis Veuillot to Élise Veuillot, July 1856, NAF 24220, f. 489.

75 In other words, Dupanloup, Bishop of Orleans, and Sibour, Archbishop of Paris. Veuillot, *Louis Veuillot*, 3:92.

76 Letter to Eugène Veuillot, 30 July 1856, ICFV, Carton 16, Envelope S.

77 Letter from Louis Veuillot to Eugène Veuillot, 25 July 1856, Veuillot *Correspondance*, 5:22.

78 Letter from Louis Veuillot to the comtesse de Montsaulnin, 28 July 1856, Veuillot *Correspondance*, 5:27.

79 Letter from Élise Veuillot to Louis Veuillot, 12 August 1856, ICFV, Carton 18, Envelope G.

80 Letter from Élise Veuillot to Louis Veuillot, 9 August (no year given, but her subsequent reference to a legal trial would suggest she is referring to the *L'univers jugé par lui même* affair), ICFV, Carton 18, Envelope G.

81 Gough, *Paris and Rome*, chapters vii, ix, and xii.

82 Comtesse de Ségur, *Livre de messe des petits enfants* (Paris, Douniol, 1858).

83 Letter from Gaston de Ségur to M Carrière, Superior at the Saint-Sulpice Seminary, 18 September 1856, quoted in Hédouville, *Mgr de Ségur*, pp. 206–207.

84 See Gough, *Paris and Rome*, chapter x.

85 Letter from Gaston de Ségur to Louis Veuillot, 20 June 1854, ICFV, Carton 16, Envelope T.

86 Letter to Olga de Pitray, 2 November 1859.

87 Price, *French Second Empire*, p. 190.

88 Letter to Olga de Pitray, 10 April 1860.

89 Letters to Olga de Pitray, 24 April 1861, 10 May 1861.

90 Letter to Olga de Pitray, 25 November 1860.

91 Letter from Louis Veuillot to Olga de Pitray, 1860, NAF 24631, f. 313.

92 Letter from Mgr de Ségur to Louis Veuillot, 1 November, c. 1860, ICFV, Carton 16, Envelope T.

93 *L'univers* was suppressed by the government 1860–67, so I use the term 'his newspaper' for brevity, when in reality the articles appeared in *L'univers* and *Le monde catholique*.

94 Louis Veuillot, 'Les Fables, par Anatole de Ségur', p. 588.

95 Anatole de Ségur, *Mgr de Ségur*, 1:304.

96 Louis Veuillot, 'Témoignages et souvenirs par M. le comte Anatole de Ségur', 25 December 1857, *L'univers*.

97 Anatole de Ségur, *Mgr de Ségur*, 2:119–120.

98 Mme la comtesse de Ségur, née Rostopchine, *Livre de messe des petits enfants* (Paris, Douniol, 1858).

99 Mgr de Ségur, *La religion enseignée aux petits enfants* (Paris, Douniol, 1857).

100 Anatole de Ségur, *Souvenirs à mes enfants* (diary 1866–67) NAF 11401.

101 John Sharp, 'Juvenile Holiness: Catholic Revivalism among Children in Victorian Britain', *Journal of Ecclesiastical History*, 35 (1984), 220–238; Bernard Aspinwall, 'The Child as Maker of the Ultramontane', in Wood, Diana (ed.) *The Church and Childhood* (Oxford, Blackwell, 1994), pp. 427–445.

102 Anderson, 'The Divisions of the Pope', pp. 29–31; McMillan, 'Catholic Christianity in France', p. 219.

103 Boudon, *Paris capitale religieuse*, p. 137.

104 Savart, *Catholiques en France*, pp. 440–442.

105 Mgr de Ségur, 'La sanctification des enfants', *Bulletin de l'Association Catholique de Saint-François de Sales pour la défense et la conservation de la foi*, February, second in a series of six articles, January–June 1867.

106 See Maurain, *Politique ecclésiastique*, pp. 371–375.

107 Quoted in Gough, *Paris and Rome*, p. 89.

108 Marcoin, *La comtesse de Ségur*, pp. 291–292.

109 Olga de Pitray, *Mon bon Gaston*, p. 158.

110 Letter to Templier, 16 February 1864.

111 Letter to Templier, 12 May 1864.

112 *Ibid.*

113 Letter to Templier, 22 March 1864.

114 Letters to Templier, 12 May 1864.

115 Letter to Templier, 20 November 1864.

116 Letter to Templier, 8 November 1866.

117 NAF 22830, ff. 58–64, 151–165.

118 *Cahiers Séguriens*, 5 (2004), reproduces two texts from Anatole de Ségur, *Le dimanche des soldats* and *Mémoires d'un troupier*, to allow comparison with *Le mauvais génie*.

119 Anatole de Ségur, *Mgr de Ségur*, 1:56–69.

120 See letters exchanged between the brothers for the period 1852–55, contained in NAF 22830, ff. 56–66, and 151–161.

121 See for example, Louis Veuillot, *La guerre et l'homme de la guerre* (Paris, Vivès, 1854), pp. 397–398; Anatole de Ségur, *Troupier*, pp. 55–56; Mgr de Ségur, *Au soldat en temps de guerre* (Paris, Tolra et Haton, n.d.).

122 For further discussion of Ségur's representations of Catholic masculinity, see my chapter 'Petits garçons modèles: la masculinité catholique à travers l'oeuvre de la comtesse de Ségur', in Régis Revenin (ed.) *Hommes et masculinités de 1789 à nos jours* (Paris, Éditions Autrement, 2007), pp. 208–219.

123 Kreyder, 'L'évangile selon Sophie de Ségur'.

124 *Ibid.*, p. 74.

125 Letter from the Cardinal Donnet, Archbishop of Bordeaux, 5 November 1865, comtesse de Ségur, *Évangile d'une Grand'mère*.

126 *Œuvres*, 1:801.

127 *Œuvres*, 1:504.

128 Veuillot, *Ça et là* (1860), quoted in Pierrard, *Louis Veuillot*, p. 125.

129 Anatole de Ségur, *Mgr de Ségur*, 1: chapter seven.

130 See letter from Louis Veuillot to Élise Veuillot, 25 November 1857; and Veuillot, review of *Témoignages et Souvenirs*.

131 Letter to Templier, 12 October 1857.

132 Letter to Templier, 16 June 1861.

133 Letter to Templier, 5 June 1869.

134 *Œuvres*, 2:504.

135 *Œuvres*, 3:3.

136 See Marcoin, *La comtesse de Ségur*, pp. 111–123.

137 Letter to Templier, 3 January 1865.

138 Letter from Anatole to Gaston de Ségur, 15 October 1852, NAF 22830, f. 56.

139 Louis Veuillot, letter to l'abbé Morisseau, 18 July 1856, in *Correspondance*, 5:12.

140 For example Veuillot's *Ça et là* (Paris, Gaume Frères et J. Duprey, 1860); for a discussion of Veuillot's politics, see Pierre Pierrard, *Louis Veuillot*.

141 Louis Veuillot, *Lendemain de la victoire* (Paris, J. Lecoffre, 1850), preface, pp. 71–72.

142 *Ibid.*, p. 75.

143 Letter from Louis Veuillot to Olga de Pitray, 25 December 1860, in *Correspondance*, 6:333.

5

Model girls and divine women: reading the comtesse de Ségur

The comtesse de Ségur's most notorious contribution to French culture has been the concept of the 'petite fille modèle', the pure, pious and obedient young miss whom she encouraged girls to emulate. The phrase has passed into French idiom. The model little girl immediately conjures up an image of girlhood under a more strait-laced era, the conservative Second Empire. These were not real children but model ones, upholding an impossible ideal to which the girls of the upper classes were forced to try to conform. Ségur's model girls have become shorthand for describing the repressive gender roles imposed upon little girls. Thus, although Ségur wrote for both boys and girls, it is her model girls that are most often associated with her work, and she is perceived popularly as writing for girls.

Why? *Petites filles modèles* is not even the title that has sold the most copies. No matter. The construction of Ségur as a 'feminine' author was largely carried out by later critics, and was only ever partial. It is in fact relatively rare to find examples of women writing about how they enjoyed reading books by the comtesse de Ségur when they were young.[1] For example, I opened this book with a quote from General de Gaulle expressing his admiration for her (albeit in a rather tongue in cheek manner). However, her reception increasingly described Ségur as an author for girls. This was in part because many of these commentators were describing what they felt to be the excessive prudishness in the education of girls from the social elites, in which girls were offered little more to read than rigorously policed children's books. For example, in 1897 the novelist Robert de Montesquiou (b. 1855) expressed this view. He deplored the pious education that meant that at fifteen, and even fifty if she was unlucky enough not to marry, girls were still reading books by Ségur and her governess colleagues.[2] Similarly, writing in 1908, the journalist Jean Ernest-Charles pitied the poor girls of the upper classes. While their brothers escaped the nursery once they reached the age of reason, 'little girls remain forever modelled on the books by the comtesse de Ségur. They have no opportunity to react.'[3] Given the reluctance of boys to read books labelled 'girly', this became a self-fulfilling prophecy.[4] In 1948, when conducting a survey on children's reading practices, the psychologist Alfred Brauner noted the very strict demarcation of reading along gender lines. In his sample of children from a mining community in northern France, boys did not borrow Ségur's books from the library, and never cited her as their favourite author, in comparison to the girls, who voted her their favourite author.[5] The idea persisted. Simone de Beauvoir's analysis of Ségur denied that she even wrote seriously about male characters. In 1967 an article in the *Quinzaine Littéraire* recorded Ségur's continuing popularity amongst children in a Parisian lycée.[6] The journalist automatically selected a girls' school. She did not feel the need to remark upon, and certainly did not justify, this choice.

This chapter on the comtesse de Ségur's legacy in France therefore focuses on her role in feminine culture. I argue that the feminisation of her readership, and the cultural significance of the model little girls, has ensured that her books helped define the contours of feminine childhood. *Les petites filles modèles* and the Fleurville trilogy have been presented to little girls to read for the past one hundred and fifty years. Today their sales continue to go from strength to strength, now packaged in sugary pink covers featuring two model little girls in voluminous dresses. In this way her books form a link between generations of girls. To study her is not only useful for the history of women; it also offers an interesting perspective on the history of girls' reading practices.

In addition, the perception of Madame de Ségur as writing only for girls provides a useful problematic for understanding interpretations of women's writing. The misconception also has its origins in the type of books that she wrote. The comtesse was a 'governess' author, which is to say that she wrote morally improving works for young children. Boys left the nursery to go on to greater things, whereas their sisters did not. Nursery literature has therefore been understood as a feminine genre, and has suffered accordingly. The term 'governess' was first used by the editor Hetzel, during his campaign in the 1860s to 'replace the dried fruit of governess literature ... with something simpler and more healthy, which might at least lead to a taste for better things'.[7] The vocabulary used to describe such books could be very cruel. Montesquiou wrote of how 'Fleuriot, Ségur, and Monniot oozed out snivelling works of puerile drivel'.[8] Ernest-Charles accused the comtesse and her hordes of imitators of confecting rancid sugary, sticky confections, the 'retrograde marmalade' of 'simple books that fought against all the great efforts of modern education'.[9] When Simone de Beauvoir remembered her maiden aunt who wrote for *La poupée modèle* in the Belle Époque, she described her as 'obese and moustachioed'.[10] Nursery books conjure up a grim picture of moustachioed old maids, writing saccharine pap. The old stereotypes of the bluestocking, of women's intellectual inferiority, and of their tendency to religious fanaticism have died hard in the case of governess authors.

Within France there has been a resurgence of interest in the comtesse from feminists, keen to reclaim her as a talented author. However, this has involved distancing her from the work of her colleagues. The current perception of Ségur's writings, and how they fit with those of other 'governesses', ought to be nuanced, because it has been coloured by a misogynistic notion that these nursery books were therefore inferior in terms of both form and content. As with all stereotypes, the oft-repeated jibes conceal a much richer and more complex culture than might be expected. The immense contribution that these women made to religious writing in the mid-century publishing boom has not yet received the attention it deserves.

The female reading public was expanding fast in the nineteenth century, generating an insatiable demand for books and education manuals designed specifically for them. The comtesse de Ségur began writing at the apogee of this incredibly fertile time for girls' print culture. The period stretching roughly from 1750 to 1830 had seen the production of books for girls grow fivefold.[11] The ensuing boom of the printing industry mid-century carried this new genre with it. Legislation enacted in 1833, 1850, 1867, and culminating in the Republican laic laws of the 1880s, expanded opportunities for schooling for girls. This was in part caused by, but also stimulated debates surrounding, the subject of their education. Female literacy rates were steadily catching up with those of men. Of the generation of women that grew up in the Second Empire, 33 per cent were unable to sign their names when they were married between 1872 and 1875, as compared to 22 per cent of their husbands. Girls were therefore doing slightly better than the national average in 1866, which was 39 per cent, and they were slowly closing the gender gap – in

1854, 31 per cent of men had been unable to sign their name, compared to 46 per cent of their wives.[12] However, as has been noted by several scholars, this is no straightforward story of an unstoppable march towards progress. Historians disagree over to what extent the expansion of education provided girls with opportunities and eventually undermined the ideal of feminine domesticity, or whether it should be seen rather as further reinforcing their socialisation along traditional gender lines.[13]

Similarly, scholars have been, and remain, divided over how to interpret the comtesse and the impact that she had on girls' culture. Was she a villainess, responsible for creating the 'petite fille modèle', and as such a crucial part of the cultural straitjacket imposed upon generations of little girls?[14] Or was she too a victim of the patriarchal order of Second Empire France? At the same time as second-wave feminists in the mid-1970s were vilifying her works and all they represent in *Les temps modernes*,[15] and the influential critic Marc Soriano in his *Guide de la littérature pour la jeunesse* was suggesting her works were too sexist to give to children,[16] Soriano was also arguing elsewhere that Madame de Ségur had in fact been a proto-feminist.[17] By the early 1980s the issue was still unresolved. One year an issue of the trade union CGT's publication for women, *Antoinette*, asked 'should the comtesse de Ségur be banned?';[18] the next, the magazine of the women's liberation front, *Des femmes en mouvement hebdo*, wondered 'the comtesse, a feminist? Who appears to murmur, as others after have done, that one is not born a woman, but becomes one?'[19] More recently, the comtesse de Ségur has been interpreted by scholars as marking an important turning point in perceptions of girlhood, and, in particular, that in 'Sophie' she created the modern little girl.[20] This assertion has been widely accepted.[21]

But is this recent scholarship now in danger of trying to square the circle? On the one hand, there is no escaping the conservatism of most of Ségur's directly stated views on girls and women. All the theories of Ségur's feminism rest upon a deeper reading of her texts (usually inspired by psychoanalysis) and generally conclude she was a feminist 'unknowingly', or 'in spite of herself', or because her texts 'fail' in their stated pedagogic aim. Furthermore, although her later books may contain some strong female characters, and even make claims which seem to struggle against the weight of cultural norms, it is the notion of the 'petite fille modèle' which has been retained in the French collective memory. On the other hand, her books really are for modern girls, in the sense that they are still read today. While fellow feminine best-sellers such as Monniot's *Journal de Marguerite*, Zulma Carraud's *Petite Jeanne*, or the works of authors like Julie Gouraud and Zénaïde Fleuriot did not survive into the twentieth century,[22] Ségur's sales went from strength to strength, and her books went on to enjoy something of a golden age between the 1930s and the 1960s, and are again being revived in the 2000s.[23] In light of these apparent contradictions, it is helpful to shift the focus slightly. Rather than trying to make Ségur into a feminist, it is more fruitful to examine instead how she constructed her identity as a woman writer, and one concerned with girls' education. She wrote at a time when girls' education, and, particularly, who had control over it, was the subject of fierce debate. The domestic space was fixed under the glare of moralists and reformers of all political backgrounds – so too were the women and girls involved in this process. There exists a wealth of sources in the form of articles, reviews, manuals and moral commentaries,[24] along with the comtesse's works and correspondence, to help us to understand where she and her little girls fit in. This chapter incorporates methodology on identity from the New Biography, as well as from the history of the book and reading, into this analysis, to try to locate the comtesse de Ségur's place in French feminine culture.

Philippe Lejeune's pioneering research on young girls' diaries has allowed historians to build an idea of the ways in which their domestic education operated, and how within such a restricted universe young girls constructed rather timorous selves in their diaries.[25] Some studies of women pedagogues are also now being produced.[26] The field of nineteenth-century authors for children, examined from this perspective, remains under-researched, with Madeleine Lassère's excellent study of Victorine Monniot[27] forming a notable exception. Literary scholarship on such authors has on the other hand been vast, and provides interesting material to work with. In particular, the work of Mitzi Myers, the saviour of English governess authors – who faced vitriolic attacks similar to those quoted above on their French counterparts – has inspired scholars of children's literature to rethink completely the way they approach such authors.[28] The comtesse de Ségur's contribution to the education of girls in nineteenth- and twentieth-century France tends to be overlooked, because she was a children's author, rather than a true pedagogue.[29] Nevertheless, this chapter argues that her books played a formative role on the upbringing of girls, so this chapter follows Mitzi Myers's lead, and locates Ségur's place in the venerable 'matrilineage' (to borrow from Myers's inventive vocabulary) of women educators.

Such an approach requires sensitivity to the problems of source material. This chapter has been greatly influenced by, and even draws its title from, the fascinating history of reading in nineteenth-century France by Martyn Lyons.[30] In this study he places his subjects in their social context by exploiting the dual meaning of 'reading'. When Lyons looks at the reading practices of workers, women, and peasants, he also asks how they were 'read' by bourgeois moralists as a social problem. This had serious implications for what books they had access to, and how they read them. Likewise, the following section asks how the comtesse and her governess colleagues were 'read', and analyses the ways in which this effected how they constructed their identities. The chapter then focuses in the second section on how young girls were supposed to read their books, so as to ask tentatively what the legacy of the comtesse de Ségur's model little girls might have been for modern girlhood.

The mother educator and 'governess' literature

Madame de Ségur's public self was a carefully crafted, and well-maintained, performance. Notions of how and why women authors ought to write, and little girls ought to read, permeated this image of the author that she created. She was entering into an already crowded marketplace. Women had for over a hundred years been prominent in the production of books for the nursery, wresting the genre from male authors such as Perrault. There were still some men writing very successfully, notably Arnaud Berquin, followed by his protégé Nicholas Bouilly, and latterly the publisher Hetzel under the pseudonym P.-J. Stahl, or Théodore Barrau, whose nom de plume was (rather tellingly) Louise d'Altemont. However, it was a genre in which there was now a strong feminine tradition. Governess literature, as it was called, had produced a clutch of celebrities, and spawned a mass of imitators. In Europe it had principally been developed together by such authors as Sarah Fielding and Madame le Prince de Beaumont, followed by Stéphanie de Genlis, Sarah Trimmer, Mary Wollstonecraft, and Maria Edgeworth, amongst many others, from the mid-eighteenth century onwards. As well as through translation, their travels as governesses provided opportunities for cross-fertilisation. The label 'governess' illustrates the close relationship between this literature and the education profession. Over a third of the women authors in France for the period 1750–1830 were governesses, or teachers of some description.[31] Most famously, Madame de Genlis had been the governess of the Duke of Orléans's children, including the future King Louis-Philippe. The defining characteristics of governess literature are that it has an educational aim; it is written for young children; it is centred upon maternal mentors (reflecting the new authority invested in motherhood); and it develops particularly 'feminine' religious or moral concerns rather than overtly intellectual ones.[32] While their work had beaten a path for successors, such women had also inevitably provoked a backlash of male ridicule at their pretensions. Similarly, the growing appetite of girls for literature was accompanied by fears as to the effects upon society. However, the new generation of governesses that emerged by mid-century had several positive images of womanhood to draw upon, as the obsession with the mother educator reached its height, and the religious revival provided celibate women with a cultural model for an active, public life.

As discussed in Chapter 3, authors like Ségur, whose reading public included young girls, were subject to intense scrutiny. They were also easy targets for ridicule. Their books were derided for being so safe as to be excruciatingly dull. Hetzel accused them of writing the literature of 'dried fruit', and Louis Veuillot echoed his sentiments. The journalist regularly complained about the authors who were giving 'good' books a bad name, 'in brief, the problem almost invariably with these sorts of books is that they are written by spinsters who know nothing of life, the world, literature, and often not even grammar'.[33] Governesses were also haunted by the spectre of the bluestocking. Rebecca Rogers's chapter on mid-century educators gives a good idea of the criticisms women pedagogues faced.[34] She reproduces Daumier's caricatures from the 1840s, which suggested that such women posed a threat to social order. His bluestockings teach their charges ideas beyond their role in life, and so produce ridiculous unsexed, unmarriageable creatures. The venom reserved for the 'spinsters' who wrote for children contrasted sharply with the exaltation of the mother educator in this same period. Writing for children was second best, suspect even. On the other hand, female pedagogues could also draw upon a more favourable discourse, as in writing for children they were operating within the boundaries imposed upon their gender. They could associate their work with that of the mother educator, and claim that their writing was an extension of their maternal role. Paradoxically, the obsession with the private sphere provided women with substantial professional opportunities. The discourse on feminine domesticity was also big business in the mid-nineteenth century, which saw a veritable boom in education manuals, cookery manuals, etiquette books, and so on.[35] The feminine private sphere was not only held up to intense scrutiny but also packaged for public consumption. Negotiating this contradiction was no easy task, but it was certainly possible.

To do so, women authors needed to distinguish themselves from the old stalwarts of governess literature, who were falling out of favour with the growing Catholic reviewing system, but also the reading public. For example, although she had dominated the market in the first half of the nineteenth century, Madame de Genlis's popularity had begun to wane.[36] Reviewers regularly complained about the dearth of appropriate reading matter available. The emphasis on rationalism and reason to be found in governess literature from the late eighteenth and early nineteenth centuries had also earned it a reputation for being rather dull. Perhaps more damning in the eyes of Catholics was that the big names were perceived to bear the taint of the Enlightenment. In the case of Madame de Genlis, this extended to accusations of libertinism (it was even suggested that her education of Louis-Philippe had included his sexual initiation).[37] They were suspected of lacking religion. Gaston de Ségur accused Madame de Genlis of being associated with the freemasons,[38] while the *Bibliographie catholique* picked her up for referring to God as the Supreme Being. The same review berated Berquin for mentioning God only very occasionally, and rejected Madame Guizot because she was Protestant.[39] Similarly, the *Journal des demoiselles* complained that Madame Guizot was 'too cold and reasonable', while Berquin, 'is not religious'.[40] While the conventions of governess literature still influenced the new generation, a perceptible shift was taking place, as the Catholic revival in France took hold. The new generation of successful women authors distinguished themselves from their predecessors because they were overwhelmingly Catholic. More than simply religious – religion had always played an important role in the pedagogy of the nursery – they were now militantly so.[41] Catholic concern about unsuitable books led to the great spurt in 'good book' production 1830–70.[42] Girls' literature was swept up and carried along by this new impetus.

It was in this context that the comtesse de Ségur sought to create her identity. The main way in which she constructed her public image was in the dedications at the front of each of her storybooks. She later fleshed out these brief sketches into a proper self-portrait in her Bible series. When Madame de Ségur introduced herself to her public in the preface to *Nouveaux contes de fées* (quoted at the beginning of Chapter 1 above), she addressed two specific girl readers, her granddaughters Camille and Madeleine. She explained that these are the stories she used to tell them, which she has now committed to paper. The two girls will be able to remember their grandmother as they read her books. Ségur drew upon a traditional image of the old woman, telling bedtime stories to a gathering of little children. The old woman storyteller had not always been reputable, but the vogue for fairy tales at the seventeenth-century court had domesticated the crone, playing down her bawdy past and associating her instead with St Anne, the holy grandmother.[43] In this role, although the author was a genuine aristocrat, Ségur drew upon this cult of the grandmother storyteller, representing herself in an intimate setting, with a small family of two granddaughters, speaking to them in an affectionate tone. She exhorted her 'dear children' to think of their 'old grandmother', who wanted nothing more than to please them. Louis Veuillot noted the strangeness of this image the illustrious aristocrat painted of herself, as an old granny, bouncing children on her knee. He was clearly impressed that 'such a cultivated mind, so lofty and proud, should stoop so charmingly to these simple and childlike tasks of a grandmother'.[44] In this way, Ségur aligned herself with the new sentimental mother figure who had replaced the distant, aristocratic mode of motherhood, and was gaining favour in elite families, including the imperial family of the current regime.[45]

The comtesse referred to her advanced age not only to recall the tradition of feminine storytelling but also to emphasise that she was fulfilling her biological role. Ségur drew attention to the fact that she was not neglecting her maternal duties, as they were over, and she had now assumed the new role of the wise old grandmother. She thus reassured readers that she was neither a spinster nor a governess. To reinforce this, Ségur's emphasis was above all on the private nature of these writings, produced only accidentally, even reluctantly, for the public sphere. Her dedications were always written for her grandchildren, rarely acknowledging that her books were written for a public audience. The image of the comtesse as a private, rather than a professional writer resonated with the ideal of humble Christian womanhood. When the monument to the comtesse was erected in the Jardin du Luxembourg in 1910, *Le Figaro* echoed approvingly the sentiments expressed by the committee on 'the almost familial character that this celebration ought to have, dedicated to a woman "who sought neither acclaim nor celebrity" and who only wanted to amuse her grandchildren, but in so doing accomplished one of the most salutary *oeuvres* of the nineteenth century'.[46]

The comtesse's humble identity was a creation she took great care to cultivate. While her prefaces offered fleeting glimpses of the author, in her Bible series she developed a full self-portrait. Ségur's 'Grandmother's Bible' series consisted of her retelling for children of abridged versions of the Gospels, *Évangile d'une grand'mère* (1866), the Acts of the Apostles,

Les actes des apôtres (1867), and the Old Testament, *Bible d'une grand'mère* (1869). In *Évangile d'une grand'mère* she introduced the reader into her 'real' home life. She did this by framing her version of the New Testament with a second narrative which featured herself as narrator, surrounded by all her grandchildren, to whom she was reading the Bible out loud. Then, the opening scene of the second in the series, *Les actes des apôtres*, depicted her room, where the famous comtesse de Ségur is writing. Her grandchildren are at her feet, playing with her books and constantly interrupting her. The author answers their questions patiently. When one child tries to read from the Acts, which she finds in her grandmother's books by her writing desk, she has difficulties with the words, and here we have the premise for the narrative to begin. 'Grandmother' promises to read it to the children tomorrow.[47] Ségur thus further emphasised the link between her profession as a writer and her biological role in life. This was made explicit in the dedication of her *Bible d'une grand'mère*, which promised her grandchildren that she would now set to writing the lives of the saints for them: 'I will have thus worked up till the end for those I love and to whom I owe the happiness of fifty years of motherhood.'[48] Moreover, these portraits made it clear that she drew her inspiration from Christian sources – her writing table is portrayed laden with holy books. It was no accident that she chose the Bible series in which to reveal herself most fully. This was the image that the comtesse wanted to be recorded for posterity.

The overwhelming insistence on writing as a selfless exercise that she engaged in only for the good of her grandchildren was an important fiction not only for her public but also for herself. This ideal of the endlessly devoted grandmother was impossible. It exhausted the comtesse, and she reproached herself for not being able to live up to her persona. Indeed, her public image was a paradox; the professional author could not write while her children played at her feet and pestered her. The whole publication process, and particularly that of the Bible series, embroiled Madame de Ségur in a series of protracted struggles to achieve the product that she wanted. Similarly, she struggled to find writing time amongst her duties as a wife, mother, and grandmother. Correspondence with her daughter was filled with references to her frustration at having to look after her husband or various grandchildren, when she had a book to finish for Hachette. When nursing her husband, the comtesse was forced to write by gaslight, after the comte had gone to bed.[49] Similarly, when looking after her newborn grandson, she complained of losing 'my best writing hours . . . for two days now I have been constantly secretly impatient at not finding one quiet hour to devote to my letters . . . my heart is pounding with impatience and my mind is becoming an inferno'.[50] Moreover, the inventory of their Paris apartment, following the death of the comte de Ségur in 1863, shows that, when she was engaged in writing her storybooks, the books beside the comtesse's writing materials were of a more profane nature than the religious books the children innocently pick up. The beady eyes of her concierge noticed a bound set of Sir Walter Scott's collected works, and Bouillet's famous encyclopaedia. He also recorded that she kept ten 'half empty' bottles of liquor by her desk, which presumably served to stimulate the comtesse's creativity further.[51]

The touching scene in her bedroom evoked in *Les actes des apôtres* was a fiction that allowed the comtesse to expiate some of the guilt that she felt for resenting her feminine responsibilities. For her public, she presented her two roles as inseparable the one from the other. In private, however, the comtesse expressed a sense of unease with another, more troubling self-image. A letter to one of her granddaughters refers to feeling that she had neglected her maternal duties. She had recently had her photograph taken, and was troubled by the woman she saw: 'it is tiresome for me, someone who has neglected her family to go down to posterity looking like a ferocious tiger or a drunken doorwoman'.[52] Although it is unclear which photograph she is referring to, most of the published images of the comtesse that portray her when she was an author show a rather weary-looking old widow, dressed in black. They contrast sharply with the joyful energy of her books (figure 4). The imagery of ferocity and drunkenness, the polar opposite of the submissive Christian mother, is echoed in the diabolic vocabulary she used to describe her urge to write, or the violent frustration she felt when prevented from writing her correspondence. The comtesse de Ségur could not always believe her fiction that she sublimated her voracious desire to write into her role of gentle grandmother, who engaged in such an activity only for the edification of her grandchildren.

Ségur's efforts to establish her reputation could also have a more playful side. She was not above engaging in rivalry with other successful 'governesses',[53] while at the same time nodding to the fact that her writings belonged to the governess genre. Her *Mémoires d'un âne* adopted the technique of using children's toys or pets as narrators. This was a classic governess genre, famously used by Mrs Sarah Trimmer, in her tale of talking birds, *The History of the robins* (1786).[54] Julie Gouraud had popularised it in France with her publishing success of the 1840s, *Mémoires d'une poupée* (1839), and she had made it her own in numerous sequels.

4 Sophie Rostopchine, comtesse de Ségur (1799–1874), original black and white
photo by Étienne Carjat (1828–1906)

Thus, in her *Mémoires d'un âne* (1860), the comtesse felt the need to nod
to Gouraud, but also make her own claim to originality. Midway through
Ségur's story, the younger girls, Henriette and Élisabeth, wonder whether
their clever donkey would one day write his memoirs, just like the doll
whose book they enjoyed reading. Their sensible cousins, Camille and

Madeleine, set them straight: 'it was a lady who wrote the doll's memoirs, and, to make the book more amusing, she pretended to be a doll, and to write like a doll . . . A doll is not a living thing, it is made out of wood, leather, and filled with air, so how could it think, see, listen, and write?'[55] Ségur gently teased her readers in this hall of mirrors – if dolls cannot write their memoirs then neither can donkeys. Gouraud, who also wrote for Hachette's *Bibliothèque Rose*, was not insensitive to such cheek. In her *Mémoires d'un caniche* (1865), Gouraud's poodle put Ségur's donkey in his place by showing how he was more mindful of the importance of Christian humility. The dog explained to readers that he was not an 'intellectual' as *some* animals writing their memoirs have recently claimed (the preface to *Mémoires d'un âne* had boldly argued that soon one will say 'clever as a donkey'):[56] 'however, I am no more stupid than another, and I do not see why I could not write my little story, following the example of dolls, little boys, even donkeys'.[57] This quarrel illustrates the thought which these governess authors put into their work, and how no small measure of pride was involved in their writing projects. Their literary pride inflected their choice of the genre itself. Both Ségur and Gouraud argued that by writing these memoirs they were giving the mute inhabitants of the domestic sphere a voice. Ségur's tale declared it would change the way people perceived donkeys, sweeping away their prejudices. (Donkeys were the chic pets for little children of the upper classes, who learned to ride on them.) Gouraud applied this logic to little girls. She followed *Mémoires d'une poupée* with a sequel in 1840, then *Mémoires d'une petite fille* (1857), *Lettres de deux poupées* (1864), and *Mémoires d'un petit garçon* (1864). The latter opens with a tussle between a brother and sister. The sister cries that she owns a book called *Mémoires d'une petite fille*, and so he won't be able to taunt her by calling girls stupid any more: 'if you are proud to learn Latin, well I am proud that a little girl has written her memoirs'.[58]

The recent school of Ségur researchers have often argued that the comtesse stands apart from her fellow governesses;[59] however, the episode above suggests that she was aware of her position within this writing tradition. In addition, the case of the Bible series should make us more cautious about concluding too quickly that the comtesse was subversive. Although the sales of Ségur's Bible works were feeble in comparison to the rest of her oeuvre, they concretised the explicitly religious aspect of her grandmother image. With this series, she associated her books with the Catholic Church, by seeking the approval of archbishops and bishops, whose letters were published at the front of *L'Évangile d'une grand'mère*. Where the comtesse, mindful of Hachette's policy of neutrality, had always remained cautious in her prefaces, the clerical authorities were keen to spell out to mothers the political importance of her books. Cardinal Donnet, Archbishop of Bordeaux asked, 'when it comes to the instruction which children require, it appears that nothing is neglected by the government. Is it possible to say the same for their moral and religious education? How many families fail to fashion the child's heart and imprint on them the love of God?' In his view, Ségur's Bible series was the answer to society's neglect of its duties.[60] Similarly, the Christian grandmother she presented in the series was an image that was received with enthusiasm by reviewers. Following the publication of her *Évangile*, the *Bibliographie catholique* declared (erroneously as it turned out): 'for a long time now we have been used to the excellent educational works from the elegant pen of Mme la comtesse de Ségur, easy and just right for the young. This new volume, approved by seven archbishops and bishops, will be one of the most widely read and appreciated, and maybe the most useful for those for whom it is written.'[61] Subsequent reviewers wrote paeans to the comtesse: 'tireless in her devotion to the young and religion, Mme la comtesse de Ségur has written the follow-up to the *Évangile d'une grand'mère* which we reviewed last year ... She is however a wise grandmother, excellent and scholarly, gentle, and patient!'[62] This portrait captured the clerical imagination – they now had a 'face to put to the name that has become so dear and familiar to children'.[63]

Madame de Ségur's fellow governesses of the Second Empire shared her militant identity. Zénaïde Fleuriot (1829–89) explained in her first book, *Souvenirs d'une douarière* (1859), 'to my readers [girls: *lectrices*], ... I dedicate these essays to you, joining those courageous writers who have accepted the mission of purifying literature, by restoring it to its two immortal bases: religion and morality.'[64] Fleuriot's energetic literary self was rather different from Ségur's. She was a governess, not a mother. She hailed from an old Breton family whose steadfast royalism had led to its ruin in the 1830s. Her father had encouraged her to read, and latterly, to write. Her Breton identity permeated her writings, which were filled with references to the sea, and her love of the raw beauty of her homeland. She wrote that, as a Breton, piety was as natural to her as breathing.[65] Fleuriot's epitaph summed her life up thus: 'I believed, so I spoke.'[66] Just as the comtesse received the support of her family and Louis Veuillot, Zénaïde Fleuriot was also part of a network of Catholic writers and publishers. She had first received help in her literary career by Alfred Nettement, a writer who collaborated closely with the publisher Jacques Lecoffre. She remained close to both men, and would eventually take over the direction of Lecoffre's magazine, *La semaine des familles*.[67] Her work received accolades in books published by Lecoffre and written by Nettement[68] and Henri Jouin,[69] both influential critics of the time. They hailed her contribution to Catholic efforts to missionise France. Fleuriot had initially been very much a product of the Lecoffre stable, as she recalled, 'I counted on him. He was going to take my literary affairs in hand, and as he was very religious and very conscientious, all I needed was to let him do so.'[70] Thus it was with reticence that Fleuriot began to write for Hachette in 1873. She was conscious that she was entering a rather different, commercial world.[71] However, like Ségur's, her work for the *Bibliothèque Rose* continued to be dominated by religious concerns.[72] Also like the comtesse, she became something of a Catholic celebrity, and was surprised by the extent to which she was fêted in Rome: 'I did not know I was so well-known'.[73] Her fiction set during the Franco-Prussian War, *Aigle et colombe* (1871), received both the Pope's blessing and the Montyon prize from the Académie Française.

Madeleine Lassère's book on Victorine Monniot brings to light another militant Catholic personality amongst these women writers. The success of her first book *Le journal de Marguerite* (1859) allowed Monniot, also a former governess, to devote all her time to writing. Hers was an austere religion, rather different to that of Ségur, or that of any of the books to be found by Gouraud or Fleuriot in the *Bibliothèque Rose*. There was to be no light entertainment in what she saw as 'the serious subject of education, childhood, and youth'.[74] Thus, most of her books were long, and not illustrated. Even the *Journal* did not receive any visual decoration until ten years later. She was a dolourist, and defiantly so in the face of critical reservations about the suitability of such an approach for little girls. The *Journal* did not flinch from describing the tragic death of a baby, or from killing off the protagonist's dearest friend. A review in *La poupée modèle* for example warned mothers not to give the book to sensitive children.[75] The preface to its sequel, *Marguerite à vingt ans*, explained to her readers, 'I warn you that this is not an amusing book. Attentive voices, friendly voices, have, in my interest, echoed the different judgements from the public on the *Journal de Marguerite*, repeating, "too sad . . . too sad . . ." to which I reply, "that is life".'[76] Monniot was also a fervent ultramontane, unflagging in her devotion to the Pope, a sentiment that underpinned all of her books. This devotion was centred on the personality cult of Pius IX. For example, in *Marguerite à vingt ans*, Marguerite is depicted praying beneath a bust of Pius IX, 'reminiscent of the adorable image of the Lord'.[77]

The governess authors were often derided as spinsters, and both Fleuriot and Monniot clearly struggled with the stigma of remaining unmarried. Although Fleuriot had been attracted to the idea of becoming a nun, the usual destiny of her literary heroines was marriage. Family disaster, or lack of physical charm, might intervene, however, and she portrayed with sympathy girls who devoted their lives to their family or charity, but this was always second best. Monniot defended her status of old maid ferociously in *Notre Seigneur Jésus-Christ, études et méditations pour les jeunes filles* (1874): 'can one ever choose to embrace the solitary and colourless life of an old maid? . . . would you have created her to be a sort of pariah in the great Christian family? No, no Lord Jesus . . . The old maid has thus this advantage over the mother and even over the nun, for her fate was decided uniquely by the hand of God.'[78] Both Fleuriot and Monniot received the endorsement of the clerical authorities, including the Pope, as well as the Académie Française. Fleuriot had even been dissuaded from taking the veil when, in 1867, she felt tired of the world. The Jesuit priest Père Olivaint told her not to, but to return instead to her desk and dip her pen in holy water. As he said, she had the spiritual wellbeing of her five hundred thousand readers to consider.[79] Their work as writers was important to the Church, and as such they carved out a positive identity for themselves.

These governesses were far from rose-water writers. They were professionals, who earned both the respect and endorsement of their masculine peers. The clerical authorities carefully spelled out to mothers the political importance of governess books. There was a constellation of at least several authors who stood out from the crowd, and the comtesse de Ségur belonged to this group. Amongst others, Julie Gouraud, Zénaïde Fleuriot, Victorine Monniot, and the comtesse de Ségur all wrote (for the most part) with their real names,[80] and constructed very recognisable and individual identities. Alongside Ségur's grandmother storyteller was the pious Breton Zénaïde Fleuriot, the proudly literary Julie Gouraud, and the dolourist Victorine Monniot. Interesting and forceful personalities, they drew upon accepted images of women (mother educator, and Catholic militant) and the notion of women's natural piety, to create public identities for themselves. It seems fitting to conclude this section with the image of Gouraud's Catherine, proudly brandishing her book, written by a little girl just like her. This proved that boys were wrong to call girls stupid. These generations of governess authors created a distinctly feminine culture, and with this came a sense of self-esteem for such women. It remains to ask how this flourishing genre – which thanks to the publishing boom was reaching more girls than ever – might have influenced girls constructing their gendered identities as they grew up reading such books.

'Well, I am proud that a little girl has written her memoirs': books for model girls

Following the publication of *Petites filles modèles* in 1858, Madame de Ségur received a letter from a young girl named Isabelle:

> In this epistle, the young correspondent asked if the two model little girls *really did* exist, because her mother told her that she should follow their example, and Isabelle could not believe that children as well-behaved could exist outside of books. My mother [the comtesse] kindly responded to this naive question, and from there began a faithful and lively correspondence between the child and the storyteller.[81]

This fragment of their correspondence – now lost – whets the historian's appetite. It provides a glimpse of how readers might have responded to her books, and engaged with the idea of the comtesse herself. It also shows that Ségur was happy to communicate with her young fan base. However, what the correspondence really demonstrates is the difficulties historians face when trying to trace the voices of readers like Isabelle, the model little girls of Second Empire France.

Not only are the sources all too often missing, but those that do exist appear only as further reflections of the same model. We might just as well ask whether we could believe that readers as well-behaved as Isabelle existed anywhere other than on paper. Her letters exemplify the intended relationship between Madame de Ségur and her readership (and this was entirely deliberately, for Isabelle's letters were the only example of the comtesse's fan mail selected for publication by Ségur's daughter, Olga). Isabelle was instructed by her mother to emulate the behaviour of Camille and Madeleine, thus replicating the scenario of the book. She was much impressed by these heroines, but despaired of ever attaining their perfection. However, as Ségur explained in the dedication to the book, 'they really do exist . . . the existence of Camille and Madeleine can be verified by all those who know the author'.[82] She practically invited the reader to check the veracity of her portraits, and so this young reader took the author up on her offer. Quite possibly it was Isabelle's mother or governess who encouraged the girl to write to the comtesse, in order to further develop the exercise of the young reader's identification with the model girls.

Olga's biography explains that the correspondence between Ségur and Isabelle then continued for many years. The second quotation from their letters that Olga provides suggests that, as the relationship between writer and reader developed, it was articulated in the religious vocabulary of the period:

> In one of her letters, Isabelle told my mother of how she had been on a pilgrimage to Notre-Dame de la Salette, and that she had been given a piece of the rock on which the 'beautiful lady' was seated, weeping! The pious girl was so excited by her souvenir that she wanted to share her treasure with her dear Madame de Ségur, and she sent her a small medallion containing half of the rock she had received. My mother was very moved by this kind gesture, she showed it to me and took great care of it.

Isabelle's description of the Virgin as a 'beautiful lady . . . weeping' is typical of the tone of the Ségur family writings. Like the young visionaries of La Salette, or the child saint Bernadette of Lourdes, and the naive rhetoric so characteristic of nineteenth-century Catholicism,[83] Isabelle represented an innocent piety. She had read this religion in the comtesse's books, and so she eagerly shared her spiritual experience with the author. Here in Isabelle's letter we find all the ingredients of how Ségur and her family hoped children would read her books, and indeed, perceive the comtesse herself.

The aim of this section is to shed some light on the reading experiences of girls of the time (and to question tentatively whether they really did flounder in the sticky 'marmalade' of nursery literature, as Ernest-Charles would have it) using the comtesse de Ségur's writings and those of her colleagues as a window on to such readers. Undertaking to analyse girls' 'real' responses to their books would be impossible.[84] Moreover, evidence concerning Ségur's young female readers directly is at best fragmentary. Apart from Isabelle, the rest of the comtesse's fan mail has been destroyed, sold, or lost.[85] Diaries (*journaux intimes*) are of little help, for those written by younger children (and they are usually written by girls) tend to simply relate facts, without much commentary.[86] They do not often mention reading Ségur, as her books are aimed at the four to twelve age group, and girls generally took up writing diaries around the time they were preparing their first communion, aged ten or eleven. Moreover, diaries were not 'secret'. They were used as a pedagogical tool, a more playful way for girls to learn their lessons and communicate their thoughts to their mothers or governesses. Mothers occasionally mention Ségur in their correspondence, as in the case of Zélie Martin, mother of the future girl saint, Thérèse Martin,[87] but this reference is brief. Then there are Sigmund Freud's patients from turn-of-the-century Vienna who, within the privacy of the doctor–patient relationship, could reveal how her books stimulated their erotic fantasies.[88] However, it seems a little dramatic to draw conclusions about her readers using the testimonies of those who sought the help of a psychoanalyst. The vast majority of descriptions of reading the comtesse's books come from subsequent generations. Such material is fascinating but immediately brings a new set of problems of interpretation. We risk skating blithely over a period of 150 years, comparing the responses of readers from wildly different contexts, and making assumptions about reactions which may well be difficult to decipher. For example, the author and right-wing anarchist Gyp (b. 1849) made several references to the comtesse in her novels. Interpreting the intended meaning of her comments, and how this may relate to her girlhood experiences, from such tiny drops in a huge oeuvre is a hazardous enterprise. The bitter description of a tomboy being forced by her French governess to write 'foolish' dictations from *Model Little Girls* as punishment, in Radclyffe Hall's (b. 1880) lesbian novel *The Well of Loneliness* (1928) is perhaps easier to understand.[89] Meanwhile Leïla Sebbar's (b. 1941) memories of reading *Petites filles modèles* to her maids, Fatima and Aïcha, in her Algerian village of Hennaya indicate that Ségur was also read in colonial contexts.[90] This is an important line of enquiry, and could no doubt shed further light on the interplay between the constructs of gender, class, and power that influence the reader, but it would require a much larger study to do it justice. Finally, the problem of interpretation is particularly acute when dealing with childhood, as sources tend to be written once the subjects are older, and so reflect adult concerns. They also, partly as a result of the tricks our memories play on us, but often consciously, draw upon accepted cultural narratives of childhood.

This chapter answers some of these difficulties by understanding the act of reading as historically specific. Martyn Lyons's emphasis on the importance of looking at how various groups were 'read' by society is useful.[91] Such an approach can be used for Ségur's books. The books children were given, how they were taught to read them, and the ways in which they related such material to the outside world were all determined by intermediaries: by adults such as teachers, parents, or clergy, but also by peer pressure, or from siblings. Since locating anything close to a 'real' response to Second Empire children's literature is impossible, this section asks instead what reading models were being presented to them? Why were authors like Ségur interested in writing books for girls? How did they want girls to interpret them?

The Christian girl was encouraged to read little and read well, according to Bishop Dupanloup's famous dictum.[92] Once boys from well-off families reached the age of reason, at seven, they left the confines of the nursery and commenced their more cerebral education. This was designed to prepare them for public life. The most important difference was the depth and intellectual rigour of such studies, and that they learned Latin. Without Latin, a student could not sit for the baccalaureate, and so girls were effectively barred from higher education. Girls' reading however, although circumscribed, was still a serious occupation. According to Dupanloup, girls ought to take notes as they read, and never leave books half-finished, but rather read and study them several times over. Most publications for girls were not as rigorous as Dupanloup in their approaches to girl readers; nevertheless, the activity was certainly taken seriously. The magazine for girls, *Poupée modèle*, instructed its readers (from toddlers up to eight-year-olds), to study carefully, and then imitate, the behaviour of the model dolls and girls represented in its publication. According to the *Poupée modèle*, even the most amusing books still had a didactic aim. Some books, like those by Mgr de Ségur, required a particularly serious approach. Even readers of a tender age were expected to follow this. Thus, the *Poupée modèle* explained how to read Mgr de Ségur's *La piété enseignée aux enfants*: 'this book is not to be read like a book of stories ... after every chapter, you must sit down with your mother or elder sister and reflect carefully on what you have just seen and learned. Then you will make the good resolution to always put into practice the wise advice that you find in this book, and you will go play or work as usual, even better than usually, if you have understood the teachings of the good priest.'[93] In contrast, his mother's volumes were presented as a treat. For example, after having reprinted a section from the Old Testament, the *Poupée modèle* introduced a passage from one of the comtesse de Ségur's books: 'as a reward for paying attention ... or getting bored, now I am going to talk to you about a charming volume by Madame de Ségur'.[94] Nevertheless, when reading the comtesse's storybooks, girls still had to make sure they learned their lessons, as the *Poupée modèle* explained: 'it is brimming with amusing and spiritual stories, and good thoughts as well. There are so many examples which are easy and charming to follow, that my friends I am persuaded you will all work hard to resemble the heroines of Madame de Ségur.'[95]

Reading was an activity that was ideally carried out together, as a family.[96] This was so that parents could police their children, and avoid the perils of solitary reading, which was of particular concern for girls and women. When Bonnie G. Smith reconstructed an average day in the life of a pious bourgeois woman of northern France, she drew it to a close with this cosy domestic scene: 'in the evening she will sit with her family listening to one of the children read from the comtesse de Ségur's *Évangile d'une grand'mère*'.[97] Still, to a certain extent, little girls were encouraged to read independently. In her first dedication to Camille and Madeleine, Ségur referred to having read her fairy tales out loud to the girls, and impressed upon them that they should think of her as they read. Ségur's correspondence with her editor indicates she wanted to help her little readers follow the story. She worried about the size of the print, and the problems children might have when opening the pages.[98] This suggests that she wanted to make it easier for children to read her books on their own. When Zélie Martin's youngest daughter was learning to read, her mother was encouraged to see her reading Ségur's books without help: 'this afternoon I watched her, very serious, reading out loud to herself *Petites filles modèles*. She thought that I could not hear her, and she gave each character their own voice.'[99] The girl was not left to her own devices; the reading was still within a familial context as the mother supervised her, but from a discreet distance.

Montesquiou's charge that governess authors were particularly guilty of writing dull 'snivelling' books must be nuanced. Governesses wanted to ensure their books were a gripping read, for several reasons. First, such women were professional authors, and had a passion for writing. Naturally they also took great pleasure in reading, and wanted to teach their readership to do the same. Fleuriot spoke of having been 'electrified' by *Swiss Family Robinson* as a girl, while Ségur's model girls often have a book in their hand, and Monniot's *Journal* regularly wrote of how enjoyable it was to read books. Second, this was missionary literature, and so to be moved by a book was considered an important response. Girls were encouraged not simply to emulate the behaviour of the characters but also to become emotionally engaged with the text. Louise L*** (b. 1850) described indulging in an orgy of tears each time she reread Monniot's *Journal de Marguerite*. After reading, on the priest's recommendation, Madame Craven's *Récit d'une sœur*, she wrote of being profoundly moved.[100] Indeed, in her diary from the 1860s, young Lucile le Verrier recorded how she felt a failure because the story of *Récit d'une sœur* failed to move her – she described pinching herself, but to no avail.[101] In her memoirs, the comtesse d'Armaillé drily observed that this was a common ploy in the religious education of the time: 'we used to cry a lot'. She recalled how the clergy were always trying to make children cry – one particularly moving sermon sent two little girls into convulsions.[102] Certainly Ségur judged her *Pauvre Blaise* was a success when it moved her granddaughter to tears.[103] The *Bibliographie catholique* commended the occasional 'salutary tears' that children would shed over Ségur's *La sœur de Gribouille*.[104] The lachrymose piety of governess literature was no doubt one of the reasons why Montesquiou dismissed them as 'snivelling', and it is also likely that this was part of the reason why they have been designated as writing 'feminine' literature. The highly emotionally charged, missionary religion of the nineteenth-century revival was denigrated by Michelet in 1845 as a cynical strategy designed by the Jesuits to appeal to women and children.[105] However, when Anatole de Ségur was writing missionary booklets to be distributed amongst soldiers, Gaston also encouraged him to try to make them cry.[106] Being moved to tears was an important part of reading religious books. Tears were the outward expression of the soul.[107] Crying was a sign that these edifying stories had moved the reader's heart. The 'heart' was an important concept in the new Catholicism which emphasised love. Such writers therefore aimed to manipulate the emotions of their audience, to encourage this piety.

The comtesse and her colleagues sought to cultivate the 'heart', but what about the mind? And how did they perceive their role as educators? In 1867, the education minister Victor Duruy caused uproar when he proposed rudimentary secondary education courses for upper-class girls – hoping to wrest them from the control of nuns.[108] The following year, Ségur advised her daughter Olga on how to oversee the education of her own daughter:

> Tutors and governesses sometimes have a mania for excessive study; which is never the making of a woman and leads her to neglect the essentials, like needlework, tidying drawers and effects etc. It is not a grand and useless instruction in different languages, or advanced scholarship that will help a woman to get on with her life in the home, rather it is the thousands of little feminine tasks, and they are a hundred times more useful than Latin, Greek, or I don't know what, which only serve to waste time and make her big-headed.[109]

Madame de Ségur had not provided her own daughters with the extensive education that she had received herself as a girl, and she did not envisage it for her granddaughters either. Ségur's argument hinged on the fact that a woman's place was in the home. Her granddaughter could not hope for anything else in her life, and so she concluded, 'do not let her become overwhelmed with work, allow her body to develop at the same time as her intelligence'. Ségur did not suggest the girl would be incapable of learning Latin or Greek, simply that they served no purpose, and as such she would be wasting her time. She agreed with Veuillot, who had written a series of articles criticising Duruy, that an education that developed a sense of self-worth in women would be dangerous.[110] In 1931 Chanoine Cordonnier cited Ségur's letter approvingly, and lamented that young women had not listened to the comtesse's sage advice.[111]

However, the comtesse's views on female education were not as prohibitive as the quotation above might suggest. Ségur submitted her final manuscript to Hachette in July 1869, *Après la pluie, le beau temps*. It is the story of how a young girl, Geneviève, is rescued from the clutches of her evil guardian, Monsieur Dormère, by an eccentric old woman, Mlle Primerose. Dormère devotes all his time to his son, Georges, and so, aged eleven, Geneviève knows nothing, and would have been left 'ignorant as an idiot'[112] if it had not been for Mlle Primerose. The whole scenario of the book, with its recurrent motif of the father privileging the son while leaving his adoptive daughter to her own devices, underlines the unfair treatment that girls receive. Governess Mlle Primrose therefore takes Geneviève under her wing, and sees that she receives a full education. Mlle Primerose upbraids the father and son for having neglected their duties, and shows them how wrong they were: 'a girl! They are of little use. An old maid on the other hand is often helpful; like myself, for example. I am giving the good little Geneviève an education; I teach her many things my dear. She knows nearly as much as you do, Georges, except Latin.'[113] Geneviève marries well, and follows her husband to Rome, where she nurses him after he is injured. In this book, Ségur's argument was close to the ideas expounded by the liberal Bishop Dupanloup in his response to Duruy's proposals for reform, *Femmes savantes, femmes studieuses* (1867). The bishop argued that the main role of women was motherhood, and as such they were educators. In this capacity, they needed some form of proper education to carry out the task in a way that would be able to combat effectively the nefarious work of the modern State.[114] A stark division between 'liberal' and 'intransigent' Catholics is perhaps unhelpful in this case, for not only was the comtesse interested in promoting some form of education for girls, even Louis Veuillot was not wholeheartedly against such an argument. His review of Dupanloup's work had concluded that it sketched out a noble plan, and that, although it needed modification, he approved of the general outlines.[115]

Ségur's contribution to the debate – and literary swansong – was also an idiosyncratic homage to the governess, for the real linchpin of *Après la pluie* is Mademoiselle Cunégonde Primerose. This straight-talking spinster plays the role of a rather unlikely fairy godmother, who engineers the education of Geneviève and her happy marriage to Jacques. When they go to Rome, she tends to the sick and provides much needed moral support to the pontifical zouaves. Through her twin contributions of teaching and nursing, the main activities in which Catholic women participated in the community, Mlle Primerose proves 'an old maid is often helpful'. Contemporary discourse had little pleasant to say about the ageing, unmarried woman. As Monniot and Fleuriot had done, Ségur was at pains to rehabilitate such women in her final book. She provided a more positive literary image of the 'governess'. Rude, outspoken, and bossy, Primerose is a burlesque creation, but she is also heroic, for she challenges Monsieus Dormère's authority in order to protect her pupil. She undermines masculine authority not only openly but also discreetly, through her learning. When angry, she quotes Virgil's *Aeneid*, in Latin.[116] This lady was not the idealised mother educator of Dupanloup's treatise, rather she was a fiercely intelligent and independent figure, whose education means that she serves the Church better, but also highlights the injustices done to women and girls by their male superiors.

The governess model of femininity was active. Referring to *The Swiss Family Robinson*, Zénaïde Fleuriot reminisced about her love of books as a child, and how those that she had really enjoyed offered little in the way of models for her gender:

> The problem with *Robinson* is that it does not include one single little girl amongst its characters; this means that the young girls who are electrified by reading it, finding no one else to copy but those little boys with their light feet and nimble hands, are forced to identify with them. From the moment I was given that blessed book, I cared for nothing but expeditions to far off lands, gymnastic exercises, savage food, caves and navigation. In a word, I became the most adventurous of all the little girls . . .
>
> . . . Is it the idea of being useful, when one is but a weak child, that makes these hardworking children living like men seem so admirable? I don't know: but I found the active labouring life of the Robinsons far more attractive than the languid life of these simpering princesses who do nothing, and are content to watch for the swish of the genie or the fairy's magic wand.[117]

Fleuriot set out to write characters for girls to emancipate them from what she felt were the pathetic heroines they were currently offered, and provide them instead with exemplary girls who led active, meaningful lives. The young heroines of Fleuriot's books channelled energies that might be tempted by stories of adventure into useful charity work instead, along with motherhood and educating children; or, if they were not married, Fleuriot's heroines acted as guardians and educators for their young relatives. Similarly, the comtesse's girls learn through emulating their mothers that they must intervene in the local community, through charitable works. Still, this model of femininity was entirely congruent with the Christian ideal of the 'femme forte', the strong, yet silent, entirely selfless wife and mother. Ségur's character Mlle Primerose formed something of an exception in her defiant attitude towards patriarchal authority. (She also featured in one of Ségur's least popular books; it was *Sophie* and the *Petites filles modèles* who have made the most impact in terms of sales (see Appendix II).) Generally, governess heroines lead active lives, but achieve this through selfless devotion to others. Sometimes this involves painful lessons where they learn to suppress their instincts. In Ségur's *Diloy le chemineau* (1868) for example, the uppity young Félicie gradually understands the importance of being charitable towards others, after the humiliating experience of being thrashed by a railway-worker to whom she was rude. Less dramatically, the whole premise of Monniot's *Journal de Marguerite* is of the struggles of Marguerite to repress her boisterous, childish behaviour, in order to become a pious, selfless, and useful young woman. Unlike Ségur's and Fleuriot's heroines, who were usually destined to marry and live happy ever after as mothers, Marguerite becomes a nun. This was rare. Generally, governess literature emphasised motherhood, and the idea that the mother educator had an important religious and social role.

A further aspect of this dynamic, social model of femininity was teaching girls about their role in modern society. The new generation of governess authors sought to cultivate in their readers the 'siege mentality' of syllabus Catholicism. This could be either through creating heroines like Mlle Primerose, who helped her protégés to go to Rome to protect the Pope, or indeed through their own identity as authors. For example, when Zénaïde Fleuriot set up a new publication in November 1868, *La famille*, described as an 'illustrated magazine devoted to fashion and domestic life', she made her intentions perfectly clear: 'this magazine will be one more soldier in the great army which defends in society the cause of all that which is admirable, good, and true; it will be one more righteous voice joining the magnificent concert of intelligences'. Presenting the domestic sphere as a battleground implicated in a wider struggle against good and evil, Fleuriot offered her readers an active model for engagement, namely that they must defend the values of religion and the family. This message was reinforced in girls' periodicals. The *Journal des demoiselles* (the older sister to the *Poupée modèle* and aimed at adolescent girls) regularly reprinted articles and poems by Louis Veuillot for example. Julie Gouraud also edited the *Journal des jeunes personnes*. In June 1859, as the Italian question meant war once more, Gouraud's editorial considered the religious justifications for war, and why she should broach this subject with her young girl readers. 'Women', she wrote, 'must be interested in all the serious questions regarding society'. Gouraud then warned her readers, however, that she was not sanctioning active political debate; rather it is a woman's role to provide support and prayer for those in need.[118] This desire to encourage active political interest, if not engagement, in their readers could be even more explicit. In 1871, horrified by the war and then the Paris Commune, Victorine Monniot, author of the best-selling *Journal de Marguerite*, exhorted her readers to act, by distributing her latest book amongst the poor: 'do it for me, join me in the struggle by distributing this novel, you who can afford to buy it'.[119]

These women formed an integral part of French upper-class and bourgeois girlhood in the second half of the nineteenth century. Lejeune notes that Monniot's *Journal* was the 'cult novel' for girls,[120] while in 1910 the novelist Jules Lemaitre referred to a girl who knew her *Bibliothèque Rose* off by heart.[121] Caroline Rouxel's research has unearthed a correspondence between two teenage girls, who discussed their love of Zénaïde Fleuriot's books and swapped notes on their favourites.[122] The religious identity of these governesses was not lost on their readers either. Isabelle, one of Ségur's young correspondents, felt sure that her 'dear Madame de Ségur' would appreciate a relic from the sacred shrine of Notre Dame de La Salette. Moreover, although neither the comtesse de Ségur or Zénaïde Fleuriot was officially made a saint after her death, in the eyes of some of their readers this minor detail was immaterial. They were women who had devoted their lives to the good of children and their families, and so were clearly people who would look favourably upon the troubles of those still in this world. Arnold Van Gennep recorded how women and girls would go to Ségur's grave to pray for a husband or a baby, or to ask for a cure. Her tomb was covered with children's crutches, babies' bonnets, and sheets from invalids' beds, left as ex-voto by grateful pilgrims. The grave of Zénaïde Fleuriot was believed to have similar powers. As Van Gennep noted, young girls prayed to these 'imitation saints' precisely because they were perceived to be protectors of children and youth.[123]

By deliberately writing heroines adapted to their day, the governesses also created a feminine culture that would be interpreted by generations of young girls. When the feminist philosopher Simone de Beauvoir (b. 1908) reread Ségur's books, she presented her as a specifically feminine author: 'it is through the eyes of men that the little girl explores the world and discovers her destiny . . . Mme de Ségur's books are a curious exception to this rule: they describe a matriarchal society where the husband is either absent or ridiculous.'[124] *Petites filles modèles* is the clearest example of such a matriarchy. The matriarch is Madame de Fleurville, a widow and mother of two daughters, who oversees Château Fleurville. She is joined by Madame de Rosbourg, whose husband is lost at sea, when her coach crashes outside the Château. These two lone women decide to live together and dedicate themselves to the education of their daughters.[125] Their decision to live together is not depicted as second best, owing of the tragic loss of their husbands; rather it is a happy fortune which allows them to live as friends. Together they create Fleurville: a utopian vision of a kind of open convent, looking after the poor and sick of the region, and with an emphasis on joy and laughter. When Simone de Beauvoir reread her girlhood, in *Mémoires d'une jeune fille rangée*, she saw this 'feminine' literature as having a profound effect upon her conception of her gendered self. Thanks to such books, she did not feel disappointed with having been born a girl: 'the heroes in the books by Madame de Ségur, Zénaïde Fleuriot were children, and adults played a subordinate role: mothers take up an important place in their books. Fathers counted for nothing.'[126] The young Beauvoir's games mimicked Ségur's *Petites filles modèles*, as she and her sister agreed that their husbands were always on holiday.[127]

This is in fact a distortion of Ségur's writings, for, as I set out in Chapters 2 and 4, Ségur set out deliberately to create positive male characters, notably the virile sea captain Monsieur de Rosbourg in *Les vacances*. Simone de Beauvoir's use of Ségur's books in *Mémoires d'une jeune fille rangée* (1958) is indicative of the importance she accorded to this literature, and of the specific use she intended for her rereading of these books. In her memoir Beauvoir wanted to examine how, and to what extent, as a girl she internalised gender norms. References to the comtesse, often subtle, appear quite frequently in the early stages of the book. She recalls how she and her sister used to imitate the Fleurville girls in their play with dolls. Should this be interpreted as an example of how effectively the gender codes set out in Ségur's books worked? Was Beauvoir's recollection of her childish games accurate? Did she really not notice the male characters? Or was she using the vocabulary of collective memory so that her readers would instantly know how to read her famous argument that one is not born a woman but becomes one? What better way to describe her relationship to her doll than as that of a 'perfect mother of a model little girl'?[128] She portrays the effects of Catholic education in the same way, detailing how she was told that the fate of France depended on her obedience and piety, concluding 'and I became a model little girl'.[129] The young Beauvoir's progress mirrors that of Sophie in the plot of *Petites filles modèles*, as she is transformed from a naughty little girl prone to tantrums into a tame, obedient girl like her model cousins. That Beauvoir applied this narrative of girlhood from the 1850s to characterise her life in the 1910s, writing it for readers in the late 1950s, is indicative of the place Ségur's girls occupied in French culture. It suggests her 'petites filles modèles' were an easily readable symbol for a particular model of female childhood, but also a model that exactly one hundred years later Beauvoir felt still needed to be repudiated.

Ségur and her female protagonists proved an awkward symbol for many women in the twentieth century. Not all were as nuanced as Beauvoir in their desire to reject Ségur's model girls, because, understandably, they were keen to distance themselves from any comparisons with them. During an interview in 1980, Marguerite Yourcenar (b. 1903) took offence when asked if she had been 'petite fille modèle' as a girl: 'no, I did not have a sense of social class at all. Neither was I a model little girl: the idea of being a model did not occur to me. I must say that I have always hated Madame de Ségur's books.'[130] As an aristocrat and a woman, her class and her gender condemned Yourcenar to this association. According to her biographer, Yourcenar received only a basic education from her governess, but this was supplemented by her father, who gave her books from his own library to read. He justified this unconventional practice by declaring, 'better Tolstoy than the comtesse de Ségur'.[131] The feminist Louise Weiss (b. 1893), in her memoirs of her Republican childhood', admitted that she had enjoyed reading the comtesse as a child. She explains however that family discussions were more important to her education: 'I have not forgotten them, while I know nothing any more of the comtesse's fables.' It is striking that Weiss too emphasised that it was her governess, not her family, who had given her the comtesse de Ségur's books to read.[132] The 'petite fille modèle' was a noxious concept to many women of Yourcenar's and subsequent generations. Michelle Perrot (b. 1928), one of the leading historians of women in France, used the 'petite fille modèle', as she put it 'with no appetite or desire', as the measure of repressed girlhood against which to compare the experience of real girls from the Second Empire.[133] Claude Langlois points out that Perrot belongs to the generation of feminists who saw the Catholic Church as being the real oppressor of women.[134] For them, the comtesse de Ségur was the embodiment of this stifling education.

There was a noticeable shift in sensibilities after the 1970s. This was no doubt due to the impact of the *écriture féminine* movement, the second-wave feminists who answered Hélène Cixous's call in 1975 for women to write 'feminine writing', free from 'phallocentric' constraints on the female body and its expression.[135] This movement generated academic interest in women writers, such as Ségur, who had hitherto been excluded from the male literary canon. Scholars began to question to what extent Ségur was really a victim of her circumstances. Could she have written any other books under the Second Empire? They set to reading between the lines of her texts, looking for hints of her feminine subversion of the established norms.[136] As noted above, Ségur's stories are somewhat contradictory on the subject of girls' education, and so, just as it was possible to castigate her for being an instrument of repression, so scholars have also been able to construct a narrative of feminine struggle in her books. Thanks primarily to the exhibition curated by Nicole Savy, *Petites filles modernes*,[137] it is now the figure of Sophie, depicted fighting against the weight of parental prohibitions, rather than Camille and Madeleine, who features in feminist discussion of Ségur. With Sophie, Madame de Ségur is credited by scholars as one of the first creators of the 'modern little girl', a psychologically complex being, imbued with a concept of her own timorous self, rather than created as a simple biological destiny (as opposed to Rousseau's Sophie). The modern boy had been a product of the eighteenth century, crystallised in Rousseau's *Émile*; Ségur's Sophie provided his female counterpart in France. Still, as I discussed in Chapter 2, Sophie is a difficult, ambiguous character, surrounded by violence and misery. Even at the close of the trilogy, she still fears that she is not as clever and well-behaved as the other girls, and so does not deserve to be loved as much.[138] The happy ending of *Les vacances* tells us that she is married. There is never any question that Sophie's destiny will be anything other than fixed in the home, and it is only by becoming 'more and more like her friends' (the model little girls) that her happiness is assured.[139]

Just as it is inaccurate to cast Ségur as a passive victim of patriarchy, so it is difficult to make her fit any concept of feminism. Such an interpretation is all too often based upon a desire to see Ségur as an exception from her counterparts. This view tacitly accepts the idea that governess authors were generally awful spinsters. Rather, as this chapter has attempted to show, Ségur and her colleagues were professional authors, engaged in the work of the religious revival, who knowingly fashioned role models for girls which they felt would be useful for the regeneration of the faith in France. On the one hand, the language of passion with which governess authors expressed their desire to free girls from simpering fairytale heroines was imbued with a sense of pride, even an urge to rival with boys in terms of being active. On the other hand, this was not the language of feminism. Such authors did not have any subversive intentions. Far from it. Fleuriot felt that it was the lack of suitable reading material for girls had led her to indulge in potentially unbecoming behaviour. By providing protagonists tailored to little girls, authors such as Ségur were further reinforcing gender roles by ensuring that girls did not have to resort to reading their brothers' books and finding inspiration therein. Reading books that were not specifically designated for them could be interpreted as a transgressive act. Anne-Marie Thiesse's survey of readers born in the Belle Époque noted that when asked about Jules Verne many women responded, 'I saw the novels of Jules Verne, but they were more for my brothers.'[140] The feminisation of Ségur's readership was a further sign of this segregation of reading. The ever-growing interest in girls' reading matter worked both for and against them. While they now had a literary universe they could call their own, it was a strictly codified and restricted one. The comtesse de Ségur's approach to the subject illustrates well the ambiguities of the governess's legacy to little girls.

Conclusion

This study of governess literature has shown how militantly religious its authors were, and how it was written by women and consumed by women and children (often given to them by governesses). In particular, writing for girls proved important for governess authors, as it provided them with an opportunity to reassess their own role in society. Drawing upon the feminine ideals of the time, these women exploited the possibilities offered by assuming the role of the mother educator, and the Catholic militant, to create distinctive public identities for themselves. They managed to defy masculine hostility, indeed, to win the unalloyed praise of 'great' Catholic men, such as Louis Veuillot, Father Olivaint, and even the Pope. In this way, they forged a dynamic role for themselves, as writers, editors, book reviewers, and militant campaigners. The laywoman governess author must be added alongside charitable ladies and consecrated sisters as a third model of Catholic femininity in the religious revival.

Furthermore, it was specifically by thinking about the type of books that girls needed that helped women like Ségur and Fleuriot to consider what they felt was important for their gender. Their own love of reading, and pride as wordsmiths, ensured that they were concerned to stimulate this same passion in their readers. Their works privileged young girls as active protagonists, which, as Nicole Savy rightly points out, makes them 'modern little girls'. However, this book agrees with Charles Sowerwine's argument that the many women who entered the public sphere did so by endorsing the ideal of domesticity, and so, paradoxically, helped to reinforce the validity of the notion of separate spheres.[141] Ségur's 'modern' heroine, Sophie, was not destined for any other roles than those of wife and mother. Other governess heroines may have been active in a wider sense, but they operated within the strict boundaries of charity and other nurturing roles. The creation of a militant feminine culture was a double-edged sword, for their representations served to further codify gendered behaviour. This was very much the intention of Ségur and her colleagues; in their zeal to protect 'traditional' values as they saw them, they set about creating role models for girls that they felt the current literature did not provide. Judging from the way that Simone de Beauvoir made use of Ségur's *Petites filles modèles* in her writings in the 1940s and 1950s, it would appear that Ségur did help to create the image of the 'modern little girl', in that she created an enduring vision of girlhood, and a femininity riddled with ambiguities. She invented a vision of 'traditional' girlhood that remains popular within some families in modern France.[142]

Notes

1 Laura Kreyder, 'Sophie, vieille enfant', *Europe*, 2005, p. 50.
2 Robert de Montesquiou, *Les roseaux pensants* (1897), pp. 18–19.
3 J. Ernest-Charles, 'La ridicule statue de la Comtesse de Ségur', *La grande Revue* 10 May 1908, 168–177, reproduced in *Les cahiers Séguriens*, 5 (2004), 96–101.

4 Siân Reynolds's study of reading in the interwar notes this phenomenon: *France between the Wars: Gender and Politics* (London, Routledge, 1996), p. 42.

5 Alfred Brauner, *Nos livres d'enfants ont menti. Une base de discussion* (Paris, SABRI, 1951), pp. 100–103.

6 Françoise Choay, 'Soixante petites filles et la comtesse', *Quinzaine Littéraire*, 15–30 April 1967.

7 Quoted in Parménie and Bonnier de la Chapelle, *Hetzel*, p. 596.

8 Montesquiou, *Roseaux pensants*, pp. 18–19.

9 Ernest-Charles, 'La ridicule statue de la comtesse de Ségur'.

10 Beauvoir, *Mémoires d'une jeune fille rangée*, p. 18.

11 Isabelle Havelange and Ségolène Le Men, *Le magasin des enfants. La littérature pour la jeunesse 1750–1830* (Montreuil, Association Bicentenaire Montreuil, 1988), p. 26.

12 Anderson, *Education*, pp. 18–19.

13 Rebecca Rogers, *From the Salon to the Schoolroom. Educating Bourgeois Girls in Nineteenth-Century France* (University Park, Pennsylvania State University Press, 2005); cf. Susan K. Foley, *Women in France since 1789. The Meanings of Difference* (London, Palgrave Macmillan, 2004), pp. 28–55.

14 Marie-Christine Vinson, *L'éducation des petites filles chez la comtesse de Ségur* (Lyon, Presses Universitaires de Lyon, 1987); Isabelle Papieau, *La comtesse de Ségur et la maltraitance des enfants* (Paris, L'Harmatton, 1999).

15 *Les temps modernes* special issue 'Petites Filles en Éducation', 378 (1976).

16 Soriano, *Guide*, pp. 473–485.

17 *La fortune de Gaspard* (1974 Pauvert edition), preface.

18 Thérèse Fournier, 'Faut-il interdire la comtesse de Ségur?', *Antoinette*, December 1980.

19 Fabienne Pascal, 'Du côté des petites filles modèles', *Des femmes en mouvement*, 7–14 May 1982.

20 Nicole Savy, *Les petites filles modernes*, Catalogue d'exposition-dossier, Musée d'Orsay (Paris, Editions de la Réunion des musées nationaux, 1989).

21 Stéphane Michaud, 'Idolâtries. Représentations artistiques et littéraires', in Duby and Perrot, *Histoire des femmes*, 4:145; Nathalie Dresse, 'Les petites filles en représentation', *Chronique féministe*, January–February 1997, 61.

22 Parinet, *Histoire de l'édition*, pp. 89–91.

23 Renonciat, 'Fortune éditorial', pp. 216–219.

24 A sample of the comtesse's and her colleagues' reception has been taken from the *Bibliographie catholique*, while further reviews of their work have been consulted from the major girls or children's periodicals of the Second Empire *Journal des Demoiselles*; its (little) sister publication, *Poupée modèle*; Hachette's *La semaine des enfants*; Lecoffre's *La semaine des familles*; *Journal des jeunes personnes*; *Journal des enfants de Marie*; 'moral commentaries' have been taken from the writings of the republican editor Hetzel; the journalist

Louis Veuillot; Mgr Dupanloup; and the big illustrated publications listed above.

25 Lejeune, *Le moi des demoiselles*. This paragraph is partially indebted to Rebecca Rogers, 'L'éducation des filles. Un siècle et demi d'historiographie', *Histoire de l'éducation*, 115–116 (2007), 37–79.

26 Isabelle Brouard-Arends and Marie-Emmanuelle Plagnol-Dieval (eds) *Femmes éducatrices au siècle des lumières* (Rennes, Presses Universitaires de Rennes, 2007); Marie-Emmanuelle Plagnol-Diéval, *Madame de Genlis et le théâtre d'éducation au XVIIIe siècle* (Oxford, Voltaire Foundation, 1997).

27 Madeleine Lassère, *Victorine Monniot ou l'éducation des jeunes filles au XIXè siècle, entre exoticisme et catholicisme de combat* (Paris, L'Harmatton, 1999).

28 See Donelle Ruwe, *Culturing the Child 1660–1830: Essays in Memory of Mitzi Myers* (Lanham, MD, Scarecrow Press, 2005).

29 Rogers, *Salon to the Schoolroom*; Mayeur, *L'éducation des filles*; Marie-Françoise Lévy's *De mères en filles: l'éducation des françaises 1850/1880* (Paris, Calmann-Lévy, 1984) promises the reality behind Ségur's books, before explaining that she is too literary for the study. Literary works by Isabelle Bricard, *Saintes ou pouliches: l'éducation des jeunes filles au XIXe siècle* (Paris, Albin Michel, 1985) and Colette Cosnier, *Le silence des filles de l'aiguille à la plume* (Paris, Fayard, 2001) mention Ségur.

30 Martyn Lyons, *Readers and Society in Nineteenth-Century France. Workers, Women, Peasants* (Basingstoke, Palgrave, 2001).

31 Havelange and Le Men, *Magasin des enfants*, p. 28.

32 Myers, 'Impeccable Governesses', pp. 34–35.

33 Louis Veuillot, 'Les contes de Madame de Ségur', p. 423; Pierrard, *Louis Veuillot*, pp. 22–24.

34 Rogers, *Salon to the Schoolroom*, pp. 83–107.

35 Lyons, 'Les best-sellers', *HEF*, 3:394–395.

36 Plagnol-Diéval, *Madame de Genlis*, introduction.

37 *Ibid.*, p. 101.

38 Hédouville, *Mgr de Ségur*, p. 548.

39 *Bibliographie catholique* 1854–55, Review of the Bibliothèque des chemins de fer.

40 Mathilde Bourdon, review of the early works of the comtesse de Ségur, *Journal des demoiselles*, May 1860.

41 Rogers, *From the Salon to the Schoolroom*, chapter three; Havelange, 'La littérature destinée aux demoiselles 1750–1830', p. 37.

42 Artiaga, 'Les catholiques et la littérature "industrielle" au XIXe siècle', chapter 2.

43 Warner, *From the Beast to the Blonde*, chapter 6.

44 'Les contes de Madame de Ségur' *L'univers*, May 1860.

45 J.-B. Margadant, 'The Duchesse de Berry and Royalist Political Culture in Postrevolutionary France', in Margadant (ed.) *The New Biography*; Havelange, 'La littérature destinée aux demoiselles 1750–1830', p. 33.

46 G. Davenay, 'Le monument de la comtesse de Ségur', *Le Figaro*, 20 June 1910.

47 Comtesse de Ségur, *Les actes des apôtres* (Paris, Hachette, 1867), Introduction.

48 Comtesse de Ségur, *Bible d'une Grand'mère* (Paris, Hachette, 1869), Dedication.

49 Letter to Olga de Pitray, 30 November 1860.

50 Letter to Olga de Pitray, 21 November 1856.

51 28 July 1863, Inventaire, AN Minutier Central, ET/ CXVII/ 1295.

52 Letter to Élisabeth Fresneau, undated, quoted in Paul Acker, 'La comtesse de Ségur, née Rostopchine', *Revue de Paris*, 1 April 1908, 589–612, p. 605.

53 Francis Marcoin, 'Autour de la comtesse', *Cahiers Robinson*, 9 (2001), 23–36, p. 30.

54 Isabelle Nières-Chevrel, 'Avant-Propos', *Revue de littérature comparée*, 4 (2002), 413–420.

55 *Œuvres*, 1:604–605.

56 *Œuvres*, 1:522.

57 Julie Gouraud, *Mémoires d'un caniche* (Paris, Hachette, 1865), p. 3.

58 Julie Gouraud, *Mémoires d'une petit garçon* (Paris, Hachette, 1864), pp. 3–4.

59 Isabelle Nières-Chevrel, 'Au miroir des écrivains français', *Europe*, 914/915 (2005), 22–38; Marcoin, 'Autour de la comtesse', p. 36.

60 Letter, 5 November 1865, published as preface to Ségur, *L'Évangile d'une grand'mère*.

61 Review of *Évangile d'une grand'mère* by V. Postel, *Bibliographie catholique*, 35, April 1866.

62 Review of *Actes des apôtres*, *Bibliographie catholique*, 37, April 1867.

63 Review of *Après la pluie, le beau temps* by A. Vissac, *Bibliographie catholique*, 45, June 1872.

64 Zénaïde Fleuriot, *Souvenirs d'une douarière* (Paris, Dentu, 1859), preface.

65 Anne le Drunot, *Mlle Zénaïde Fleuriot, 1829–90* (1990), pp. 30–33.

66 *Ibid.*, p. 25.

67 Fleuriot-Kerinou, *Fleuriot*, chapters 4, 15.

68 Alfred Nettement, *Le roman contemporain. Ses vicissitudes, ses divers aspects, son influence* (Paris, Librairie Jacques Lecoffre, 1864).

69 Henri Jouin, *Mademoiselle Z. Fleuriot. Du rôle des femmes dans la littérature populaire* (Paris, Librairie Jacques Lecoffre, 1871).

70 Letter from Zénaïde Fleuriot to her sister Marie, 19 January 1866, Fleuriot-Kerinou, *Fleuriot*, p. 140.

71 Caroline Rouxel, *Zénaïde Fleuriot ou Le parcours d'un écrivain catholique pour la jeunesse au XIXe siècle*, Mémoire de Master de littérature jeunesse, Université du Maine, septembre 2005, Unpublished, p. 66.

72 Chupeau, 'L'école des premiers livres'.

73 Letter from Zénaïde Fleuriot to the Reverend Mother of the Auxiliatrices Marie de la Providence, 1 March 1870, Fleuriot-Kerinou, *Fleuriot*, p. 282.

74 *Simples tableaux de l'éducation maternelle*, introduction, quoted in Lassère, *Monniot*, p. 35.

75 Review of *Le Journal de Marguerite*, *La poupée modèle*, March 1864.

76 Victorine Monniot, *Marguerite à vingt ans*, preface, quoted in Lassère, *Monniot*, p. 34.

77 Lassère, *Monniot*, pp. 88–89.

78 *Ibid.*, p. 25.

79 Le Drunot, *Fleuriot*, pp. 16, 7.

80 Gouraud began her career writing under the pseudonym Louise d'Aulnay; Fleuriot wrote as Anna Edianez de L*** de S-B until 1866.

81 Quoted in Olga de Pitray, *Mon bon Gaston*, pp. 159–160.

82 *Œuvres*, 1:119.

83 Gibson, *Social History of French Catholicism*, chapter 8.

84 Jacqueline Rose, *The Case of Peter Pan, or The Impossibility of Children's Fiction* (London, Macmillan, 1984).

85 There is no mention of fan mail in subsequent biographies, or in the *Cahiers Séguriens*. The Hachette archives do not contain any such letters, even from more recent readers.

86 Philippe Lejeune and Catherine Bogaert, *Le journal intime. Histoire et anthologie* (Paris, Textuel, 2006), p. 158.

87 Zélie Martin, *Correspondance familiale 1863–87* (Paris, Office de Lisieux, 1958).

88 Freud, *A Child is Being Beaten*.

89 Radclyffe Hall, *The Well of Loneliness* (London, Wordsworth Classics, 2006), p. 47.

90 Leïla Sebbar, *Voyage en Algéries autour de ma chambre, Abécédaire* (Saint-Pourçain-sur-Sioule, Bleu autour, 2008), pp. 158–159. I would like to thank Alexandra Gueydan for bringing this reference to my attention.

91 Lyons, *Readers and Society*.

92 Françoise Mayeur and Jacques Gadille (eds) *Éducation et images de la femme chrétienne en France au début du XXème siècle* (Lyon, Éditions l'Hermès, 1980), p. 32.

93 *Poupée modèle*, March 1865.

94 *Poupée modèle*, May 1864.

95 Review of *Les bons enfants*, *Poupée modèle*, June 1864.

96 Roger Chartier and Jean Hébrard, 'Les imaginaires de la lecture', *HEF*, 4:535.

97 Smith, *Ladies of the Leisure Class*, p. 53.

98 See letters to Templier, 2 March 1858; 20 February 1861.

99 Letter from Zélie Martin to her sister, October 1875, *Correspondance*.

100 Lejeune, *Moi des demoiselles*, pp. 204–205.

101 Lucile le Verrier, *Journal d'une jeune fille Second Empire 1866–78* (Paris, Zulma, 1994), p. 46.

102 D'Armaillé, *Quand on savait vivre heureux*, p. 58.

103 Letter to Olga de Pitray, 30 November 1860.

104 Review of *La sœur de Gribouille*, by Ch. Laval, *Bibliographie catholique*, 27, April 1862.

105 Jules Michelet, *Du prêtre, de la femme, de la famille* (Paris, Comptoir des Imprimeurs-Unis, 1845).

106 See my article, 'Petits garçons modèles'.

107 Alain Lanavère, 'Le bonheur selon Madame de Ségur', *Mélanges offertes à M. le Professeur Jacques Robichez. Cent ans de la littérature française 1850–1950* (Paris, SEDES, 1987), pp. 23–30.

108 Rogers, *Salon to the Schoolroom*, pp. 202–205.

109 Letter to Olga de Pitray, 2 June 1868.

110 Veuillot, 'M. Duruy sous le voile', 16 December 1867, *Mélanges*, 2, pp. 278–286.

111 Cordonnier, *Silhouettes familiales*, pp. 97–98.

112 *Œuvres*, 3:953.

113 *Œuvres*, 3:957.

114 Rogers, *Salon to the Schoolroom*, pp. 218–221.

115 Veuillot, 'M. Duruy sous le voile', pp. 282–283.

116 *Œuvres*, 3:1015.

117 Fleuriot-Kerinou, *Fleuriot*, pp. 50–51.

118 *Journal des jeunes personnes*, 1 June 1859.

119 Lassère, *Monniot*, p. 42.

120 Lejeune, *Moi des demoiselles*, p. 19.

121 Inauguration ceremony speech for the monument to the comtesse, 19 June 1910, *Les Contemporains. Études et portraits littéraires. Huitième série* (Paris, Oudin, 1918).

122 Rouxel, *Fleuriot*, p. 74.

123 Arnold Van Gennep, *Manuel de folklore français contemporain* (Paris, Éditions Auguste Picard, 1943), 1:243.

124 Beauvoir, *Le deuxième sexe*, 2: 36–37.

125 Ségur, *Œuvres*, 1:129.

126 Beauvoir, *Mémoires d'une jeune fille rangée*, p. 77.

127 *Ibid.*, p. 78.

128 *Ibid.*, p. 78.

129 *Ibid.*, p. 42.

130 *Les yeux ouverts*. Entretiens avec Matthieu Galey, quoted in Kreyder, *L'enfance des saints et des autres*, pp. 222–223.

131 Quoted in Josyane Savigneau, *Marguerite Yourcenar: Inventing a Life* (Chicago, University of Chicago Press, 1993), p. 42.

132 Louise Weiss, *Souvenirs d'une enfance républicaine* (Paris, Denoel, 1937), p. 37.

133 Perrot, 'Une jeune fille du faubourg Saint Germain', p. 174.

134 Claude Langlois, 'Le catholicisme au féminin revisité', in Corbin et al., *Femmes dans la cité*, pp. 139–149, p. 143; cf. the revisionist view, for example James F. McMillan, who argues in *France and Women 1789–1914: Gender, Society and Politics* (London, Routledge, 2000) that republicans were equally active in ensuring women remained in their place.

135 Hélène Cixous, *Le rire de la Méduse et autres ironies* (Paris, Galilée, 2010, originally published as a special issue of *L'Arc*, 1975).

136 Doray, *La comtesse de Ségur*; Beaussant, *La comtesse de Ségur ou l'enfance de l'art*; Strich, 'Critique génétique d'un manuscrit: La Bible d'une grand-mère (1869)'.

137 Savy, *Petites filles modernes*.

138 Ségur, *Œuvres*, 1:512.

139 Ségur, *Œuvres*, 1:520.

140 Anne-Marie Thiesse, *Le roman du quotidien. Lecteurs et lectures populaires à la Belle Époque* (Paris, Chemin Vert, 1984), p. 41.

141 Sowerwine, 'Women's Citizenship', pp. 25–26.

142 Catherine Monnot, *Petites filles d'aujourd'hui. L'apprentissage de la fémininité* (Paris, Éditions Autrement, 2009), pp. 61–64.

Conclusion

This book has studied the comtesse de Ségur as a cultural icon. In restoring her to the original context of the religious antagonisms of Second Empire France, it has highlighted a neglected aspect of the culture wars, namely the important contribution made by women authors such as Ségur to the massive surge in devotional print culture. By examining the workings of one small and highly influential network involved in leading this literary offensive, and by reconstructing the role played by the comtesse in their politico-religious campaign, it has provided a case study in the political engagement of a Catholic woman.

Madame de Ségur's personality meant that she would not readily accept being sidelined. Her gender excluded her from any direct involvement in politics; as a woman, Ségur was not only disenfranchised but also, in theory at least, she was not meant to be involved in political life at any level. Nevertheless, the informal nature of intransigent ultramontane politics provided the comtesse de Ségur with a real opportunity to join in their battles. Once age released her from many of the cumbersome tasks of motherhood she was free to become a writer, and earn an independent income; and so the comtesse discovered that she had a 'voice'. She joined the extreme right-wing *Veuillotiste* camp and entered the fray with all the enthusiasm of a new convert.

As a member of the Ségur family literary dynasty, she participated in their efforts to refashion the French nobility according to the ideals of intransigent ultramontanism. The journalist Louis Veuillot applauded their efforts, which responded exactly to his own hopes for the French nation. The comtesse struck up a close friendship with Veuillot, and became his correspondent. It was in these letters that she refined her ideas. The Ségurs and Veuillot formed part of a wider network of writers, clerics, and politicians who met regularly for dinners where they debated, discussed, and shaped the ideas of their political community. As the government and sections of the ecclesiastical authorities in France became increasingly hostile towards their activities, the intransigents were forced to rely upon such private forums. Madame de Ségur doubly ensured she was not relegated to the sidelines both by hosting dinners in her capacity as the Ségur family matriarch and through her correspondence with Veuillot.

It was imperative that the Ségur family's conversion to this new Catholicism be made public, as ostentatiously as possible, for, as Margaret Lavinia Anderson has explained, high-profile conversions amongst the European intellectual elite played a key role in the religious revival, by showing that 'the terrain is habitable'. Their defiant stance gave others further down the social scale the 'cultural self-confidence' needed to practise their religion when many were deserting it.[1] In the French case, the need for religious revival in the aftermath of 1789, and renewed fears of revolution following 1848, meant that the more extreme Catholics like the Ségurs and the Veuillots were driven by a sense of embattlement. Men in nineteenth-century France in particular felt that they risked ridicule if they dared to practise their faith in public. The Ségur family was part of the move to reverse this trend, and as part of this, their own lives had an important, representative function. That they were one of the oldest noble houses in France was all the better: Veuillot saw it as poetic justice that it should be the French nobility that led the nation back into the fold. It followed that the nature of the writings that were published under this famous name 'Ségur' was crucial. Their books were produced within the context of this shared mission, evidenced by the significant level of intertextuality in their collective oeuvre. This also extended to their life stories that were published in the public domain.

Madame de Ségur immortalised their ideal of the family in her books, creating an illusion that her stories were based upon the lives of her children and grandchildren. She fashioned an attractive image of the Catholic family which was warmly received by Veuillot in particular, but also other organs of the Catholic 'good books' movement. However, although this book has emphasised the importance of reading the comtesse through the optic of her role as part of the Ségur family, it has also argued that in her work the comtesse developed her own idiosyncratic version of the Ségur family mission. The romanticised religion of the 'new Catholicism' rejected the fearsome God of eighteenth-century Jansenism, and replaced it with a religion of love. Madame de Ségur aligned this new religion with modern ideas on parenting. In particular she used her vision to denounce the continued practice of corporal punishment within French families (her own included). Thus, although the Ségur family and subsequent religious campaigners harnessed her life stories to the cause, they were never really able to reduce Madame de Ségur to the ideal of Christian womanhood. Her obsessions, eccentricities, and powerful personality have ensured that accounts of the 'nation's grandmother' have always been contradictory. She was a committed militant, but on her own terms.

Catholics proved highly enterprising in their efforts to disseminate the new devotions, using pamphlets, newspapers, and cheap literature to complement grassroots missionary work. Veuillot's newspaper and Mgr de Ségur's best-selling opuscules played a large part in this. In the era of Napoleon III's plebiscite politics, reaching a wide audience was crucial – as the Monsignor remarked to Élise Veuillot, 'I wrote my *Réponses* for senators and cooks.'[2] Madame de Ségur was also shrewd in her approach to the market. She had cut her teeth in these matters by helping to launch Gaston de Ségur's first book, *Réponses*, in 1850. Thus, when the comtesse set to getting her own books published, she was determined to construct a commercially viable name for herself. Madame de Ségur was very conscious of the new ideas on children, how to write for them, and how to appeal to her young readership. She understood that her power lay in her commercial success. Financial gain was of course welcome, but what really mattered to the comtesse was the size of her readership. Healthy sales figures gave her bargaining power with her editor, and ensured that men like Louis Veuillot took her seriously. Income gave her independence, but it was her audience which gave her authority. She was aware of the importance of using the possibilities offered by commercial culture. Just as historians now recognise that men like Veuillot were a part of the crucible of modern European political culture, so it is important to include Madame de Ségur and other authors of 'improving' literature in the narrative of 'modernisation'.

The sentimentalised religion of the 'New Catholicism', with its cult of suffering, obsession with the childlike, and noisy rejection of the modern world, has been argued by some writers to have the greatest appeal to women because it was a creed of the powerless.[3] Women often appear far removed from the great political questions that occupied male Catholic intellectuals. Madame la comtesse de Ségur née Rostopchine did not see herself in these terms. In her view, dolourism was an excellent doctrine for the lower classes, to keep them in their place. She was a woman of letters and the matriarch of the Ségur/Veuillot family network of writers, and, as such, she had important work to do. The comtesse saw herself as part of the literary vanguard of the culture wars, and she was received as such by her contemporaries. She expressed her faith in highly militant, politicised terms. Ségur was not manipulated by her male superiors (despite attempts by her family and publisher): Chapter 3 has shown just how ferocious she could be when her artistic interests were threatened. Furthermore, although the comtesse may have been a singularly determined lady, she was by no means the only woman author to be engaged in militant ultramontanism. There were in fact large numbers of women involved in writing books, in journalism, and in editing magazines for Catholic publishers, or with stated religious aims. This feminine print culture flourished in the publishing boom, and many were celebrities. They were held in great respect by fellow writers and critics, and their work was recognised by influential clerics, even by the Pope. Catholic women could interact with the male elite on terms that are simply not covered by the vocabulary currently used in historiography to describe their experience.

Still, the view of the role of such women authors in the public sphere must be qualified. Even though they were conservative women, seeking to reinforce rather than to challenge the structures of patriarchal society, the 'governess' authors were still bound by many restrictions because of their sex. Using the methodology of the New Biography, this case study of the comtesse de Ségur has illustrated the effect of the cultural pressures that weighed upon her construction of her self, her life, and her actions. She was still the 'pygmy' at the 'giant' Veuillot's feet. Female authors such as Ségur who wrote children's literature faced particularly harsh ridicule. They risked being derided as spinsters and bluestockings. Later generations would add accusations of bigotry and religious fanaticism to the list of insults. Their troubles were exacerbated by the contemporary perception of little girl readers as being incredibly vulnerable; the purity of these young innocents had to be preserved at all costs. Any material that was to be put into their hands had to be rigorously vetted before it could go to press. All women had to construct their public identities with the utmost care, and the 'governess' authors were no exception. The construction by Madame de Ségur of her grandmother image was in this respect a masterpiece, drawing on accepted ideas of the old woman storyteller, and the new obsession with the mother educator, to create a reassuring brand. Similarly, her maternal headship of the Ségur family was an excellent justification for the comtesse's involvement in the ultramontane network.

I have argued that Madame de Ségur's experiences reveal the contribution a woman author could make to intransigent Catholicism. Only a small minority of women in the Second Empire were prepared to speak out against the repression of their sex. Many more were energetically involved in the Church. What this book has done is to bring to light one woman who worked within an important sector of this activity, which might be termed Catholic women's 'voice'. It is important to recognise that the involvement of women in political activities was not just in left-wing feminism, but also right-wing anti-feminism. As Elizabeth MacKnight has argued, the narrative of feminism does not make sense if we do not incorporate into it the stories of the many women who were not feminists, or who were anti-feminists – not least because this diminishes the courage of the few who did speak out. Thus, this means studying books such as *Petites filles modèles*, because they played a significant role in the construction of gendered identity of girls. Although the impact of the comtesse de Ségur on the generations of girls who grew up reading her books may well have been negative, as can be inferred from the ambivalence of many women to her in their autobiographies and memoirs, still it is interesting to note that, more recently, Madame de Ségur's semi-autobiographical character 'Sophie' has been reclaimed by modern feminists in France. They see in her stories an account of resistance to, and finally painful acceptance of, society's restrictions. However, this has all too often been accompanied by an attempt to 'sanitise' her, by glossing over Ségur's political engagement, and casting her as a passive victim of the excesses of her era. This book has attempted to redress the balance. Ségur is no feminist heroine, but neither is it helpful for us to dismiss her as a villainess and ignore her.

Notes

1 Anderson, 'Divisions of the Pope', pp. 26–27.
2 Olga de Pitray, *Ma chère maman*, p. 176.
3 Di Giorgio, 'La bonne catholique'; Smith, *Ladies of the Leisure Class*.

Appendix I
The collected works
of the comtesse de Ségur

Sources: Claudine Beaussant (ed), Ségur, *Œuvres*, 1:xliv–liii; Laura Kreyder, *L'enfance des saints*, pp. 233–239; *Cahiers Séguriens*, 2000–7; Hachette Catalogues, IMEC; *Bibliographie de la France. Journal générale de l'imprimerie et de la librairie* (*BF*) 1856–71 (this journal announces the date of the legal registration of the book, and could often be several months later or earlier than the actual publication); *La Semaine des enfants* 1856–74; BN-Opale catalogue

1855

La santé des enfants, Hachette, Bibliothèque des chemins de fer.

1857

Nouveaux contes de fées, Hachette, Bibliothèque des chemins de fer. Beaussant dates its publication December 1856, Kreyder suggests January 1857. A volume by Madame de Ségur entitled *Contes à mes petites filles*, which was the provisional title, is advertised in the Hachette catalogues in October 1856, but does not appear under the definitive title until January 1857. The *Semaine des enfants* serialisation begins 3 January 1857.

1858

Petites filles modèles, Hachette, Bibliothèque Rose illustrée. Beaussant dates publication 12 October 1857 however, there is no mention in the Hachette catalogues until March 1858, and it is first announced 15 May 1858 in the *BF*.

Livre de messe des petits enfants, Douniol.

1859

Les malheurs de Sophie, Hachette, Bibliothèque Rose illustrée. Announced *BF* 8 January 1859, probably appeared for the New Year. Some episodes serialised in the *Semaine des enfants*, July–October 1860, and December 1862.

Les vacances, Hachette Bibliothèque Rose illustrée. Announced 10 September 1859, *BF*.

1860

Mémoires d'un âne, Hachette, Bibliothèque Rose illustrée. Serialised in the *Semaine des enfants*, 17 December 1859. Advertised in the Hachette Catalogue October 1860. Announced 21 July 1860, *BF*.

1861

Pauvre Blaise, Hachette, Bibliothèque Rose illustrée. Announced 23 November 1861, *BF*. Serialisation in the *Semaine des enfants* begins 13 July 1861.

1862

La sœur de Gribouille, Hachette, Bibliothèque Rose illustrée. Advertised November 1861 Hachette Catalogues. Announced 28 December 1861, *BF*. Kreyder dates publication January 1862. Serialisation in the *Semaine des enfants* begins 22 March 1862.

1863

Les bons enfants, Hachette, Bibliothèque Rose illustrée. Announced 6 December 1862, *BF*. Serialisation in the *Semaine des enfants* begins 13 August 1862. Kreyder dates publication late 1862, Beaussant 1863. First edition BN dated 1863 (1862 dépôt légal stamp in red on the first page, next to the publisher's date of 1863).

Les deux nigauds, Hachette, Bibliothèque Rose illustrée. Announced 28 December 1862, *BF*. Serialisation in the *Semaine des enfants* begins 4 October 1862. Kreyder dates publication late 1862, Beaussant 1863. First edition BN dated 1863.

L'auberge de l'ange gardien, Hachette, Bibliothèque Rose illustrée. Serialisation in the *Semaine des enfants* begins 8 April 1863.

Le Général Dourakine, Hachette, Bibliothèque Rose illustrée. Announced 19 December 1863, *BF*. Serialisation in the *Semaine des enfants* begins 14 November 1863.

1864

François le bossu, Hachette, Bibliothèque Rose illustrée. Announced 14 January 1865, *BF*. Serialisation in the *Semaine des enfants* begins 4 May 1864.

1865

Un bon petit diable, Hachette, Bibliothèque Rose illustrée. Serialisation in the *Semaine des enfants* begins 14 December 1864.

Comédies et proverbes, Hachette, Bibliothèque Rose illustrée. Serialisation in the *Semaine des enfants* begins 30 August 1865.

1866

Jean qui grogne et Jean qui rit, Hachette, Bibliothèque Rose illustrée. Announced 16 December 1865, *BF*. Hachette Catalogues advertise this book under the title *Jean le bon et Jean le mauvais* until 1866.

Évangile d'une grand'mère, Hachette, albums illustrés. Kreyder dates the publication 1866, Beaussant 1865. Announced 9 December 1865, *BF*. (The BN copy has an 1865 dépôt légal stamp in red on the first page, next to the publisher's date of 1866.)

La fortune de Gaspard, Hachette, Biobliothèque Rose illustrée. Serialisation in the *Semaine des enfants* begins 25 April 1866.

1867

Quel amour d'enfant! Hachette, Bibliothèque Rose illustrée. Announced 24 November 1866, *BF*. Kreyder dates publication 1866. Copy of first edition BN dated 1867 (1866 dépôt légal stamp in red on the first page, next to the publisher's date of 1867).

Le mauvais génie, Hachette, Bibliothèque Rose illustrée. Serialisation in the *Semaine des enfants* begins 7 August 1867.

Les actes des apôtres, Hachette, albums illustrés. Announced 5 January 1867 *BF*.

1868

Diloy le chemineau, Hachette, Bibliothèque Rose illustrée. Serialisation in the *Semaine des enfants* begins, under the title *Le chemineau*, 11 April 1868.

1869

Bible d'une grand'mère, Hachette, albums illustrés.

1871

Après la pluie, le beau temps, Hachette, Bibliothèque Rose illustrée.

Appendix II
Editions of the collected works of Madame de Ségur, published by Hachette 1855–1941

Sources: Legros, *De l'histoire à l'Histoire*; Renonciat, 'Fortune éditorial de la comtesse de Ségur'; Livre de magasin B 1853–1910, Registre états des stocks en magasin: HAC132, IMEC. The copyright on Ségur's works expired in 1930. These figures include the great drive by Hachette to expand her market in the 1930s, and compete with rival publishers. NB – Early figures are based on partial records of copies sent out to kiosks and sellers, so they can provide only a rough estimate.

Name of book	Number of editions	Total printed
Mémoires d'un âne	59	1,144,209
Les malheurs de Sophie[1]	53	1,111,085
Un bon petit diable	55	1,085,220
Les petites filles modèles	52	1,000,668
L'auberge de l'ange gardien	47	933,230
Le Général Dourakine	48	867,471
Les vacances	49	845,712
Les deux nigauds	42	798,520
La sœur de Gribouille	38	711,068
François le bossu	38	627,865
Jean qui grogne et Jean qui rit	44	623,650
Après la pluie, le beau temps	35	606,054
Pauvre Blaise	43	602,510
Nouveaux contes de fées[2]	38	563,618
Diloy le chemineau	37	560,710
Quel amour d'enfant!	35	554,350
Les bons enfants	36	548,000
Le mauvais génie	36	536,050
La fortune de Gaspard	33	533,640
Comédies et proverbes	26	332,350
Évangile d'une grand'mère	17	195,300
Bible d'une grand'mère	10	150,800
Les actes des apôtres	3	103,500
La santé des enfants	6	8,800

Notes

1 Renonciat and Mistler rank *Les malheurs de Sophie* as the most popular work by the comtesse de Ségur. Legros's calculations suggest that *Mémoires d'un âne* was slightly more popular. Given the nature of the evidence available, this remains a moot point.

2 In the 1930s, the *contes* were published individually. For the sake of brevity I have not included them in this table. However, they went into thirty editions between 1930 and 1939. Renonciat, 'Fortune éditoriale', p. 219.

Select bibliography

Manuscript sources

BIBLIOTHÈQUE NATIONALE DE FRANCE

Ségur and Rostopchine family papers and correspondence.
NAF 22830-34 Ségur family papers.
NAF 22834 Rostopchine Family papers.
NAF 11401 Anatole de Ségur, *Souvenirs à mes enfants*, diary 1866–67.
Veuillot family papers and correspondence, 1831–82.
NAF 24220 to 24233 and NAF 24617 to 24632.

INSTITUT DE MÉMOIRES DE L'EDITION CONTEMPORAINE

Hachette Archives.
Hachette Catalogues 1855–81: Bound inside several volumes of these catalogues (volumes 15, 17, 28, and 30) is the History of MM. Louis Hachette & Co., 1828–68, and the documents relative to this history, as written and compiled by Alphonse Langlois, former employee. The most useful is *Notice historique et statistique sur l'origine, la formation et le développement de la librairie de MM. Hachette 1828–68 par Alphonse Langlois*, in volume 15, 1868.
Livre de magasin B, 1853–1910, Registre états des stocks en magasin.
Contracts and receipts, 1856–69: Cecile Petit's dissertation below reproduces several contracts from private collections.
Correspondance de la Comtesse de Ségur avec Émile Templier HAC 154.116: This correspondence is published in the front of Ségur, *Œuvres*.
Les Archives Iconographiques (S26).
First editions of Hachette Bibliothèque Rose Collection.

HACHETTE LIVRE ARCHIVES

Iconography.
Library of first editions.

ARCHIVES DE L'INSTITUT CATHOLIQUE

Fonds Veuillot.
Carton 16 Letters to Louis Veuillot.
Carton 18 Letters to and from Louis Veuillot from various members of his family.

ARCHIVES NATIONALES

Minutier Central.
Marriage Contract M. le Comte de Ségur & Mademoiselle la Comtesse Rostopchin, 13 July 1819, ET/ CXVII/ 1098.
Last will and testament, and liquidation of estate, of the comtesse de Ségur, 11 February 1874, Reserve 1018, ET/ CXVII/1361.
Liquidation and Succession of the estate of Eugène de Ségur, 6 May 1864, Minutier Central ET/ CXVII/ 1301, and inventory, ET/ CXVII/ 1295.

Published primary sources

Comtesse de Ségur, *Œuvres*, 3 volumes, edited and annotated by Claudine Beaussant, preface by Jacques Laurent (Paris, Robert Laffont, 1990).
Livre de messe des petits enfants (Paris, Douniol, 1858).
Évangile d'une Grand'mère (Paris, Hachette, 1866).
Les actes des apôtres (Paris, Hachette, 1867).
Bible d'une grand'mère (Paris, Hachette, 1869).
Lincoln, Harold, *The Sea and the Savages, A Story of Adventure* (Edinburgh, William P. Nimmo, 1872): English translation of the Crusoe story in Ségur's *Les vacances* (1859).

FAMILY BIOGRAPHIES

Mgr Louis-Gaston de Ségur, *Ma mère. Souvenir de sa vie et de sa sainte mort* (Paris, Tolra, 1875).
Olga, Vicomtesse de Simard de Pitray, *Mon bon Gaston, souvenirs intimes et familiers par sa sœur Olga* (Paris, Gaume, 1887).
Olga, Vicomtesse de Simard de Pitray, *Ma chère maman (Comtesse de Ségur, née Rostopchine) pour faire suite à Mon bon Gaston* (Paris, Gaume, 1891).
Anatole de Ségur, *Mgr de Ségur. Souvenirs et récit d'un frère* (Paris, Bray et Rétaux, 1882) and Anatole de Ségur, *Souvenirs et causeries du soir* (Paris, J. Lefort, [1900]) transcribes letters from the Count Rostopchine to his wife and daughter.
Pierre de Ségur, 'La comtesse de Ségur', *Bulletin de la société normande de géographie*, 1912.
Paul de Pitray interview with Maurice Noel, 'Quand le Bon Petit Diable a 72 ans', 29 December 1934, *Le Figaro.*
Arlette de Pitray, *Sophie Rostopchine, Comtesse de Ségur, racontée par sa petite-fille* (Paris, Albin Michel, 1939) also see *Miroir de l'histoire*, July 1963.
Nathalie Narichkine, née Rostopchine, *1812 Le comte Rostopchine et son temps* (Saint Petersbourg, Société R. Golicke et A. Willborg, 1912).

Lydia Rostoptchine, *Les Rostoptchine* (Paris, Balland, 1984 [1919]).

André Rastaptchine [Rostopchine], *Russie anecdotique, bibliographique, biographique, géographique, historique, littéraire, statistique et, contrairement à l'ordinaire, véridique* (Brussels, M.-J. Poot et Cie, 1874).

PUBLISHED CORRESPONDENCE

Vicomtesse de Simard de Pitray, née Olga de Ségur, sa fille (ed.) *Lettres de la comtesse de Ségur née Rostopchine au vicomte et à la vicomtesse de Pitray* (Paris, Hachette, 1891).

Vicomtesse de Simard de Pitray, née Olga de Ségur (ed.) *Lettres d'une grand'mère la comtesse de Ségur à son petit-fils Jacques de Pitray* (Paris, Librairie H. Oudin, 1898).

Vicomtesse de Simard de Pitray, née Olga de Ségur, reprints letters from Gaston in her biography *Mon bon Gaston*, and letters from the comtesse de Ségur to Louis Veuillot in her biography *Ma chère maman*.

Louis Veuillot, *Œuvres complètes* XV, deuxième série, *Correspondance* mis en ordre, et annotée par François Veuillot, volumes 1–12 (Paris, P. Lethielleux, 1931–32): his letters to the comtesse de Ségur are in volumes 4–9.

Correspondence concerning the comtesse de Ségur and M.M.L. Hachette et Cie, published in *Œuvres*, 1: lxi–cxlvi.

Strich, Marie-José (ed.), with a preface by Michel Tournier, *1799–1874 La comtesse de Ségur. Correspondance* (Paris, Scala, 1990).

Acker, Paul, 'La comtesse de Ségur, née Rostopchine', *Revue de Paris*, 1 April 1908, 589–612, reproduces letters to her granddaughter Elisabeth Fresneau.

Letters reproduced in *Les amis de la comtesse de Ségur, Les Cahiers Séguriens, Au Pays de l'Argentelles, L'Orne de la comtesse de Ségur*, catalogues of exhibitions put on at the Musée de la comtesse de Ségur.

Two letters partially reproduced in *La comtessse de Ségur, née Rostopchine (1799–1874)* Catalogue no. 29, Librairie Thierry Corcelle, Paris, 1999 [Consulted at the *Bibliothèque L'Heure Joyeuse*].

FAMILY CORRESPONDENCE

Lettres de Mgr de Ségur à ses fils spirituels, publiées par le Marquis de Ségur (Paris, Bray et Rétaux, 1897) which is a revised edition of *Lettres de Mgr de Ségur de 1854 à 1881, Publiées avec une introduction et des notes par le Marquis de Ségur* (Paris, Bray et Rétaux, 1882).

Marthe de Hédouville, *Les Rostopchine. Une grande famille russe au XIXè siècle* (Paris, Éditions France-Empire, 1984).

MEMOIRS AND BIOGRAPHIES

Armaillé (née Ségur) comtesse d', *Quand on savait vivre heureux (1830–60) Souvenirs de jeunesse, Publiés par la comtesse Jean de Pange* (Paris, Plon, 1934).

Baille, Charles, *Souvenirs sur Mgr de Ségur* (La Chapelle-Montligeon, Imprimerie de Notre Dame de Montligeon, 1901).

Chaumont, Abbé Henri, *Monseigneur de Ségur Directeur des âmes* (Paris, René Haton, 1884).

Moussac, le Marquis de, *Mgr de Ségur* (Paris, Librairie des Saints-Pères, 1906).

Veuillot, Eugène, and Veuillot, François, *Louis Veuillot*, 4 volumes (Paris, Victor Rétaux, 1899–1913).

(Various) *Monsieur Émile Templier 1821–91* (Paris, Imprimerie D. Dumoulin et Cie, 1892).

RECEPTION

Bibliographie catholique

(Where no author is indicated, the review was anonymous).

Review of *Petites filles modèles*, 18, February 1859.

Review of *Les malheurs de Sophie*, and *Nouveaux contes de fées*, by Maxime de Montrond, 22, October 1859.

Review of *La sœur de Gribouille*, by Ch. Laval, 27, April 1862.

Review of *Les bons enfants*, by V. Postel, 32, November 1864.

Review of *L'auberge de l'ange gardien* and *Pauvre Blaise*, by Gustave Robert, 33, April 1865.

Review of *Évangile d'une grand'mère* by V. Postel, 35, April 1866.

Review of *Actes des apôtres*, 37, April 1867.

Review of *Le mauvais génie*, 40, July 1868.

Review of *Diloy le chemineau*, 41, May 1869.

Review of *Après la pluie, le beau temps*, by A. Vissac, 45, June 1872.

La poupée modèle / Journal des demoiselles.

Review of *Les bons enfants*, *Poupée modèle*, June 1864.

Review of *Évangile d'une grand'mère*, *Poupée modèle*, December 1868.

Review of *Les malheurs de Sophie*, *Les vacances*, *Les petites filles modèles*, and *Nouveaux contes de fées*, by Mathilde Bourdon, *Journal des Demoiselles*, 28, May 1860.

L'univers / Revue du monde catholique.

Veuillot, Louis, 'Les contes de Madame de Ségur', 31 December 1859, *L'univers*, reproduced in Veuillot, *Mélanges*, 8, 422–426.

Veuillot, Louis, 'Témoignages et souvenirs par M. le comte Anatole de Ségur', 25 December 1857, *L'univers*, reproduced in *Mélanges*, 7, 293–298.

Veuillot, Louis, 'Les Fables, par Anatole de Ségur', 10 December 1865, *Revue du monde catholique*, reproduced in *Mélanges*, 8, 585–588.

THE MONUMENT CAMPAIGN

Acker, Paul, 'La comtesse de Ségur, née Rostopchine', *Revue de Paris*, 1 April 1908, 589–612.

Anon., 'Le Monument de la comtesse de Ségur', *L'Illustration*, 1er semester 1910, 560.

Davenay, G., 'Le monument de la comtesse de Ségur', *Le Figaro*, 20 June 1910.

Ernest-Charles, J., 'La ridicule statue de la Comtesse de Ségur', *La grande revue*, 10 May 1908, reproduced in *Les cahiers Séguriens*, 5 (2004), 96–101.

Lemaitre, Jules, 'Madame de Ségur', Speech delivered at the inauguration ceremony, 19 June 1910, *Les contemporains. Études et portraits littéraires. Huitième série* (Paris, Oudin, 1918), 201–206.

Maricourt, André de, 'La comtesse de Ségur', *Le correspondant*, 25 June 1910, 1185–1198.

Montesquiou, Robert de, 'Le Balzac de l'enfance', *Le Figaro*, 7 September 1907, see also *Les Roseaux pensants* (1897).

Prévost, Marcel, 'La comtesse de Ségur: l'aïeule conteuse', *Le Figaro*, 19 May, 1907, reprinted in *Marcel Prévost et ses contemporains. Critiques littéraires, portraits, correspondances, inédits*, vol. 1 (Paris, Les Éditions de France, 1943).

NEWSPAPERS AND JOURNALS

Bibliographie catholique.
Journal des demoiselles.
Journal des jeunes personnes.
La poupée modèle.
La semaine des enfants.
La semaine des familles.
L'univers.

WRITINGS OF SÉGUR'S MILIEU

Ségur, Louis-Gaston Adrien de, *La Religion enseignée aux petits enfants* (Paris, Douniol, 1857).

—— *Réponses courtes et familières aux objections les plus répandues contre la religion* (Paris, J. Lecoffre, 1851).

—— *La Révolution expliquée aux jeunes gens* (Paris, Tolra et Haton, 1861).

Ségur, Anatole de, *Le dimanche des soldats* (Paris, J. Lecoffre, 1850).

—— *La caserne et le presbytère. Contes et récits* (Paris, Bray, 1853).

—— *Les mémoires d'un troupier* (Paris, Bray, 1858).

—— *Les martyres de Castelfidardo* (Paris, Tolra, 1861).

—— *Fables* (Paris, Hetzel, 1863) (first two books published 1847, full collection, 1863).

—— *Souvenirs et causeries du soir* (Paris, Bray, 1857).

Veuillot, Louis, *La guerre et l'homme de la guerre* (Paris, Vivès, 1854).

—— *Mélanges*, 7–10, 1856–71.

—— *Lendemain de la victoire* (Paris, Victor Palmé, 1850).

'GOVERNESS' LITERATURE

Balzac, Honoré de, *Correspondance inédite avec Madame Zulma Carraud (1829–50)* (Paris, Armand Colin, 1935).

Carraud, Zulma, *La petite Jeanne ou le devoir* (Paris, Hachette, 1852).

—— *Maurice ou le travail* (Paris, Hachette, 1855).

Fleuriot, Zénaïde, *Souvenirs d'une douarière* (Paris, Dentu, 1859) [Published under the pseudonym Anna Edianez de L**** de S-B].

—— *Raoul Daubry, Petit chef de famille* (Paris, Hachette, 1881).

Fleuriot-Kerinou, Francis, *Zénaïde Fleuriot: sa vie, ses œuvres, sa correspondance* (Paris, Hachette, 1897).

Genlis, Madame de, *Essais sur l'éducation des hommes, et particulièrement des princes, par les femmes. Pour servir de supplément aux lettres sur l'éducation* (Amsterdam, 1782).

—— *Les veillées du château ou cours de morale à l'usage des enfants*, 4 volumes (Maastricht, Dufour & Roux, 1784).

Gouraud, Julie, *Mémoires d'une poupée. Contes dédiés aux petites filles* (Paris, Ébrard, 1839).

—— *Mémoires d'un caniche* (Paris, Hachette, 1865).

—— *Mémoires d'un petit garçon* (Paris, Hachette, 1864).

Monniot, Victorine, *Le Journal de Marguerite ou les deux années préparatoires à la première communion* (Paris, Périsse frères, 1859).

Diaries, memoirs, and correspondence

Beauvoir, Simone de, *Mémoires d'une jeune fille rangée* (Park, Gallimard, 1958).

Brame, Caroline, *Le journal intime de Caroline Brame*, Annotated and with essays by Michelle Perrot and Georges Ribeill (Paris, Editions Montalba, 1985).

Cabanis, José, *Plaisir et lectures* (Paris, Gallimard, 1964) volume 1, 121–129.

Laurent, Jacques, *Histoire égoïste* (Paris, La Table Ronde, 1976).

Lenéru, Marie, *Journal de Marie Lenéru* (Paris, Grasset, 1945).

Le Verrier, Lucile, *Journal d'une jeune fille Second Empire 1866–78* (Paris, Zulma, 1994).

Martin, Zélie, *Correspondance familiale 1863–87* (Paris, Office de Lisieux, 1958).

Mauriac, François, *Mémoires intérieurs* (Paris, Flammarion, 1959).

Pange, comtesse Jean de, *Comment j'ai vu 1900* (Paris, Grasset, 1962).

Weiss, Louise, *Souvenirs d'une enfance républicaine* (Paris, Denoel, 1937).

Reading governess literature

Bethléem, L'abbé Louis, *Romans à lire & Romans à proscrire. Essai de classification au point de vue moral des principaux romans et romanciers de notre époque (1800–1911) avec notes et indications pratiques* (Nord, Librairie Oscar Masson & Bureaux de Romans-Revue, 1911).

Bonheur, Gaston, *Qui a cassé le vase de Soissons? L'album de famille de tous les Français* (Paris, Robert Laffont, 1963).

Bourdon, Mme, *Les servantes de Dieu. Vies édifiantes des dames les plus pieuses et les plus charitables* (Paris, Putois-Cretté, 1861).

Brauner, Alfred, *Nos livres d'enfants ont menti! Une base de discussion* (Paris, SABRI, 1951).

Enfance. Psychologie, pédagogie, neuro-psychiatrie, sociologie (Published in collaboration with the CNRS) Edited by Henri Wallon. May–June 1956: special issue dedicated to children's literature.

Freud, Sigmund, *A Child Is Being Beaten. A Contribution to the Study of the Origin of Sexual Perversions* (1919) Reproduced in Ethel Spector Person (ed.) *On Freud's 'A Child Is Being Beaten'* (New Haven, Yale University Press, 1997).

Jouin, Henry, *Mademoiselle Z. Fleuriot. Du rôle des femmes dans la littérature populaire* (Paris, Librairie Jacques Lecoffre, 1871).

Nettement, Alfred, *Le roman contemporain. Ses vicissitudes, ses divers aspects, son influence* (Paris, Librairie Jacques Lecoffre, 1864).

P.E. Marquigny de la Compagnie de Jésus, *Une femme forte. La comtesse Adelstan. Étude biographique et morale* (Paris, Jacques Lecoffre, 1873).

Soriano, Marc, *Guide de littérature pour la jeunesse: courants, problèmes, choix* (Paris, Flammarion, 1975).

Soriano, Marc, preface to *La fortune de Gaspard* (Paris, Jean-Jacques Pauvert, 1972).

Secondary sources

Anderson, Robert D., *Education in France 1848–70* (Oxford, Clarendon Press, 1975).

Artiaga Loïc, *Des torrents de papier: catholicisme et lectures populaires au XIXe siècle* (Limoges, PULIM, 2007).

Aspinwall, Bernard, 'The Child as Maker of the Ultramontane', in Wood, Diana (ed.) *The Church and Childhood* (Oxford, Blackwell, 1994), pp. 427–445.

Atkin, Nicholas, and Tallett, Frank (eds) *Catholicism in Britain and France since 1789* (London, The Hambledon Press, 1996).

—— (eds) *Religion, Society and Politics in France since 1789* (London, The Hambledon Press, 1991).

Au pays d'Argentelles, La revue culturelle de l'Orne, 7 (1983), 121–139, and 9 (1985), 134–142.

Beaussant, Claudine, *La comtesse de Ségur ou l'enfance de l'art* (Paris, Robert Laffont, 1988).

Becchi, Egle, and Julia, Dominique (eds) *Histoire de l'enfance en occident* (Paris, Seuil, 1998).

Boudon, Jacques-Olivier, *Paris capitale religieuse sous le Second Empire* (Paris, Les éditions du Cerf, 2001).

Bricard, Isabelle, *Saintes ou pouliches: l'éducation des jeunes filles au XIXe siècle* (Paris, Albin Michel, 1985).

Brown, Penny, *A Critical History of French Children's Literature 1600–Present* (London, Routledge, 2008).

Calvet, Jean, *L'enfant dans la littérature française* (Paris, F. Lanore, 1930).

Chartier, Anne-Marie, and Hébrard, Jean, *Discours sur la lecture (1880–2000)* (Paris, Fayard / BPI-Centre Pompidou, 2000).

Cholvy, Gérard, and Hilaire, Yves-Marie, *Histoire religieuse de la France contemporaine 1800/1880* (Paris, Privat, 1985).

Clark, Christopher, and Kaiser, Wolfram (eds) *Culture Wars. Secular–Catholic Conflict in Nineteenth-Century Europe* (Cambridge, Cambridge University Press, 2003).

Constant, Paule, *Un monde à l'usage des demoiselles* (Paris, Gallimard, 1987).

Corbin, Alain, Lalouette, Jacqueline, and Riot-Sarcey, Michèle (eds) *Femmes dans la cité 1815–71* (Grâne, Créaphis, 1997).

Cordonnier, Charles, *Silhouettes familiales. La comtesse de Ségur l'idéale grand'mère* (Paris, Librairie J.-M. Peigues, 1931).

Cosnier, Colette, *Le silence des filles de l'aiguille à la plume* (Paris, Fayard, 2001).

Cunningham, Hugh, *Children and Childhood in Western Society since 1500* (Harlow, Pearson Education, 1995, 2005).

Curtis, Sarah A., *Educating the Faithful. Religion, Schooling, and Society in Nineteenth-Century France* (De Kalb, Northern Illinois University Press, 2000).

Darrow, Margaret H., 'French Noblewomen and the New Domesticity', *Feminist Studies*, 5 (1979), 41–65.

Dauphin, Cécile, Lebrun-Pézerat, Pierette, and Poublan, Danièle, *Ces bonnes lettres. Une correspondance familiale au XIXe siècle* (Paris, Albin Michel, 1995).

De Maeyer, Jan, Ewers, Hans-Heino, Ghesquière, Rita, Manson, Michel, Pinsent, Pat, and Quaghebeur, Patricia (eds) *Religion, Children's Literature and Modernity in Western Europe 1750–2000* (Leuven, Leuven University Press, 2005).

Diesbach, Ghislain de, *La comtesse de Ségur, née Rostopchine 1799–1874* (Paris, Perrin, 1999).

Doray, Marie-France, *La comtesse de Ségur: une étrange paroissienne* (Lyon, Rivages, 1990).

Driskel, Michael, *Representing Belief: Religion, Art and Society in Nineteenth-Century France* (University Park, Pennsylvania State University Press, 1992).

Duby, Georges, and Perrot, Michelle (eds) *Histoire des femmes en occident* (Paris, Plon, 1991), volume 4, *Le XIXe siècle*.

Dufour, Hortense, *La comtesse de Ségur née Sophie Rostopchine* (Paris, Flammarion Collection Grandes Biographies, 1990).

Duroselle, Jean-Baptiste, *Les débuts du catholicisme social en France (1822–70)* (Paris, PUF, 1951).

Ergal, Yves-Marie, and Strich, Marie-José, *La comtesse de Ségur* (Paris, Perrin, 1990).

Europe, Revue littéraire mensuelle, 914/915 (2005).

Foley, Susan K, *Women in France since 1789. The Meanings of Difference* (London, Palgrave Macmillan, 2004).

Ford, Caroline, *Divided Houses. Religion and Gender in Modern France* (Ithaca, Cornell University Press, 2005).

Fourment, Alain, *Histoire de la presse des jeunes et des journaux d'enfants (1768–1988)* (Paris, Éditions Éole, 1987).

Gibson, Ralph, *A Social History of French Catholicism 1789–1914* (London, Routledge, 1989).

Gildea, Robert, *Education in Provincial France, 1800–1914: A Study of Three Departments* (Oxford, Clarendon, 1983).

—— *Children of the Revolution. The French 1799–1914* (London, Allen Lane, 2008).

Glénisson, Jean, and Le Men, Ségolène (eds) *Le livre d'enfance et de jeunesse en France* (Bordeaux, Société de Bibliophiles de Guyenne, 1994).

Gough, Austin, *Paris and Rome: The Gallican Church and the Ultramontane Campaign 1848–53* (Oxford, Clarendon Press, 1986).

Grand album comtesse de Ségur (Paris, Hachette, Collection 'Grandes Œuvres', 1983).

Grenby, M.O., *Children's Literature* (Edinburgh, Edinburgh University Press, 2008).

Guénel, Jean, *La dernière guerre du pape. Les zouaves pontificaux au secours du saint-siège 1860–70* (Rennes, Presses Universitaires de Rennes, 1998).

Harris, Ruth, *Lourdes. Body and Spirit in the Secular Age* (Harmondsworth, Penguin, 1999).

Harrison, Carol E., *The Bourgeois Citizen in Nineteenth-Century France. Gender, Sociability and the Uses of Emulation* (Oxford, Oxford University Press, 1999).

—— 'Zouave Stories: Gender, Catholic Spirituality, and French Responses to the Roman Question', *The Journal of Modern History*, 79 (2007), 274–305.

Havelange, Isabelle, and Le Men, Ségolène, *Le magasin des enfants. La littérature pour la jeunesse 1750–1830* (Montreuil, Association Bicentenaire Montreuil, 1988).

Hecquet, Michèle (ed.) *L'éducation des filles au temps de George Sand* (Arras, Artois Presses Université, 1998).

Hédouville, Marthe de, *La comtesse de Ségur et les siens* (Paris, Editions du Conquistador, 1953).

—— *Mgr de Ségur, sa vie – son action 1820–81* (Paris, Nouvelles Editions Latines, 1957).

Hesse, Carla, *The Other Enlightenment. How French Women Became Modern* (Princeton, Princeton University Press, 2001).

Heywood, Colin, *Childhood in Nineteenth-Century France: Work, Health and Education among the classes populaires* (Cambridge, Cambridge University Press, 1988).

—— *Growing Up in France: From the Ancien Régime to the Third Republic* (Cambridge, Cambridge University Press, 2007).

Horaist, Bruno, *La dévotion au pape et les catholiques français sous le pontificat de Pie IX (1846–78) d'après les archives de la Bibliothèque Apostolique Vaticane* (Rome, École Française de Rome, Palais Farnese, 1995).

Hunt, Peter, *Children's Literature* (Oxford, Blackwell, 2001).

Ivereigh, Austen (ed.) *The Politics of Religion in an Age of Revival* (London, Institute of Latin American Studies, 2000).

Knibiehler, Yvonne, Bernos, Marcel, and Ravoux-Rallo, Elisabeth, *De la pucelle à la minette. Les jeunes filles de l'âge classique à nos jours* (Paris, Temps Actuels, 1983).

Kreyder, Laura, *L'enfance des saints et des autres. Essai sur la comtesse de Ségur* (Milan, Schéna-Nizet, 1987).

Kselman, Thomas, *Death and the Afterlife in Modern France* (Princeton, Princeton University Press, 1993).

—— *Miracles and Prophecies in Nineteenth Century France* (New Brunswick, Rutgers University Press, 1983).

La Comtesse de Ségur au Château des Nouettes à Aube de 1821 à 1872 (Aube, Musée de comtesse de Ségur, Undated).

Lamberts, Emiel, *The Black International (1870–78) The Holy See and Militant Catholicism in Europe* (Brussels, Rome, Institut Historique Belge de Rome, 2002).

Lanavère, Alain, 'Le bonheur selon Madame de Ségur', in *Mélanges offertes à M. le Professeur Jacques Robichez. Cent ans de la littérature française 1850–1950* (Paris, SEDES, 1987), pp. 23–30.

Langlois, Claude, *Le catholicisme au féminin. Les congrégations françaises à supérieure générale au XIXe siècle* (Paris, Les Éditions du Cerf, 1984).

La revue des livres pour enfants, 131/132 (1990).

Lassère, Madeleine, *Victorine Monniot ou l'éducation des jeunes filles au XIXè siècle, entre exoticisme et catholicisme de combat* (Paris, L'Harmatton, 1999).

Laurent, Jacques, 'Étrennes noires', *La table ronde*, January 1949, 157–167.

Lejeune, Philippe, *Le pacte autobiographique* (Paris, Éditions du Seuil, 1975, 1996, new, revised edition).

Le Roc'h Morgère, Louis (ed.) *L'Orne de la Comtesse de Ségur. Actes des colloques d'Alençon et de Cérisy-la-Salle* (Alençcon, Archives Départmentales, 1991–92), 2 volumes.

—— *Le moi des demoiselles. Enquête sur le journal de jeune fille* (Paris, Seuil, 1993).

Les amis de la Comtesse de Ségur (1990–99) in 2000 became *Les Cahiers Séguriens.*

Les petites filles modèles (Aube, Musée de la Comtesse de Ségur, 1997).

Lévy, Marie-Françoise, *De mères en filles: l'éducation des françaises 1850–80* (Paris, Calmann-Lévy, 1984).

Lloyd, Rosemary, *The Land of Lost Content: Children and Childhood in Nineteenth-Century French Literature* (Oxford, Clarendon Press, 1992).

Loyrette, Paul, and Strich, Marie-José, *Sur les pas de la comtesse de Ségur. Le voyage en Russie de Louis-Gaston de Ségur* (Paris, Gallimard, 2005).

Luc, Jean-Noël, *L'invention du jeune enfant au XIXe siècle. De la salle d'asile à l'école maternelle* (Paris, Belin, 1997).

Luton, Lisette, *La Comtesse de Ségur, A Marquise de Sade?* (New York, Peter Lang, 1999).

Lyons, Martyn, *Readers and Society in Nineteenth-Century France: Workers, Women, Peasants* (Basingstoke, Palgrave, 2001).

Mainardi, Patricia, *Husbands, Wives and Lovers. Marriage and Its Discontents in Nineteenth-Century France* (New Haven, Yale University Press, 2003).

Marcoin, Francis, *La comtesse de Ségur ou le bonheur immobile* (Arras, Artois Presses Université, 1999).

—— *La librairie de jeunesse et littérature industrielle au XIXe siècle* (Paris, Honoré Champion, 2006).

Margadant, Jo Burr (ed.) *The New Biography. Performing Femininity in Nineteenth-Century France* (Berkeley and Los Angeles, University of California Press, 2000).

Martin, Henri-Jean, Chartier, Roger, and Vivet, Jean-Pierre (eds) *Histoire de l'édition française*, volumes 3 & 4 (Paris, Promodis, 1985–86).

Maurain, Jean, *La politique ecclésiastique du Second Empire de 1852 à 1869* (Paris, Librairie Félix Alcan, 1930).

Mayeur, Françoise, *L'éducation des filles en France au XIXe siècle* (Paris, Hachette, 1979).

Mayeur, Françoise, et Gadille, Jacques (eds) *Education et images de la femme chrétienne en France au début du XXème siècle. Entretiens de La Combe de Lancey (Isère) 8, 9, 10 octobre 1978 à l'occasion du centenaire de la mort de Mgr Dupanloup* (Lyon, Éditions l'Hermès, 1980).

Mayeur, Jean-Marie, 'Catholicisme intransigeant, catholicisme social, démocratie chrétienne', *Annales ESC* (1972), 483–499.

McMillan, James F., 'Catholic Christianity in France from the Restoration to the Separation of Church and State, 1815–1905', in Gilley, Sheridan, and Stanley, Brian (eds) *World Christianities c. 1815–1914* (Cambridge, Cambridge University Press, 2006), 217–232.

—— *France and Women 1789–1914: Gender, Society and Politics* (London, Routledge, 2000).

—— 'Louis Veuillot, *L'univers* and the Ultramontane Network in Nineteenth-Century France', in Bates, David, and Gazeau, Véronique (eds) *Liens personnels, réseaux, solidarités en France et dans les îles Britanniques (XIe–XXe siècles)* (Paris, Publications de la Sorbonne, 2006).

—— 'Rediscovering Louis Veuillot: The Politics of Religious Identity in Nineteenth-Century France', in Harkness, Nigel, Rowe, Paul, Unwin, Tim and Yee, Jennifer (eds) *Visions/Revisions Essays on Nineteenth-Century French Culture* (Bern, Peter Lang AG, 2003), 305–322.

Mension-Rigau, Eric, *L'enfance au château. L'éducation familiale des élites françaises au vingtième siècle* (Paris, Rivages, 1990).

Misrahi, Colette, *La comtesse de Ségur ou la mère médecin* (Paris, Éditions Denoël, 1991).

Mistler, Jean, *La librairie Hachette de 1826 à nos jours* (Paris, Hachette, 1964).

Mollier, Jean-Yves, 'Éditer la comtesse de Ségur ou les ruses de la raison policière', *Cahiers Robinson*, 9 (2001), 14–22.

—— (ed.) *Histoires de lecture XIXe–XXe siècles* (Bernay, Société d'histoire de la lecture, 2005).

—— 'La comtesse de Ségur et la Bibliothèque Rose', *L'auteur et son éditeur, à travers les collections de l'institut mémoires de l'édition contemporaine* (Caen, IMEC, 1998), 15–26.

—— 'Les femmes auteurs et leurs éditeurs au XIXe siècle: un long combat pour la reconnaissance de leurs droits d'écrivains', *Revue Historique* (2006), 313–333.

—— *Louis Hachette (1800–64) Le fondateur d'un empire* (Paris, Fayard, 1999).

Monicat, Bénédicte, *Devoirs de l'écriture. Modèles d'histoires pour filles et littéature féminine au XIXe siècle* (Lyon, Presses Universitaires de Lyon, 2006).

Musée Goya, Les petites filles modèles (Paris, Exposition Ville de Castres, Presses Artistiques, 1957).

Myers, Mitzi, 'Impeccable Governesses, Rational Dames, and Moral Mothers: Mary Wollstonecraft and the Female Tradition in Georgian Children's Books', *Children's Literature* 14 (1986), 31–58.

Nières-Chevrel, Isabelle (ed.) *La comtesse de Ségur et ses alentours*, Special issue of Cahiers Robinson, 9 (2001).

—— (ed.) *La comtesse de Ségur et ses illustrateurs* (Rennes, Bibliothèque Municipale, 1999).

Ottevaere-van Praag, Ganna, *La littérature pour la jeunesse en Europe occidentale (1750–1925)* (Berne, Peter Lang, 1987).

Pannier, Daniel (ed.) *Mgr de Ségur, 1820–21* (Paris, Via Romana, 2008).

Parinet, Élisabeth, *Une histoire de l'édition à l'époque contemporaine XIXe–XXe siècle* (Paris, Seuil, 2004).

Parménie, A., and Bonnier de la Chapelle, C., *Histoire d'un éditeur et de ses auteurs: P.J. Hetzel (Stahl)* (Paris, Éditions Albin Michel, 1953).

Perrot, Michelle, *Femmes publiques* (Paris, Les Éditions Textuel, 1997).

—— (ed.) *A History of Private Life* (Cambridge, MA, The Belknap Press of Harvard University Press, 1990), volume 4, *From the Fires of Revolution to the Great War*.

Pierrard, Pierre, *Louis Veuillot* (Paris, Beauchesne, 1998).

Piquard, Michèle, *L'édition pour la jeunesse en France de 1945 à 1980* (Paris, enssib, 2004).

Plagnol-Diéval, Marie-Emmanuelle, *Madame de Genlis et le théâtre d'éducation au XVIIIe siècle* (Oxford, Voltaire Foundation, 1997).

Popiel, Jennifer J., *Rousseau's Daughters. Domesticity, Education, and Autonomy in Modern France* (Durham, University of New Hampshire Press, 2008).

Poulat, Émile, and Laurant, Jean-Pierre, *L'antimaçonnisme catholique* (Paris, Berg International, 1994).

Price, Roger, *The French Second Empire. An Anatomy of Political Power* (Cambridge, Cambridge University Press, 2001).

Rogers, Rebecca, *From the Salon to the Schoolroom. Educating Bourgeois Girls in Nineteenth-Century France* (University Park, Pennsylvania State University Press, 2005).

—— 'L'éducation des filles. Un siècle et demi d'historiographie', *Histoire de l'éducation*, 115–116 (2007), 37–79.

Savart, Claude, *Les catholiques en France au XIXe siècle. Le témoignage du livre religieux* (Paris, Beauchesne, 1985).

Savy, Nicole, *Les petites filles modernes*, Catalogue d'exposition-dossier, Musée d'Orsay (Paris, Editions de la Réunion des musées nationaux, 1989).

Schlafly, Daniel, 'De Joseph de Maistre à la "Bibliothèque Rose" le catholicisme chez les Rostopcin', *Cahiers du monde russe et soviétique*, 11 (1970), 93–109.

Scott, Joan Walloch, *Only Paradoxes to Offer. French Feminists and the Rights of Man* (Cambridge, MA, Harvard University Press, 1996).

—— *Gender and the Politics of History* (revised edition, New York, Columbia University Press, 1999).

Seeley, Paul, 'O sainte mère: Liberalism and the Socialisation of Catholic Men in Nineteenth-Century France', *The Journal of Modern History*, 70 (1998), 862–891.

Smith, Bonnie G., *Ladies of the Leisure Class: The Bourgeoises of Northern France in the 19th Century* (Princeton, Princeton University Press, 1981).

Smith Allen, James, *In the Public Eye: A History of Reading in Modern France, 1800–1940* (Princeton, Princeton University Press, 1991).

Thiesse, Anne-Marie, *Le roman du quotidien. Lecteurs et lectures populaires à la Belle Époque* (Paris, Chemin Vert, 1984).

Vinson, Marie-Christine, *L'éducation des petites filles chez la comtesse de Ségur* (Lyon, Presses Universitaires de Lyon, 1987).

Warner, Marina, *From the Beast to the Blonde: On Fairy tales and Their Tellers* (London, Chatto and Windus, 1994).

Zeiller, Jacques, *La comtesse de Ségur* (Paris, Bloud, 1913).

Zeldin, Theodore (ed.) *Conflicts in French Society: Anticlericalism, Education & Morals in the 19th Century* (London, George Allen & Unwin, 1970).

—— *France 1848–1945* (Oxford, Oxford University Press, 1979–80).

Theses and dissertations

Bauland, Marc, *Les collections de romans pour la jeunesse de la Librairie Hachette (1945–1980)*, D.E.A., Université de Versailles-Saint-Quentin-en-Yvelines, octobre 1997, Unpublished.

Mouranche, Marielle, *Les livres pour l'enfance et la jeunesse de 1870 à 1914*, thèse, École Nationale des Chartes, 1986, Unpublished.

Legros, Valérie, *De l'histoire à l'Histoire. Lire la comtesse de Ségur*, thèse de doctorat, Université de Rennes II, 1996, Unpublished.

Petit, Cécile, *La comtesse de Ségur et l'édition. Étude de sa correspondance avec Émile Templier, son éditeur*, Mémoire de DEA, Université Paris IV-Sorbonne, 2004, Unpublished.

Rouxel, Caroline, *Zénaïde Fleuriot ou Le parcours d'un écrivain catholique pour la jeunesse au XIXe siècle*, Mémoire de Master, Université du Maine, septembre 2005, Unpublished.

Index